*Peerless Science*

**SUNY Series in Science, Technology, and Society**

*Sal Restivo, Editor*

# *PEERLESS SCIENCE*

## *Peer Review and U.S. Science Policy*

**Daryl E. Chubin**
**and**
**Edward J. Hackett**

STATE UNIVERSITY OF NEW YORK PRESS

Published by
State University of New York Press, Albany

© 1990 State University of New York

For information, address State University of New York
Press, State University Plaza, Albany, N.Y., 12246

**Library of Congress Cataloging in Publication Data**

Chubin, Daryl E.
    Peerless science : peer review and U.S. science policy / Daryl E.
    Chubin and Edward J. Hackett.
        p.    cm. — (SUNY series in science, technology, and society)
    Includes bibliographical references.
    ISBN 0–7914–0309–2. — ISBN 0–7914–0310–6 (pbk.)
    1. Science—Government policy—United States—Evaluation.
    2. Peer review—United States.    I. Hackett, Edward J., 1951–    .
    II. Title.    III. Series.
    Q127.U6C48   1990                                        89–21855
    338.97306—dc20                                            CIP

10 9 8 7 6 5 4 3 2 1

*Dedicated to*
*Vicki Bluestone, Rand, and Jessica Chubin*
*Jocelyn J. Hackett and Sharon L. Harlan*

# Contents

# Preface and Acknowledgments

Peer review is not a popular subject. Scientists, federal program mangers, journal editors, academic administrators, and even our social science colleagues become uneasy when it is discussed. This occurs because the study of peer review challenges the current state of affairs. Most prefer not to question the way things are done—even if those ways at times appear illogical, unfair, and detrimental to the collective life of science and the prospects of one's own career. Instead, it is more comfortable to defer to tradition, place faith in collective wisdom, and hope that all shall be well.

Because peer review is such a sensitive subject, we feel it is especially important to thank all those who sustained us—intellectually and otherwise—during our mounting obsession with science as a social enterprise and peer review in particular. The work on peer review began innocently a decade ago, when Chubin coauthored with Ian Mitroff an analysis of peer review at the National Science Foundation that called into question how it was done and how it was studied. Two years ago, Chubin approached Hackett with the invitation to collaborate on the manuscript in progress that became the book in your hand. Fresh from a study of scientists' reactions to the research funding system, Hackett was eager to think more comprehensively about allocative mechanisms and science policy. We first worked together in the mid-1970s at Cornell, and had kept in touch through a dizzying succession of job changes. Looking backward, we thank Bob McGinnis for his support in those early years of science studies and for introducing us to one another and to the friends we respect for their minds and cherish for their hearts. To us, they will forever be associated with Cornell because history, not current affiliation, makes it so: Carl B. Backman, the late Dick Campbell, Helen Hofer Gee, Gerry Gordon, Scott Long, the late Nick Mullins, Dot Nelkin, the late Derek Price, and Robin M. Williams, Jr.

Chubin's sabbatical, in 1983–4, at Cornell's Science, Technology, and Society Program and Department of Sociology, expanded this circle to include others who contributed to the development of the manuscript: Gil Gillespie, who took charge of the National Institutes of Health survey data reported in chapter 3; Mike Brown, who was the most indulgent office-mate any visiting professor could hope for, and especially Sheila Jasanoff, with whom Chubin co-edited a 1985 special issue of *Science, Technology, and Human Values* on "peer review and public policy." Chewing over many issues with her was hearty preparation for this volume.

Hackett's work on this volume was greatly facilitated by the time, resources, and patient encouragement provided him by the chair of his department, Shirley S. Gorenstein.

Many others have provided one or both of us the kind of stimulation that makes scholarship such a satisfying process. At Georgia Tech, these people included Stan Carpenter, Jeff Franklin, Jon Johnston, Mel Kranzberg, Alan Porter, Dave Roessner, and Fred Rossini. At RPI, this role was played by Linnda Caporael, Tom Carroll, Susan Cozzens, Teri Harrison, Deborah Johnson, and Ned Woodhouse. Deserving special mention is a valuable resource on numerous issues for both of us: Sal Restivo, who founded and edits the series in which this book appears.

Others' writings and, more important, their conversations over the years have seeped into the pages that follow. We thank them for—wittingly or not—enriching our effort: John Andelin, Bill Blanpied, Larry Busch, Nancy Carson, Chris Caswill, Ellen Chu, the late Gene Frankel, Tom Gieryn, Peter Healey, Lisa Heinz, Chris Hill, David Hull, Rachelle Hollander, Carlos Kruytbosch, Karin Knorr-Cetina, Marcel LaFollette, Bill Lacy, Wil Lepkowski, Jim McCartney, Jim McCullough, Willie Pearson, Jr., Arie Rip, Rusty Roy, Henry Small, Samantha Solomon, Tom Stossel, Al Teich, Steve Turner, Ron Westrum, Pat Woolf, the late Christopher Wright, and John Ziman.

Thanks for material support of various kinds go to George Kurzon for allowing Chubin to participate in his legal appeal, recounted in chapter 3 (some of which appeared in the *Bulletin of Science, Technology, and Society* (vol. 2, 1982, pp. 423–432, c. Pergamon Press), which led to the survey described in that chapter; to David Edge and Roy MacLeod who provided access, via Nigel Gilbert, to their editorial files at *Social Studies of Science* (the fruits of this access appear in chapter 4); to the National Science Foundation which, through Work Order No. 83–GB–0032G (and the scheming of Chuck Herz and Alex Morin) supported Chubin's project to synthesize what was known "back then" about misconduct in scientific research (revisited in chapter 5), and to the Office of Technology Assessment's Contract No. 633–1310, which permitted Chubin (*before* he became a federal employee) to draft what was first excerpted in the 1986 OTA technical memorandum, *Research Funding as an Investment: Can We Measure the Returns?* and later revised as "Research Evaluation and the Generation of Big Science Policy," published in *Knowledge: Creation, Diffusion, Utilization* (vol. 9, 1987, pp. 254–277, c. Sage Publications) before being overhauled for use in chapter 6. The Office of Technology Assessment provoked and supported some of Hackett's thinking on the issues presented in this book through its Contract No. H3–4075.1, which led to his report, "Science in the Steady State: The Changing Research University"; the National Science Foundation also supported Hackett's writing through Grant No. BBS 87–11341.

A blanket acknowledgment is also owed to the editors, program managers, and anonymous referees we have encountered over a combined professional life of nearly thirty years. They have given us ample opportunity to try our hands at the roles of reviewer and reviewee. They have also heightened our sensitivity to the process of proposal and manuscript appraisal. Most of all, they have fed us a rich diet of participant observation in outrage, provocation, and political maneuvering. Our files are engorged with the products of their sharp minds and sharper tongues. Although neither of us systematically examined this personal documentation of "peer" behavior, we will carry its benefits and scars for many years. We have tried to incorporate the distilled wisdom of this experience in these pages. While we owe debts of gratitude and more to the above mentioned people and organizations, we alone are responsible for the views recorded here.

Rosalie Robertson, our editor at the Press, was patient beyond words with a manuscript that was always on its way but seemed never to arrive.

Finally, our spouses and children have had to accommodate our preoccupations and immersions in this venture. We love them for those and other reasons and, as small thanks, we dedicate this book to them.

# 1

# *The Centrality*

## *of*

# *Peer Review*

A profession which seeks the truth must consider whether silence about motives and restraint in expression serve, on balance, to enhance or suppress it.

Harold Orlans (1975)

The special properties of scientific knowledge are often attributed to the special circumstances of scientific work. Good science is predicated on a self-regulating community of experts, some contend, and peer review is the mechanism of self-regulation in science. Indeed, peer review has been well institutionalized: it is strongly bound into the structure and operations of science and supported by a network of values, beliefs, and myths. Yet there is mounting evidence that peer review in the United States is not functioning well, and there is growing concern among scientists and policymakers about the soundness of the peer review system.

## What Is "Peer Review"?

The synonyms are many: peer advice, peer evaluation, peer

1

judgment, quality control, peer censorship, merit review, refereeing, and so forth. We will use "peer review" as a generic term encompassing all these, recognizing key differences between particular implementations of the idea where the need arises. Briefly defined, peer review is an organized method for evaluating scientific work which is used by scientists to certify the correctness of procedures, establish the plausibility of results, and allocate scarce resources (such as journal space, research funds, recognition, and special honor).

The practice of peer review is familiar but not benign. Scientists are well acquainted with it, frequently alternating between the roles of performer and evaluator, of defendant and juror. Peer review is not only a routine component of the scientific role, but it is also fundamental to the institution of science, defended as symbol and guarantor of the autonomy of science. Thus peer review is built so deeply into the brickwork of science that many refuse to examine and improve it, fearing that any significant change would weaken the entire edifice. In some minds, to question peer review is to question science itself, and to question science is to challenge deeply held values about progress and the prospects for society.

As we approach the final decade of the twentieth century, there are murmurings from many quarters—federal research agencies, journal editors, scientific societies, and Congress—that peer review is in need of repair or rebuilding. Perhaps it now bears far more weight than was ever intended. The burden placed on grants peer review, for example, may have become unreasonable as the importance of obtaining research support, the competition for support, and the sheer volume of proposals have increased in recent decades. Perhaps the peer review process has been pressed to serve so many distinct purposes that it serves none well. In various forms, peer review has been employed to allocate discipline-based and interdisciplinary research grants to individuals and groups (such as centers and programs), to judge the publishability of manuscripts, to award fellowships and other support to individuals, to confer honors, and, most recently, to adjudicate cases of scientific misconduct. Perhaps peer review has been overextended, applied to so many dissimilar procedures that it has lost meaning or, in what amounts to the same thing, has acquired a range of diverse meanings for diverse speakers and audiences. Some "peer groups" are composed of expert scientists, while others include leaders from outside the scientific community. In some cases these peers decide; in others, they advise or endorse.

Whatever the cause of these strains on peer review, they have the consequence of making the organizational components of science seem deficient in mutual understanding and unity of purpose. Thus the "community of science" exhibits far less solidarity than many suppose, with internal competition for resources and power rising to the surface. The attentive public then may recognize that scientific research is an uncertain process with indefinite outcomes that must be packaged skillfully to retain public commitment and the investment of federal and state funds. And with this recognition may come reluctance to invest money or moral energy in science.

Peer review simultaneously serves several values that are not entirely in harmony. As a *process*, peer review is expected to operate according to values of fairness and expediency, yet its *product* is to be trustworthy, high-quality, innovative knowledge. There is no assurance that the process will yield the product; to the contrary, the process may interfere with efforts to secure the product. Other values may intervene as well, imposed by the institutional context of science. For example, accountability and due process are bureaucratic requirements of a particular governance system that may envelope peer review. Or national needs may be asserted: in different fields of science at different times research has been supported to provide solutions to specific problems in space exploration, health, social welfare, and economic competitiveness. Finally, these values are not always clearly expressed. For example, at the same time that the federal government invests so much in basic science, it also expresses through its funding policy a preference for short-term "mission-oriented" science that serves specific public purposes.

Peer review is paradoxical: as a decision-making process within science it allocates resources, monitors ongoing work, and validates products, preserving the professional autonomy of science through apparently rigorous self-regulation. The imprimatur of peer review labels the products of science "new," "important," and "useful." But at the same time that peer review functions to preserve professional autonomy it serves as a conduit for forces in the social environment that make the profession accountable to a larger constituency. Thus peer review forms a bridge between the mysterious and esoteric content of science and the mundane world of resource allocation. As Marcel La Follette writes,

A common fiction is that science is one thing and science policy another. According to this interpretation, what scientists do to maintain the quality and reliability of scientific knowledge is independent from influence by or on science policy; only the funding (input) or the knowledge (output) can be said to interact with political values. . . . Such a position, however, represents beliefs that are not just inaccurate but naive. And this is particularly true for the peer review system.[1]

## Symbolism and Chauvinism

The symbolism of peer review is also a powerful social lubricant. It deflects criticism by asserting the autonomy and authority of science. It also makes new knowledge claims more credible to the nonscientist because those claims bear the approval of the scientific community. But peer review drives a wedge between nonscientists and the process of claims-making, for scientists jealously guard their power to accept or reject the findings of their peers. Moreover, they are implacable in sequestering this process from the public view, as the legal proceedings described in chapter 3 make clear. In this sense scientists are chauvinistic, forcefully asserting their special prerogatives to produce and evaluate new knowledge.

Such enclaves of expertise are not unusual in societies characterized by a complex division of labor. In fact, we usually delegate to experts the authority for making decisions in areas we do not understand or have not been trained to know. We trust the expert to bear our best interests in mind. We hope that if our trust is misplaced the expert's own profession will take swift and decisive corrective action on our behalf. But is this an appropriate relationship between science and a democratic society? Is it flexible enough to serve the times of rapid change in science? Is it sturdy enough for a society increasingly dependent on science?

According to Prewitt, "democratic culture" features public control and accountability instead of peer control and autonomy; public scrutiny in place of internalized standards of conduct; checks and balances and critical public opinion supplant self-regulation and self-evaluation.[2] Yet peer review intervenes in this process, at once serving as a mechanism of scientific self-regulation that preserves the autonomy of science and as a symbol of professional accountability that insures democratic control of science. Thus our decisionmakers frequently use

peer review as an indicator of the quality and reliability of published information. On the strength of that stamp of legitimacy, policy-makers use scientific information to support decision-making—in regulation, in funding decisions, in promotion or tenure cases.[3]

These symbolic uses of peer review reinforce scientists' chauvinism and increase the distance between science and society. As experts pass judgment on one another's ideas, guided by disciplinary criteria of importance and quality, the intrinsic "rightness" of peer review is sustained and the self-assurance of professional self-regulation verges on self-deception. Alternative allocation mechanisms are viewed as threats to the autonomy of the profession and the integrity of its products. In this sense, peer review is the flywheel of science, lending stability to an enterprise that is buffeted by shifting external demands, variable resources, and strong competitive pressures.

In a larger sense science is not an independent institution but, as research costs have grown, one that has become increasingly dependent on society for resources. At the start of every budget cycle the case for supporting science is argued, connecting scientific success with national objectives for health, economic competitiveness, defense, transportation, agriculture, and the like. On the one hand, science is firmly in service of other societal goals, but on the other it systematically denies this dependence. Under such circumstances is it possible to remain assured of financing the best science? And can peer review, at the center of the profession's claim to autonomy and the society's demand for accountability, continue to serve as a mechanism of allocation and control?

Peer review is the focus of tensions between science and other social institutions.[4] When the public doubts science or resents the risks created by science, it is the process of peer review that is called into question. Scientists invoke peer review in their own defense. The media and the Congress scrutinize and investigate it. Peer review is often under siege and yet, remarkably, while the peer review *system* may absorb severe damage, the peer review *concept* emerges with renewed support from all parties. When the disputatious moment has passed, the system returns to business as usual.

This book will argue that U.S. science cannot afford to conduct "business as usual." To do so would yield an ordinary science guided by safe policies financed in unexceptional ways—hardly the prescription for the research excellence or the economic "competitiveness" so vigorously sought by national policymakers. The complacency of U.S. science, we contend, is revealed in the methods through which it disburses its scarce resources and in the idiosyncratic way it defends those methods.

U.S. science has generally been decentralized, despite early and recurring proposals to create a single organizational home for all basic research. Unlike their European counterparts, U.S. scientists both benefit and suffer from the competition and opportunity afforded by multiple funding sources, each with its own rules and strategies for research success. But as growth in the national science budget is pinched by fiscal constraints, and as other nations attain prominence in areas of scientific research once viewed as our private preserve, U.S. scientists and science policymakers ask again: Who gets supported and who does not? How do we evaluate research productivity? How do we recognize and reward quality? These are old questions that require new perspectives, new thoughts, new criteria; perhaps new answers will follow.

## Approach to a Dialogue

Does this mean we advocate dismantling the systems that administer "grants peer review?" No, but we are certain that those systems can and must be made more responsive, and less cumbersome, burdensome, and risk-averse. Do we doubt the efficacy of "journal peer review?" At times we do. Scholarly journals serve a variety of purposes: insuring the accuracy of results, providing rapid communication of new findings, disseminating new knowledge to a wide audience, and informing public policy, among others. It is unlikely that a single review mechanism would serve every purpose and every audience equally well.

We are also populists at heart. Demystify what professionals do and the public can understand and participate intelligently in decisions that affect the common good. People need not understand the minutiae of space science, particle physics, or human molecular genetics to participate responsibly in public debate about the relative merits of these high-ticket science initiatives.

Instead, people must understand the basic prospects and purposes of these areas of research. They also must become "science-literate"—knowledgeable about how modern science operates as a social enterprise, including awareness of life in the laboratory, the career patterns of scientists, the role of instruments in research, the institutional processes that favor funding one sort of science over another, and the myriad uncertainties that stand between scientific research and consumer benefit.

People should be given more opportunity to learn about science as an intellectual and social enterprise and to exercise this knowledge through participation in decisions. Science must be taken down from its pedestal and placed in a social context constructed (some might say *controlled*) by journalists, politicians, and an informed, active citizenry. The call for a moratorium on recombinant DNA research in Cambridge, Massachusetts, and the community responses to environmental hazards in Woburn, Massachusetts, Love Canal, New York, and in eastern Pennsylvania, near the Three Mile Island nuclear power plant, are examples of these groups' power when they choose to exercise it. But why must public participation be born of crisis? Is it possible willingly to recognize the public as a legitimate stakeholder in such matters?[5] We view these not as romantic or radical notions but as prerequisites for a healthy participatory democracy.

In the following chapters we will probe the relationship of peer review to science, policy, funding, publishing, and democratic principles in the United States. We have chosen to place ourselves intrusively in the narrative: separating the third-person analyst from the first-person actor is a chore hardly worth doing any more. It is artificial and incomplete; it shrouds analysis in jargon and the protentions of "value-neutral" discourse, yet provides no assurance of value neutrality. Some even say that the appearance of value neutrality provides a convenient cloak for partisanship.

In our view, if one rejects the proposition that there is a single, objective, definitive account of an issue, then one must be prepared to entertain multiple and sometimes competing accounts.[6] This is not as radical as it may first appear, for one must always ask why one account prevails over the others. In effect, this is the day-to-day work of policy analysts and policymakers, who must sort and evaluate competing accounts and then act, often with unwarranted decisiveness, in the face of uncertainty. Our approach thus recognizes that analysts, policymakers, and scientists inhabit different cultures and view the world through culturally determined perspectives.

## Five Axioms about the Culture of Science

The perspective on science that underlies the argument we shall present is grounded in the social studies of science literature. To avoid a lengthy review of that research and its relationship to other views of science, we shall instead present its essential principles as a set of five axioms.[7]

1.  Scientific research is a social act. It is not a solitary struggle between "nature" and the human mind, as accounts of the heroic scientist would lead us to believe, but instead entails relations within a community of scientists and a community of minds seeking recognition and consensus.

2.  Science is done in a nested set of contexts—countries, cultures, disciplines, organizations, laboratories, and so forth—and characteristics of the contexts shape the direction and content of scientific work.

3.  Scientific work is performed by individuals whose efforts are influenced by culture, specialized training, diverse motivations, varied intellectual skills and interests, values, biases, and prejudices. Science is not performed by white coats in an asceptic environment—a sort of intellectual clean room—free of human society and human failings. To the contrary, it is an intensely human and social activity, and bears the marks of its context and performers.

4.  In the process of doing research, scientists do not merely operate on reality, they *construct* it, trying to persuade others to accept these constructions.

5.  Science can be seen as the product of multiple realities, only one of which is generally accepted at a given time among a particular community of researchers. (In those rare instances where competing constructions are held by competing communities of scientists, memorable controversies erupt.) The prevalence of a certain socially constructed reality is called "consensus," "authority," "knowledge," or perhaps even "nature" or "truth." Thus scientific truths are, at bottom, widely accepted social agreements about what is "real," arrived at through a distinctively "scientific" process of negotiation.

## The Policy Context

Throughout the history of institutionalized science, which began in the seventeenth century, the concept of peer evaluation has been invoked by the scientific community as a mechanism of quality control.[8] In practice, peer review is presumed to distinguish inferior, misguided, flawed, or bogus research reports or proposals from sound, innovative, meritorious ideas. But this is hotly disputed by at least some vocal scientists. Fragmented as the scientific community may be, most of its members are likely to agree that peer review serves three functions: (1) insuring that scientists are accountable for the public funds they receive; (2) preserving the professional autonomy of the scientific community; and (3) certifying the soundness of new developments in science and technology.[9]

Today the social mechanisms that authorize and channel peer review (as it is practiced in federal agencies, universities, or journals) are shaped as much by considerations of public policy as by the technical criteria of the scientific community. The importance of policy considerations is openly acknowledged in many ways. For example, an NSF advisory committee coined the term "merit review" to recognize that "technical excellence is a necessary but not fully sufficient criterion for research funding. To reach such goals as increasing the practical relevance of research results, or improving the nation's infrastructure for science and engineering, additional criteria are needed."[10] Or consider the two-stage review process at NIH, which begins with an assessment of scientific merit by an Initial Review Group of scientists (also called a Study Section, described in the next chapter), then proceeds to a level of programmatic and policy review by a National Advisory Council (which includes nonscientists). In practice the second level of review typically makes awards in line with the technical ratings, with only a small proportion of proposals funded "out of order" (or "specialed"). Nonetheless, the National Advisory Councils have the authority to act more independently if they choose.

Such criteria of utility make great sense in these pragmatic times, but they reflect a sharp change from the original "contract" between science and society envisioned by Vannevar Bush in 1945. In an oft-quoted passage, Bush asserted that

> Scientific progress on a broad front results from the free play of free intellects, working on subjects of their own choice, in the manner dictated by their curiosity for the exploration of the unknown.[11]

Bush thought that colleges, universities, and research institutes were

> uniquely qualified by tradition and by their special characteristics to carry on basic research ... [because these institu-

tions offer scientists] . . . an atmosphere which is relatively free from the adverse pressure of convention, prejudice, or commercial necessity. At their best they provide the scientific worker with a strong sense of solidarity and security, as well as a substantial degree of personal intellectual freedom. All of these factors are of great importance in the development of new knowledge, since much of new knowledge is certain to arouse opposition because of its tendency to challenge current beliefs or practices.[12]

Perhaps times have changed, or perhaps free intellects were never so freely at play in well-funded laboratories. However that may be, today's free intellects do not play freely, but instead find themselves tethered to national goals for health, defense, economic competitiveness, and the like. Colleges, universities, and research institutes have come to depend on federal research support, a dependence that is transmitted (and perhaps amplified along the way) to the scientists and scholars they employ, further limiting intellectual "free play." New ideas must pass through the filter of peer review, which stimulates opposition and encourages applicants to be cautious, if not conservative, in their proposals.

Thus peer review is a chimera, a powerful and somewhat frightening creature composed of incongruous parts, that affords scientists both freedom and accountability, simultaneously insulating them from social pressures and expressing those very pressures. As a tool of public policy, peer review justifies the flow of public funds and the establishment of collective priorities:

In the long-standing relationship between government and science in the United States, major responsibility for funding basic scientific research has settled upon the government partner. For its part, the scientific community has accepted primary responsibility for defining research needs and opportunities and providing assurance that public funds are allocated on a priority basis, through peer review. For either partner to breach its responsibility carries serious risk to the solidarity of what has proved an extraordinarily effective partnership.[13]

But breaches do occur, precisely because peer review is burdened with inconsistent responsibilities. And when they do, the ambivalent rhetoric of scientists and nonscientists alike clouds our understanding of peer review practices. Commentators are torn by their ambivalence, simultaneously supporting and criticizing the peer review system. Advocates invoke peer review to defend the scientific integrity of policy decisions:

> The genius of the approach of the National Institutes of Health and the National Science Foundation to federal research is that awards are based on merit and that proposals are given fair consideration by acknowledged peers in the field.[14]

Or consider the Food Safety Modernization Act of 1983, which provides that

> the Secretary shall by regulation establish procedures for receiving advice from a scientifically qualified staff of individuals ... in cases in which the Secretary determines with respect to the safety of a substance in food that there is a substantial scientific issue the resolution of which may be materially facilitated by independent scientific peer review.[15]

But others are less sanguine, questioning whether "good" and "bad" science can be distinguished, whether science and values can be separated in the course of public decision-making, whether peers can be identified for most scientific work, and whether gatekeepers exercise good faith in their use of peer review. Some critics claim that peer-reviewed decisions are based mainly on an ideology which protects the "old boy network" from scrutiny by peers.[16] In many cases these reviews are merely input to decisions that are made behind closed doors.

Some commentators propose that different funding mechanisms are suited to different types of science. Harvey Brooks contends that peer review may be helpful in selecting research designed to discover "truths" about nature but is ill suited to make judgments about the utility of research.[17] Deborah Shapley and Rustum Roy assert that our society's dependence on peer review, which has endured for thirty years, resulted from a combination of arrogance, inertia, and fear. A generation of scientists has experienced no other means of obtaining research funding and thus feel their careers at risk whenever questions about peer review are raised.[18] Shapley and Roy's observations demand careful consideration. Perhaps their claim that grants peer review is not working seems harsh because for many the rituals of peer review are taken as axiomatic, habitual, and beyond debate. Yet this degree of uncritical commitment to peer review resembles the mystique that surrounds a sacred ritual or icon and prevents believers from examining it analytically. As Shapley and Roy explain:

> The term "peer review" in the context of science policy has acquired a deep symbolism within the science community. It is repeated like a mantra or used as a talisman to shield any activity, put it above reproach, so to speak.[19]

They go on to recite the litany of peer review's evils: it is a ritual that impedes good science, wastes time, and diffuses responsibility; it is doomed to fail because "peers" cannot be identified and, if identified, have conflicts of interest that hopelessly bias their judgments; it sometimes depends on judgments about work not yet performed, ignoring the important roles of chance and serendipity and giving free rein to conservatism and groupthink; it is demoralizing.[20]

Finally, some commentators are critical *and* supportive of peer review in the same breath. Early in the course of a scathing article about peer review one scientist writes:

> I can scarcely find words to describe such a questionable, dastardly, and potentially libelous process. The issue before us is not peer review. The issue is one particular system of peer review applied to that tiny promissory segment of a scientist's portfolio called "the proposal," with a heavy-handed impact that can cripple his morale and career. . . . we must have a system in which human frailties and their evil consequences are checked more closely. . . . We must now strive for superior application of the noble principle of peer review.[21]

Sociologists have heard all this before. The problem, according to the scientist quoted above, lies not in our systems but in ourselves. Yet sociologists are trained to be skeptical of analyses that center on the "evil consequences" of "human frailties," particularly analyses that call for a powerful system to remedy matters. Rather than lament human frailties, let us examine social systems.

## Studying Grants Peer Review

Evidence is sorely lacking on peer review practices, largely because the reviews themselves, which reside in the files of journals and funding agencies, were obtained under assurances of strict confidentiality and are not readily available for analysis. Studies of grants peer review at NIH and NSF have generally concluded that peer review operates fairly to identify and support the best science.[22] This result, however, is easy to anticipate, and much that matters has been obscured or ignored in the studies cited above. In a commentary on such research, Arie Rip observes that "because everybody [involved in the science funding system] is so concerned about fairness, the system will be reasonably fair, and the studies commissioned to check its fairness will come up with results showing just that."[23] And Roy points out that the form of peer review varies as much across programs within an agency as it does across agencies. Most programs use "*ad hoc* mail reviewers"; some use those reviews as data for panels that undertake a second level of review; still others confine decision-making to program managers and a few in-house agency advisors. Thus the peer review system is more accurately viewed as a family of closely related procedures that have some similarities and marked differences.[24]

Other studies have discerned in grants peer review an unmistakable bias toward conservatism in the name of quality control.[25] Reviewers' tolerance for innovativeness is bounded: unorthodox ideas and techniques are more welcome from those with impressive credentials, such as a prestigious academic background and an extensive track record. But sometimes established scientists who reach beyond "conventional wisdom" or propose to work outside their areas of acknowledged competence are rebuffed (for example, Luis Alvarez, Richard Muller, and Albert Szent-Gyorgi).

The inherent difficulties of grants peer review have been exacerbated in recent years by budget constraints and by the further bureaucratization of science.[26] Some fear the "incipient dismantling of the peer review system" brought about by research fraud, university lobbying for "pork-barrel" grants, disputes over intellectual property, and increased secrecy in scientific research.[27] These phenomena, discussed at greater length in chapter 5, remind us that peer review is neither a scientific procedure insulated from environmental conditions nor a mysterious rite shrouded in secrecy and ceremony. It is instead a social and political process that turns on issues of privacy, efficiency, safety, and fairness.

Despite the problems enumerated above, few alternatives to current procedures or criteria for grants peer review have been advanced. When they are, they inevitably become entangled in value conflicts: for example, processing submissions more efficiently versus choosing more carefully; continuing established investigations versus promoting promising but risky new work.[28] Suffice it to say here that an innovation such as formula funding might streamline the review process, but it would operate chiefly by narrowing the field of scientists eligible for such awards. Considering the array of difficulties that confound peer evaluations of proposals and manuscripts, the most likely outcome of formula funding is to increase the magnitude of errors by increasing the magnitude of the "prize" awarded by the process and decreasing the number of awards made and competitors allowed to participate.

In the absence of data, how does one examine these criticisms? How does one argue that block grants to labs and centers, set-asides based on track record alone, or lengthening of the standard funding period from three to five years will give us better research or less bureaucratized science? How does one overthrow the oppressive burden of tradition—the arrogance, inertia, and fear noted above—and begin to address the more fundamental questions about the fit between science and society raised by Prewitt and by LaFollette? Richard Atkinson and William Blanpied pose these larger issues precisely:

> Should peer review operate only to evaluate merit or should it also help establish priorities? Can it or should it be effective in changing the direction of a program, in allocating resources among programs within agencies themselves? These questions are significant because they challenge the assumption that peer review is the best possible way to allocate resources in the best overall interests of both science and society.[29]

### Summary: A Study of Policy and Practice

This book could be read as substantiating and articulating the challenge to the assumption that peer review is the best way to allocate resources and express diverse interests. It is also a manifestation of the continuing tension between science and other social institutions over matters of resources, quality, and the direction of scientific work. To quote Atkinson and Blanpied again:

> The assumption that research is a sacrosanct activity that government must continue to support adequately has lulled much of the scientific community into a state of political apathy and has allowed government to treat science as if it were, in fact, just another special interest.[30]

There is a role for social and policy scientists in jarring the apathy out of scientists, a need for research on scientific rituals, and an imperative to translate professional practice into terms amenable to social intelligence and science policy. While peer review remains a concern in Washington, initiatives to "study" and "fine-tune" the system need not emanate solely from the National Science Foundation, the National Academy of Sciences, and the Congress.[31] Indeed, we intend to inform such initiatives by offering new perspectives on peer review as a form of professional self-governance. We wish to contribute to the ongoing dialogue about peer review and, more ambitiously, to help shape an action agenda that clarifies the multiple meanings of peer review and leads to changes in its practice.

# 2

## *Peer Review*

### *in*

## *Theory and Practice*

Science policy is turning out to be rather more difficult than science itself. Some of the difficulties may be arising because we are not sufficiently aware of the influence of science policy on the way research is done.

John Ziman, 1983

In the Spring of 1975, the Acting Director of the National Institutes of Health (NIH) established the NIH Grants Peer Review Study Team. This group, composed largely of NIH staffers, was charged to "conduct a detailed and comprehensive study of the NIH peer review system" and to "examine in critical detail the entire process of peer review."[1] The team issued a three-volume Phase I report in December 1976.

As is the practice in such reports, the front matter of the first volume included a "Summary of Conclusions and Recommendations." The first conclusion offered is that "the NIH grants peer review system is and has been extremely effective in identifying

biomedical research activities of high quality." The reader is re-
ferred to page 4 of the report for further discussion of this important conclusion.

On page 4 one learns that

> the Study Team *feels* that peer review exercises the single
> most powerful influence on the continued high quality of the
> Nation's biomedical research effort. . . .
> Furthermore, the Study Team *believes* that confidence in the
> system is justified and has evolved primarily from the stead-
> fast position maintained by NIH that it is, first and foremost,
> the high scientific quality of the supported research, *as de-
> fined by the peer review system,* which should govern the na-
> tional biomedical research effort. . . .
> The Study Team further *believes* that the NIH research pro-
> grams constitute a critical national resource, and that the
> quality of this resource has been successfully *defined* in the
> public interest by the unique administrative device of the
> peer review system.[2]

Notice that the team "feels" and "believes" things about the
peer review system; it does not "demonstrate" or "support" them.
That is, the language used to discuss the peer review system in
"critical detail" is not the disinterested language of analysis, inference, and proof, but is the language of persuasion, emotion, and
conviction. Notice also that the *conclusion* that peer review identi-
fies high quality science is based, tautologically, on quality "as defined by the peer review system." By that self-referential standard
peer review could hardly fail to promote high quality research; nor
could any other selection mechanism judged by its own standards.

A decade later, Rustum Roy asserted that "even without systematically analyzed comparative data, the failure of review by
peers as a way of deciding which projects and which scientists
should receive grants seem to be very evident."[3] In fact, the failures of peer review were so evident to Roy that he presented no
evidence whatsoever in support of his remarks. Thus, this criticism of the peer review system is no more firmly based on empirical evidence or logical analysis than was the NIH team's
impassioned affirmation. One may agree with one or another position for anecdotal, philosophical, or rhetorical reasons, but no
compelling evidence has been generated to fortify either viewpoint.

Some judgments of peer review fall between these extremes, acknowledging the system's weaknesses while pledging continued commitment to peer review as the best allocative mechanism. For example, the NSF Advisory Committee on Merit Review, in the first paragraph of its Final Report, offers this overall assessment of peer review:

> Technical (peer) review is a cornerstone of Federal agency arrangements for research project selection. The Committee found that by and large the system is functioning well. No evidence was found that standards of technical excellence were being compromised in the review processes of the various Federal agencies, including the National Science Foundation, although improvements are possible and desirable.[4]

Or, more briefly stated in the words of Eugene Garfield, "in spite of all the complaints and all the faults hinted at, peer review is still considered the best method by which society places its bets on the most fruitful research."[5]

What is this system of evaluating research proposals that elicits such diverse and powerful reactions from commentators and committees alike? Where did it come from and how does it work? What do we know about it, what do scientists think about it, and what should we as informed citizens ask about it and of it? These are among the questions that will concern us in this chapter.

## PEER REVIEW: ORIGINS AND CURRENT PRACTICES

The practice of peer review originated with the founding of the *Philosophical Transactions* of the Royal Society in 1665. In authorizing its publication, the council of the Royal Society directed that the *"Philosophical Transactions* . . . be licensed under the charter of the Council of the Society, being first reviewed by some members of the same."[6] Thus was born the gatekeeping function of scientists' passing judgment on the quality of other scientists' work. Over the centuries this practice has evolved into the system of journal refereeing, the topic of chapter 4, and has branched into the proposal peer review system, our present concern.

Peer review was established as a mechanism for the allocation of research support in the U.S. during the 1940s and 1950s, as the current science bureaucracy was conceived, took its present shape, and grew. Peer review of proposals in the federal govern-

ment is generally thought to have begun with the establishment of
the National Advisory Cancer Council in 1937, which "was autho-
rized to review applications for research funding and to certify approval to the Surgeon General for projects that had the potential
of significantly contributing to knowledge about cancer."[7] This
council undertook the review of applications that was mandated
by statute as a precondition for research support from the National Cancer Institute, and it became the model for the National
Advisory Councils which today must approve NIH funding decisions.

In the late 1940s another variant of peer review began as an
informal practice at the Office of Naval Research.[8] A grants manager, having full authority to make a decision on his own, might
choose to send a copy of a proposal to a colleague for a second opinion. The practice may have been transferred from the Office of Naval Research to the National Science Foundation by Alan T.
Waterman, the first director of NSF.[9] Importantly, there is no
mention of peer review in the statutory authority for the NSF, although, in the words of J. Merton England, "no doubt everyone understood that there would be some sort of peer review."[10] These
differences in the origins of the two main types of grants peer review have persisted to the present. Peer review at NIH is a formal,
well-specified mechanism, whereas at NSF, while there is strong
commitment to the concept of peer review, the process has taken a
variety of forms.

## Peer Review at the National Institutes of Health

NIH peer review occurs in two stages. The first stage is performed by an Initial Review Group (IRG) of fourteen to twenty
nongovernmental scientists (sometimes called a "Study Section")
who have "national stature in a particular discipline" and who
"constitute the true scientific peers of the person submitting research grant applications." Approximately 2,300 scientists serve
on IRGs at any one time, each with a term of about four years.[11]
IRG members read the proposals in advance, then meet to discuss
and evaluate them.

At the meeting, each research grant application is presented
and discussed individually, in detail, by particular assigned
reviewers, after which there is general discussion leading
eventually to the development of a consensus. Each application is assessed for such factors as: the objectives of the re-

search; the research protocol; the capabilities of the investigator and his or her associates; the research environment; the probability of success; the appropriateness of the budget to the tasks described; and the scientific significance of the proposed research.[12]

The IRG decides by majority vote whether to approve, disapprove, or defer action on each grant application. Disapproved applications cannot receive support; deferred applications are returned to the investigator for more information. (In practice, the vast majority of applications are approved: in 1985, over 90 percent of all project [or "R01"] proposals submitted to NIH were approved.) For each approved application, members privately assign a priority score ranging from 1.0 (excellent) to 5.0 (poor). These individual scores are then averaged to represent the IRG's collective recommendation about a grant application, and the application, along with the IRG's critique, recommendation (approved, disapproved, deferred), and priority score (for approved applications) are forwarded to the National Advisory Council for a second stage of review.

Whereas IRGs are constructed to represent fields of science (or created ad hoc under special circumstances to review a particular class of proposals), each Institute is required, by legislation, to have a single National Advisory Council composed of twelve or more members drawn from both the scientific and lay communities. While IRGs are supposed to represent the interests of "science" and scientists, National Advisory Councils purportedly bring broader concerns of public health and national policy to bear on the decision process. In the words of one NIH official:

> The Council's responsibility is to review the appropriateness of the initial review [by the IRG] and to make final recommendations, in addition, related to program relevance and significance of the scientific endeavor and the priority of that research in relationship to the Institute's overall mission. By means of this dual system, there is a mandatory separation, therefore, of the assessment of projects purely regarding merit from the subsequent policy recommendations as to the scientific areas of importance in which projects will be awarded and the level of resources to be allocated to those areas.[13]

In effect, this is a modest system of checks and balances: an Institute may not award a research grant without Advisory Council approval, and an Advisory Council may not approve an application that has not first been approved by an IRG. In theory, then, a grant application must meet both scientific and programmatic criteria before it is supported.

In practice, however, the character and contribution of the second level of review is less clear. Grace Carter points out that while "Advisory Councils influence the policy decisions such as program funding levels, they only rarely make decisions at the individual grant level. A General Accounting Office study (1980) of four institutes showed that the Advisory Councils changed the priority ranking of less than one percent of 1978 applications."[14] It must be understood that the Advisory Councils' actions are recommendations, not directives. Institute Directors make the final decisions for the award of grants that have "survived" the IRGs' and Advisory Councils' reviews because "there are never enough funds to support all the recommendations of the Advisory Councils."[15] Moreover, administrators "are not bound by law to follow the priority order of applications recommended for approval by Advisory Councils, but in practice they do so with only few exceptions."[16]

Thus the NIH awards process is hardly one of "dual review," for the second stage rarely considers the merits of individual proposals (or, if they do so, their consideration makes essentially no difference in the final rankings). Rather, it is a decision system characterized by veto power vested at three levels, with substantial free play built into the IRG, Advisory Council, and administrative award levels. This does not imply that the system necessarily makes bad allocation decisions, but it does imply that the intrinsic "goodness" of the "dual review" mechanism, in itself, is not sufficient to guarantee good decisions. The quality of the decisions is an empirical issue that cannot be determined from the allocation mechanism alone.

## Peer Review at the National Science Foundation

As many have remarked, peer review at the National Science Foundation is not one system but many variants on a theme, each customized to suit the type of award (e.g., an individual project grant, a center grant, or support for an interdisciplinary center), the field of science or engineering, the preferences and proclivities of NSF staff and their client scientists, and the tradition-based expectations of all parties concerned.[17]

There are two main varieties of peer review at NSF: ad hoc mail reviews and panel reviews (often supplemented by ad hoc mail reviews). In the physical and mathematical sciences, individual project grants are usually evaluated by as many as ten ad hoc mail reviews, solicited from a " 'custom' set of reviewers for each proposal to provide a balanced view of the various aspects of the work."[18] These reviews are advisory to the responsible program officer, who "writes analyses of the reviews, and relates them to his recommendation to the Division Director."[19]

Mail reviews follow an established format, which includes instructions about the program's objectives, a review form with explicit criteria for evaluation, and five-point rating scales for summary evaluations. A recent copy of the NSF's "Information for Reviewers" is reproduced as figure 1. It makes explicit the criteria to be used, the substantive meaning of the summary ratings, and the conflict of interest and confidentiality policies. Notice that investigator's competence, the intrinsic merit of research, and utility are the primary criteria, although no precise weight is given them. The consequences for scientific infrastructure are given a secondary place in the ratings scheme. While all four criteria are presented to the reviewer, the review form itself does not give structure to the reviewer's comments—it simply provides a large blank space with five check off boxes for summary ratings.

In contrast to this mail-only format, decisions in the biological, behavioral, and social sciences are usually based on the advice of a standing panel of scientists, analogous to an IRG in the NIH system, whose expertise is supplemented by a set of about five or six mail reviews. Panels allow differences of opinion to be aired (and perhaps resolved), and they have the potential of producing more balanced and innovative perspectives on the proposed research. However, panels are also subject to the vagaries of group dynamics, including dominance by forceful personalities, "groupthink," bandwagon effects, and the like.[20]

Variations on these main methods of review and alternatives to them—such as an ad hoc panel—may be employed in special circumstances.[21] Through all of these mechanisms, in fiscal year 1985 NSF asked nearly 60,000 people to participate in its review processes.[22] However this peer input is solicited, in all cases the recommendation to fund a proposal is made by the responsible program officer, who takes into consideration the review ratings and comments, his or her own judgment of scientific merit, and other factors (such as researcher characteristics, riskiness of the

**NATIONAL SCIENCE FOUNDATION**
**INFORMATION FOR REVIEWERS**

In meeting its statutory responsibilities, the National Science Foundation seeks to support the most meritorious research, whether basic or applied. Mail reviews play a key role in the National Science Foundation's evaluation of the merit of research proposals. Please provide both written comments and a summary rating on this Proposal Evaluation Form using the criteria provided below.

**PROPOSAL EVALUATION CRITERIA**

1. *Research performance competence*—Capability of the investigator(s), the technical soundness of the proposed approach, and the adequacy of the institutional resources available. Please include comments on the proposer's recent research performance.

2. *Intrinsic merit of the research*—Likelihood that the research will lead to new discoveries or fundamental advances within its field of science or engineering, or have substantial impact on progress in that field or in other scientific and engineering fields.

3. *Utility or relevance of the research*—Likelihood that the research can contribute to the achievement of a goal that is extrinsic or in addition to that of the research field itself, and thereby serve as the basis for new or improved technology or assist in the solution of societal problems.

4. *Effect of the research on the infrastructure of science and engineering*—Potential of the proposed research to contribute to better understanding or improvement of the quality, distribution, or effectiveness of the Nation's scientific and engineering research, education, and human resources base.

Criteria 1, 2, and 3 constitute an integral set that should be applied in a balanced way to all research proposals in accordance with the objectives and content of each proposal. Criterion 1, research performance competence, is essential to the evaluation of the quality of every research proposal; all three aspects should be addressed. The relative weight given Criteria 2 and 3 depends on the nature of the proposed research: Criterion 2, intrinsic merit, is emphasized in the evaluation of basic research proposals, while Criterion 3, utility or relevance, is emphasized in the evaluation of applied research proposals. Criterion 4, effect on the infrastructure of science and engineering, permits the evaluation of research proposals in terms of their potential for improving the scientific and engineering enterprise and its educational activities in ways other than those encompassed by the first three criteria.

**SUMMARY RATINGS**

*Excellent:* Probably will fall among top 10% of proposals in this subfield; highest priority for support. This category should be used only for truly outstanding proposals.

*Very Good:* Probably will fall among *top 1/3* of proposals in this subfield; should be supported.

*Good:* Probably will fall among *middle 1/3* of proposals in this subfield; worthy of support.

*Fair:* Probably will fall among *lowest 1/3* of proposals in this subfield.

*Poor:* Proposal has serious deficiencies; should not be supported.

**CONFLICT OF INTERESTS**

If you have an affiliation or financial connection with the institution or the person submitting this proposal that might be construed as creating a conflict of interests, please describe those affiliations or interests on a separate page and attach it to your review. Regardless of any such affiliations or interests, unless you believe you cannot be objective, we would like to have your review. If you do not attach a statement we shall assume that you have no conflicting affiliations or interests.

**CONFIDENTIALITY OF PROPOSALS AND PEER REVIEWS**

The Foundation receives proposals in confidence and is responsible for protecting the confidentiality of their contents. For this reason, please do not copy, quote, or otherwise use material from this proposal. If you believe that a colleague can make a substantial contribution to the review, please consult the NSF Program Officer before disclosing either the contents of the proposal or the applicant's name. When you have completed your review, please destroy the proposal.

It is the policy of the Foundation that reviews will not be disclosed to persons outside the Government, except that verbatim copies without the name and affiliation of the reviewer will be sent to the principal investigator. The Foundation considers reviews to be exempt from disclosure under the Freedom of Information Act (5 USC 552) but cannot guarantee that it will not be forced to release reviews under FOIA or other laws.

**Figure 1**

research, and the level of research activity at the applicant's organization). Before an official decision is made, the program officer's recommendation is reviewed at the section and/or division level, or, for especially large awards, by the National Science Board.[23]

## Trends in Proposal Volume and Award Rates

A proposal for an individual research project has about a one-in-three chance of receiving support at NIH or NSF. In fiscal year 1985, NIH made decisions on 15,496 individual project proposals (R01s in the NIH coding scheme), of which thirty-two percent received support, fifty-nine percent were approved but not funded, and nine percent were disapproved.[24] At NSF in the same fiscal year, action was taken on 24,403 proposals: thirty-three percent awarded, sixty-four percent declined, and four percent withdrawn (often because the proposal had been supported by another agency).[25] As problematic as odds of two to one against may be, there are even stronger reasons for concern about scientists' prospects for research support which are revealed when changes over time and results for smaller areas of science are examined.

Table 1 shows the outcomes for new and competing renewal proposals submitted to NIH for selected years since 1965. The two strongest trends are that the number of proposals has increased, nearly doubling over the twenty-year period, and that the proportion of disapproved proposals has declined steadily and substantially in the period. The increasing number of proposals reflects several trends, including growth in the number of scientists, greater research activity, resubmission of declined applications, and the increased importance of funding for research and for student support. The declining proportion of disapproved applications may result from changes in the review standards of scientists combined with real improvements in the quality of proposals.

The probability that a proposal will be supported does not show any clear trend over time. Although roughly half of all proposals were funded in 1965, this dropped to thirty-three percent by 1970 and, with some fluctuations, is currently at about that level. In all years, applications for renewal of an ongoing project are roughly twice as likely to succeed as are applications to start a new project. One consequence of the low funding rate is that amended applications—revisions of proposals that had been declined once or more—have become a substantial and growing fraction of total submissions at NIH. In 1975, amended applications were fourteen percent of the total; by 1985 they had become nearly twenty-five percent of the total.[26]

Looking beyond such aggregate probabilities of success, some areas of science and engineering have much better funding prospects than others. For example, while the NSF-wide success rate in fiscal year 1985 was thirty-six percent, certain divisions funded

**Table 1**

NIH Funding Outcome by Year and Type of Proposal, Selected
Years 1965–1985

| Year | Funded | Approved/ not funded | Disapproved | Total # of Proposals |
|------|--------|----------------------|-------------|----------------------|
| | | NEW APPLICATIONS | | |
| 1965 | 39.6% | 13.8% | 46.7% | 5444 |
| 1970 | 23.7 | 33.8 | 42.6 | 4717 |
| 1975 | 37.1 | 31.8 | 31.1 | 6988 |
| 1980 | 25.4 | 48.8 | 25.8 | 9858 |
| 1982 | 21.1 | 58.8 | 20.1 | 10473 |
| 1985 | 24.0 | 64.6 | 11.4 | 11037 |
| | | COMPETING RENEWAL APPLICATIONS | | |
| 1965 | 70.0% | 10.2% | 19.7% | 2686 |
| 1970 | 49.2 | 33.1 | 17.7 | 2676 |
| 1975 | 63.4 | 26.0 | 10.6 | 2659 |
| 1980 | 54.7 | 38.6 | 6.6 | 3206 |
| 1982 | 45.5 | 50.5 | 4.0 | 4687 |
| 1985 | 53.1 | 45.1 | 1.8 | 4459 |
| | | ALL APPLICATIONS | | |
| 1965 | 49.6% | 12.6% | 37.8% | 8130 |
| 1970 | 32.9 | 33.5 | 33.6 | 7393 |
| 1975 | 44.4 | 30.2 | 25.4 | 9647 |
| 1980 | 32.6 | 46.3 | 21.1 | 13064 |
| 1982 | 28.6 | 56.2 | 15.1 | 15160 |
| 1985 | 32.4 | 59.0 | 8.6 | 15496 |

Source: Computed from NIH Peer Review Trends, 1988, p. 15.
Note: Award rates are somewhat inflated for the years 1970 through 1985 because
amended applications—those resubmitted after an unfavorable decision—replace
the original application if they are submitted in the same fiscal year.

less than thirty percent of the proposals they acted on (e.g., Mechanics, Structures, and Materials Engineering; Cellular Biosciences; Behavioral and Neural Sciences) while at other divisions
more than sixty percent of all decisions were favorable (e.g., Astro-
nomical Sciences, Atmospheric Sciences, and Physics).[27] Perhaps
even more important for scientists are the success rates for spe-

cific programs within divisions. In fiscal year 1981, for example, the success rates in the Social and Developmental Psychology Program and the Cellular Biosciences Program were seventeen percent and eighteen percent, respectively; by 1985 those rates had risen only slightly, to twenty percent and twenty-four percent.[28]

If the success rate in these programs becomes much lower we may approach an absurd state first imagined by Leo Szilard (in 1961!). He reasoned that, if it takes roughly a month to prepare a proposal, then when the award rate declines to about 10% scientists would have to write proposals full-time in order to remain supported. Of course, this would leave no time for such "peripheral" activities as teaching, writing articles, mentoring students, or doing research. In some areas of science, funding rates are uncomfortably close to the "Szilard point." And Szilard did not anticipate several distinctive features of contemporary science that reinforce the trends he saw at work, intensify their effects, and bring the Szilard point ever closer. For example, proposal writing is only one component of the peer-review burden: proposals beget reviews, panel meetings, and administrative actions within the funding agency. These take time. And today federally-funded research requires a substantial amount of paperwork to insure fair hiring, ethical treatment of human and animal subjects, proper handling and disposal of hazardous materials, and adequate accounting for research expenditures. In many senses an hour or a dollar spent on research doesn't go as far as it once did, so science may be uncomfortably close to gridlock.

Competition for NIH and NSF research support is intense, and while it is difficult to argue from these data that competition has become more severe than before, one certainly cannot argue that competition has lessened. (If other matters are considered, such as the "buying power" of a research grant when compared with the cost of research, faculty salaries, student support, reporting requirements, and the like, it may be fair to say that scientists now work harder than before to sustain a given level of research.) Funding competition is much greater in some areas of science than in others, and an area may experience changes in its funding rate over time. Taken together, these conditions for research support are well suited to cause distress among applicants; after all, disappointment is the most common consequence of an application for support. Generally high ratings of proposals, and high approval rates at NIH, coupled with differential funding rates across fields of science, exacerbate the problem. Thus it is not surprising that the peer review system has come under sharp criticism. But the intensity and diversity of criticisms, and the slim base of systematic evidence upon which they are based, are surprising indeed.

## CRITICISMS OF PEER REVIEW: MORE THAN SOUR GRAPES

The complex character of peer review is revealed clearly in the criticisms leveled against it. Administrators and politicians, on the one hand, and scientists on the other, offer contrasting complaints about the operations and results of the peer review system; these complaints derive from their distinct locations, roles, purposes and values, and reflect the different demands they make of the system. For example, James W. Symington and Thomas R. Kramer, reporting on the 1975 House Science, Research, and Technology Subcommittee hearings, summarize the Subcommittee's central concerns in these terms:

> Four interrelated questions encompass the important issues of peer review at the NSF. Does the NSF support high-quality research? Are all the people involved in the decision-making process performing the proper functions, and are they performing them well? How open and fair is the system of granting awards? Does a desirable distribution of monies result from the decision-making process?[29]

The Subcommittee found that "the NSF has indeed fostered advances in basic research over the past twenty-five years," and therefore did support much high-quality research.[30] However, "substantial changes in the operation of NSF's peer review systems have been proposed which possibly could lead to improvements in the systems' effectiveness for consistently selecting the best proposals, and in the acceptability of the systems to potential applicants, the scientific community, and Congress."[31] The Subcommittee also recommended opening up the review process as much as possible, consistent with preserving its efficacy as an evaluation tool, and urged NSF to undertake further study of peer review.

The Subcommittee's orienting questions, as posed by Symington and Kramer, blend political/administrative considerations about how the decision-making process operates and the distribution of funds that results with concerns that scientists might share about the effectiveness, openness, and fairness of peer review systems. The distinctly political/administrative themes are stated far more sharply in an Office of Management and Budget memorandum that criticizes peer review on five grounds:

1. It [peer review] takes the decision-making power out of the hands of elected officials and their appointees and puts it into the hands of people who are not accountable to the public.

2. It enables the scientific community to use public funds for its own purposes, that is, "pure" research, while ignoring the pressing needs of society that might benefit from "applied" research.

3. It discriminates against scientists working in small science departments at low-prestige universities and colleges.

4. It does not weight adequately the opinions of nonacademic scientists on the merits of proposals.

5. It fails to screen out proposals of questionable merit.[32]

Similar issues were raised, in gentler language, during hearings held by the Task Force on Science Policy of the House Committee on Science and Technology (April 8–10, 1986). Consider just a few of the questions addressed to an NIH representative by committee members:

I guess much of the discussion about project selection has been on how you best review for scientific merit. To what extent does that bring in other factors such as the cost, the relevance to technology development or institutional needs, or the geographical distribution of funds?[33]
The question from the congressional standpoint is how do you go about meeting the needs of constituency groups? For example, the legislation with regard to spinal cord injury was a simple effort to get the Institutes to spend twice as much money on spinal cord injury research. The initial response [from the Institutes] was we know how much ought to be spent and it's exactly right and we don't want you tinkering with it, which is the common response we get when we attempt to tinker.[34]

How vulnerable are they [Advisory Council members] to political pressures once they're appointed and once they're doing their review and making recommendations?[35]

In general, such comments chiefly reflect concerns about the
responsiveness of peer review to society, including removal of control from elected officials to scientists (and cronyism among the
scientific decisionmakers), diversion of support to scientific rather
than societal purposes, elitism, and ineffectiveness in solving practical problems (which may be a proxy for differences in standards
for evaluating whether a project has been effective).

In contrast to such political/administrative concerns, scientists' criticisms of peer review proceed from a different view of the
relationship between science and society and thus tend to empha-
size a different array of failings and foibles. David Baltimore, for
one, has stated the principle of *laissez rechercher* most emphatically:

I wish to argue that the traditional pact between society and
its scientists, in which the scientist is given the responsibility
for determining the direction of his work, is a necessary relationship if basic science is to be an effective endeavor. This
does not mean that society is at the mercy of science, but
rather that society, while it must determine the pace of basic
scientific innovation, should not attempt to prescribe its
directions.[36]

But Baltimore makes a sharp distinction between science and
technology:

The arguments [about self-direction] pertain to basic scientific research, not to the technological applications of science.
As we go from the fundamental to the applied, my arguments
fall away. There is every reason why technology should and
must serve specific needs. Conversely, there are many technological possibilities that ought to be restrained.[37]

Rosalyn Yalow, another Nobel laureate, explains in greater
detail the sorts of freedom a scientist "needs," contending that the
peer review system interferes with this need for freedom.

The very nature of revolutionary research makes it impossible to predict if a problem has a solution, what experiments
will lead to the solution, the timetable for its accomplish-

ment, or whether a completely unexpected finding will divert the entire effort in a new direction. Thus, there is an inherent conflict between the "Peer Review System" for research funding and the need to promote scientific revolutions.[38]

Yalow is pointing out a conflict between imposing measures to insure scientific accountability, a political/administrative concern, and the freedom that she believes is necessary to perform creative scientific research. Of course, her comment assumes that the purpose of research funding is to serve the internal needs of science, particularly by supporting (indeed, inducing) scientific revolutions.

The distinction between basic research and technology, so important to Baltimore's and Yalow's arguments, may have little weight among members of Congress and policymakers. If basic research is to serve society, they argue, then society's elected officials and their appointed representatives must see that research is appropriately channeled (into spinal cord research, for example). To do this, mechanisms to insure freedom *and* accountability must be in place.

Shortly after being awarded two prestigious prizes, Richard Muller pointed out that the research cited in the awards was turned down for support by NSF, and used this example, of (retrospectively) flawed decisionmaking as the foundation for a critique of funding practices that was published in *Science*. He argues that the present funding process stifles innovation through regulations that, individually, do " 'unmeasurably' small harm"; that funding agencies are unwilling to take risks by funding young scientists or scientists working outside their fields; and that compartmentalization of agencies into narrow programmatic areas impedes interdisciplinary work and frustrates scientists. The sharp disjuncture between the scientist's and the administrator's perspectives is apparent in Muller's remarks:

A funding agency must not be judged by its mistakes or by its "waste" of money any more than Babe Ruth should be judged by his strikeout record. . . .

My own best work was begun during periods when it might have looked to an outsider that I was wasting time. A physicist's career is judged by his peers on the basis of his accomplishments, not his efficiency.[39]

Innovative science, like a small child, can be guided and encouraged, but well-meaning attempts to force it in precon-
ceived directions can be counterproductive. The goal of the
funding agencies should be to facilitate research, not to direct
it.[40]

One could take exception to the principles underlying
Muller's comments. For example, well-respected baseball analysts
today *do* judge a batter by his strikeout record, and more highly
regarded batters tend not to strike out in close games with run-
ners in scoring position. Perhaps strikeouts are not the sole criterion, but well-known power-hitters as diverse as Dave Kingman
and Bo Jackson have been roundly criticized for striking out too
often.

More seriously, Muller also presupposes that peer judgment
is what matters most. While one's *peers* may evaluate accomplishments, not efficiency, one's benefactors and sponsors may legiti-
mately apply different criteria. And it is far from a settled issue
that science can only be "facilitated," not directed. Thus, while we
may agree with Muller's sentiments, we recognize that they are
not supported by evidence or principled argument.

Baltimore, Yalow, and Muller are top-level scientists whose
interests in advancing scientific research are at odds with politicians' and administrators' concerns for efficiency, accountability,
and societal direction of science. Scientists would weaken the grip
of science administrators, whereas OMB worries that decision-
making power is being taken "out of the hands of elected officials";
scientists want public funds to instigate scientific revolutions,
whereas OMB complains that peer review allows scientists to use
public funds for their own purposes. Yet one of the purposes of peer
review is to reconcile the contrasting roles of scientists and policymakers, to draw scientists into the administration of science.
Forty years ago, C. P. Rhoads observed that peer review is a
"somewhat complex mechanism for the reception and review of applications," but that there are two advantages to using it. First,
and most obviously, it might improve the quality of research by
exposing proposals to the critical scrutiny of good scientists. But a
more subtle purpose,

and perhaps a more important one, was to draw in, as participants in policy, not as supplicants for largesse, the best
investigative minds available. It was believed that if this
were accomplished, cancer research would gain something be-

yond price—the devoted, determined attention of outstanding representatives of this country's science.[41]

On the current evidence this has not yet been accomplished, at least among vocal, elite scientists. On the contrary, scientists may be increasingly excluded from key decisions. For evidence, one need look no further than the diminishing influence of scientific advisors in presidential decisions.

The concerns of Baltimore, Yalow, and Muller should not be considered representative of all scientists. For example, when a scientist of David Baltimore's stature argues that society reduce the *level* of scientific activity but not direct or limit the *substance* of research, he does so knowing that his share of national research funds is more or less secure. Scientists less certain of research support might accept some guidance or limitations in exchange for the resources they need to do research, and other scientists might have different concerns about the peer review system. Consider, for example, this bitter complaint:

Right now, the system stifles innovative research, feathers the nest of large coastal institutions, discriminates against those without scientific-political connections, often funds mediocre research because of "club" affiliations, destroys potentially productive careers, wastes large amounts of money on study sections, has severely imbalanced funding schemes, and funds the most faddish research rather than the best (molecular biology being in the spotlight today).[42]

While Baltimore and Yalow and Muller are mainly concerned about whether peer review adequately fuels scientific discovery for its own sake, this scientist raises questions of fairness and efficiency. Certainly all would join in deploring cronyism and the workings of an "old boys' network," but their definitions of network members and their motives for complaining would probably differ. What one scientist might see as appropriate support for a proven researcher another may damn as cronyism, just as scientific autonomy may appear to a politician as wasteful misappropriation of public funds.

These criticisms of peer review are frustrating and unsatisfying. They are frustrating because they reflect limited viewpoints or special interests that do not provide a comprehensive perspective. They are dissatisfying because, in their brevity, they address issues selectively and offer scant empirical or logical support. Even the best of them are but a lone scientist explaining how he or she has been mistreated, then generalizing from that experience to a set of universal principles.

Viewed from a different perspective, however, our frustration with the comments of politicians and scientists about peer review is ultimately healthy, for it means that their views are in appropriate disagreement. There would be far more reason for concern if politicians conceded that science must operate independently of political control, or if scientists accepted that science must always and immediately serve national ends (e.g., cure AIDS, bolster defense, protect the environment, and spur the economy), for either concession would signal a dangerous loss. If politicians relinquish their responsibility to direct and oversee science, then the bridge between science and society would be damaged. If scientists concede their claims to autonomy, then the societal benefits of scientists' judgments about the direction and possibilities of science would be lost. In other words, the contrasting criticisms of peer review sketched above may be considered healthy expressions of pluralism. We should recognize them as limited political statements and use them as such.

## Rustum Roy's Critique

No survey of critical writings about peer review would be complete without considering the writings of Rustum Roy, a materials scientist, educator, and science policy commentator who has offered articulate, incisive, and persistent criticisms of the grants peer review system for more than twenty years. Presented at professional conferences and Congressional hearings, published in several articles and a book, his perceptive remarks demand close scrutiny, for they purport to stand apart from the camps of "political/administrative" and "scientific" critique. Because his views have been expressed so widely, and because his sweeping claims are so forcefully asserted, we shall take an especially close and critical look at his work.

Roy has little use for agencies' self-studies of peer review and other such limited analyses. In his view,

The issues raised in the discussion of scientific choice [conducted in the pages of *Minerva* by Carter, Maddox, Polanyi, Toulmin, and Weinberg during the early 1960s] reappeared in the 1970s in connection with "peer review." Unfortunately, the entire focus of the argument was shifted from the important problem of the best way to distribute the total funds for the support of research, to an analysis of one of the less significant methods of deciding how funds should be allocated [that is, peer review].[43]

Apart from failing to address the central question of resource distribution, such studies have lesser failings as well, for they do not

compare such review [by peers] with other systems of allocating funds for research by scientists of similar qualifications; there has been no comparison with the "strong manager" method used by the United States Department of Defense, or with the formula system. No effort has been made to examine the "efficiency" of the system in terms of the costs and time required for each grant, or the efficacy of the system in support of genuine innovation.[44]

Thus, in his view, the policy community has not been addressing the key issues of peer review. What are those issues? Summarizing his several published critiques of the grants peer review system, Roy argues that the system has at least six major failings: (1) there is no evidence that good research can be predicted from a proposal; (2) a large fraction of scientists' time is wasted in preparing (and reviewing) proposals; (3) innovative research is not and cannot be supported by the peer review mechanism; (4) the system encourages dishonesty, particularly in today's tight funding climate; (5) program managers can manipulate the system to deliver the recommendations they prefer by shrewdly choosing reviewers; (6) the system resists even minor improvements.[45]

If it is so badly flawed, why has grants peer review endured? Roy offers three reasons:

First, the inherent elitism of the hard sciences and its arcane linguistic barriers have enabled some scientists to claim that science should play by special rules. . . . Second, there is now a generation of scientists who have experienced no other means of obtaining research funding and hence feel their entire research career to be at risk when any questions are raised about the peer review system. Third, the social scientists occasionally commissioned to examine the system have been co-opted by the paradigm of the "hard" science community and have yet to formulate even the most obvious questions that should be asked about any public system for distributing funds.[46]

Stated in fewer words, the age and power structure of science, in combination with complaisant social scientists hired for the purpose, have conspired to shore up the otherwise unjustifiable and impractical grants peer review system.

So far, all has been assertion and opinion without supporting analysis and evidence, and one is hard-pressed to find much empirical support in any of Roy's writings. For example, in one prominent paper Roy complains of the "glaring deficiencies" of peer review and invites us to "examine a recent example."[47] The case in point has to do with a Defense Department program that allocated $30 million to allow universities to purchase large pieces of equipment. To make this allocation, the "Department of Defense deviated from the procedures used by many of its own subdivisions" and

in an effort to gain public favour, it issued an invitation for proposals to all universities. . . . This resulted in a fiasco. Over 2,200 proposals were received for a sum of $625 million. The success ratio was less than 1:60. The time required for the preparation and submission of each proposal may be estimated at one month's work of one person . . . or nearly 200 years of scientific work. . . . *Fortunately, scientific peers were not used to evaluate the process.*[48]

What does this say about peer review? Absolutely nothing, because the proposals did not undergo peer review. It is surely a sad tale: expending 200 person-years of effort, worth roughly $16 million, to award $30 million for equipment is extraordinarily wasteful. But this example tells us much more about the desperate need for scientific instrumentation on university campuses and the willingness of scientists and administrators to take any chance, however remote, to increase their scientific capital, than it does about peer review. Granted, it is an inefficient way to allocate resources. But why should the peer review system be held responsible for universities' decisions to apply *en masse* for funds? To us, the internal finances of universities and their strategies and tactics for securing resources are far more likely explanations. While it is deplorable that so many applied for support with little prospect of success, this case tells us nothing about peer review.

Moreover, this case is the only bit of fresh empirical evidence presented in the entire thirteen-page paper, though Roy does refer, dismissively, to the Coles' study of NSF peer review, and also mentions a study of manuscript refereeing practices in journals and one of his own investigations into citation counts. By any standard this is not a strong case, and it is certainly unlikely to withstand the scrutiny of even mildly critical peers.

## Roy Redux

Other of Roy's contentions about peer review contradict or ignore well-established facts and generally accepted findings in the science studies literature. Moving from this particular example to more general principles, Roy asserts, in a most telling passage, that

> only the most sanguine advocate unfamiliar with the literature would claim that there is any basis for expecting a correlation between a scientist's ability to present an essay [that is, a proposal] and the actual future production of the "best science." The weak links in a "theoretical" sense are that we have no definition of what constitutes the "best science." With the total confusion between the terms "basic" and "applied" and over the value of relevance, and the very major psychosocial differences in perceptions and values, between—let us say—civil engineers and theoretical physicists, the entire system of review by peers is one of reinforcements of the idiosyncrasies or the ruling paradigms of any group which is constituted and supported as a unit.[49]

There is much to puzzle over in this passage. For example, Roy provides exactly one reference to make the "sanguine advocate unfamiliar with the literature" more aware of the futility of expecting an "essay" to predict the "actual future production of the 'best science' "—and that is to a research article about the refereeing of a *manuscript* submitted for journal publication. Again, this is not very illuminating of the *proposal* review process, even to a saturnine skeptic familiar with the literature.

Moreover, Roy's complaint is sociologically naive, for while he is reluctant to base a scientist's future funding on a hard-to-evaluate "essay" called a proposal, he would instead let it depend upon another hard-to-evaluate essay called a scientific paper. Ironically, a main finding of research on the peer review of manuscripts, and a core message of the science studies literature of the past decade, is that the collective judgment about the quality of a piece of work depends at least as much on the values, standards, interests, and proclivities of the judging scientists as it does on the manuscript itself. In other words, judgments about the quality of a scientific paper are as problematic as judgments about a proposal. They are indeed two different accounts, and perhaps the paper is nearer to the ultimate ends of science than the proposal. But a paper is not a window on a scientist's ability or the quality of his or her work.

Roy's "weak links in a 'theoretical sense'" would plague any allocation system, not peer review alone; we would acknowledge them as real differences in perspectives and values, not "confusions" that might be removed at some point. For example, as long as the distinction between basic and applied research resides ultimately in the mind of the researcher, we will never have a prospective, objective measure that will work in all cases. More importantly, disputes about the value of relevance and "psychosocial differences" between different types of scientists would not go away if grants peer review were terminated tomorrow. Instead, such differences would continue to exert pressure on our allocation decisions. There is no reason to think that any alternative to peer review would do anything but reinforce "the idiosyncrasies or ruling paradigms of any group which is constituted and supported as a unit." Such groups, if they have any influence at all, will affect not only the decisions of peer review panels but the decisions of referees, industrial sponsors, prospective graduate students, and policymakers, as well.

Shapley and Roy prescribe that:

> U.S. science should be reorganized to give equal weight to undirected basic research, purposive basic research, applied science, engineering, and technology.[50]

The argument they are making has three components: a value judgment, a theoretical speculation, and a factual assertion. The value component has to do with the relative merits of basic and applied research, with Shapley and Roy arguing that applied research should be more highly valued than it is now. (They would allocate basic research funds as "overhead" on applied research support.) Rather than engage in the dispute about values here, we would only note that the issue is hardly obvious and should be considered open to debate. Closely related to this value judgment is a theoretical speculation about the connection between basic research and economic development. While it is sensible to argue that directed or applied basic research would have more immediate payoffs than undirected basic research, the ultimate benefits of various sorts of research have been contested for years, without clear resolution.[51]

As evidence for their claim that applied research deserves primacy, Shapley and Roy draw on a lecture Derek Price gave at the AAAS meetings in 1983 (shortly before his untimely death) in which he disputed the view "that science can in some mysterious way be applied to make technology," arguing instead that "the arrow of causality historically is largely from the technology to the science."[52] But the cases in point that Shapley and Roy offer as evidence are not entirely convincing.

For example, the invention of radar is discussed in this ambiguous language: "While radar *could not have been invented without Hertz and Guglielmo Marconi,* the outstanding feature of the story is not that their discoveries trickled into the applied arena, but how the imperative of the war pulled the development of the technology."[53] Perhaps the "pull" of the war was the "outstanding feature"; after all, world wars are outstanding events, but this can hardly diminish or discredit the basic science of Hertz and Marconi. Indeed, although the war may have "catalyzed" basic science into an invention, one can hardly recommend waging war as responsible policy for science or the economy. Similarly, the Manhattan Project is cited as an example "of what can be accomplished when the highest quality, most basic scientists are organized and motivated to work on applications."[54] But this example tells us only that good scientists, when placed under conditions of intense urgency, limitless spending, and paramilitary organization, can become good engineers. Today, in contrast, sharply limited spending for science is among the initial conditions under which policy must be formulated and no one would seriously advocate a return in peacetime to the repressive organization of the Manhattan Project. Also, Shapley and Roy are curiously silent about the foundation of basic science—the work of Bohr, Curie, Einstein, Fermi, Hahn, the Joliot-Curies, to name just a few—on which the development of atomic weapons was based. And they aptly note Einstein's lifelong interest in applied problems, his work at the Zurich Patent Office, and his service as a consultant on torpedo detonation during World War II, while wholly ignoring the accidents of career impediments, history, and xenophobia which helped put Einstein in such unlikely positions.[55]

**Table 2**

Federal Obligations for Basic Research, Applied Research, and Development

Selected Years 1967–1988
in billions of 1982 dollars

| Year | BASIC RESEARCH Defense | Non-defense | APPLIED RESEARCH Defense | Non-defense | DEVELOPMENT Defense | Non-defense |
|---|---|---|---|---|---|---|
| 1967 | 0.8 | 4.3 | 3.6 | 4.1 | 18.0 | 15.1 |
| 1970 | 0.8 | 3.9 | 2.4 | 4.7 | 14.5 | 10.6 |
| 1975 | 0.5 | 4.0 | 2.0 | 5.2 | 13.2 | 8.2 |
| 1980 | 0.6 | 4.9 | 2.0 | 6.1 | 13.8 | 7.8 |
| 1985 | 0.8 | 6.2 | 2.1 | 5.4 | 23.8 | 5.0 |
| 1988* | 0.7 | 6.7 | 2.0 | 5.2 | 31.9 | 5.0 |

Source: *Science and Engineering Indicators* 1987, table 4–7, p. 265.
* Estimate

Perhaps the "real" lesson of Price's examples is that the connection between basic science and technological application is not a property of the science as such but instead depends upon the historical context in which the discovery is made. Thus the exigencies of a world war will elicit applications from even the most esoteric science, and will mightily stimulate scientists to produce such applications. Other historical contexts may not encourage such close connections between science and technology, and may even discourage scientists from seeking applications for their work.

There is also a factual aspect to Shapley and Roy's contention: Are federal expenditures increasingly skewed in favor of basic research? This is a difficult matter to evaluate, for at bottom the definitions of "basic" and "applied" research have to do with the intentions of scientists, their sponsors, and their employers, which are difficult to assess, especially on a sufficiently large scale to provide information useful for policy. Yet by examining recent trends in federal obligations for basic research, applied research, and development, presented in table 2, we can evaluate the central point of Roy's argument.

The data do not support the claim that applied research and development are being neglected for basic research. Considering first only nondefense expenditures, it appears that very nearly "equal weight" is given to basic research, applied research, and development ($6.2 billion, $5.4 billion, $5.0 billion, respectively, in 1985). Granted, there has been a great decline in both the proportion and amount of R&D obligations for nondefense development, but this decline has been accompanied by a compensating increase in defense development.

Of course, these categories are certainly much cruder than those in Roy's work, so these may not be the most useful divisions for him. Yet at the level of national policy it would be difficult to obtain more refined categorizations, because the distinction between, say, "undirected" and "purposive" basic research—two of Roy's categories—resides within the mind of the researcher (or within the reconstructions of the analyst). However crude the data, they hardly hint at the sort of imbalance of emphasis that might motivate Roy's strident complaint. Perhaps the long-term reduction in the level of nondefense development obligations gave Shapley and Roy the impression of neglect and imbalance. Whatever their reason, a principled argument against the long-term decline of civilian development or the current distribution that favors defense development must address the civilian benefits of defense-related R&D (the "dual use" or spin-off issue) and the classic choice of "guns or butter."

Roy's critique of peer review is not grounded in evidence, just as the NIH Grants Peer Review Study Team did not base its affirmation of peer review on empirical evidence. So we must look elsewhere to find the basis of Roy's argument. On closer scrutiny, his case rests on implicit and unexamined value positions concerning, for example, the primacy of applied science, the importance of allocative efficiency, the dysfunctions of elitism in science, the appropriateness of public support for private economic development, and a technocratic orientation to political decisions. There is nothing inherently objectionable about any of these value positions: we ourselves agree with some (e.g., an anti-elitist bias) and others have recently become popular rallying cries (e.g., economic development and national economic competitiveness). But we do object to basing a critique of peer review on such value positions, especially if the values are not made explicit and are not considered in comparison to alternative positions. In the paragraphs below, as an example of the hyperbole and passion surrounding the public

discourse on peer review, we offer an analysis of the value under-
pinnings of Roy's work.

In his account of Defense Department expenditures for scientific instrumentation, discussed above, Roy implies that the allocation would have been more efficient if the sponsor had "selected
for those universities working with the Department the articles of
equipment most needed."[56] Of course this would have spared unsuccessful applicants the bother of preparing proposals, but selecting recipients at random would also have saved time. Allocation
mechanisms cannot be evaluated by their administrative efficiency
alone.

Roy also complains that "the entire operation further exacerbated the differences between the successful and the unsuccessful
applicants, since the unsuccessful universities wasted their efforts,
while those with the more successful applicants gained even
more."[57] The egalitarian sentiments expressed in this criticism are
laudable, but we have no evidence that the schools that received
equipment also tended to be successful in other ways, so we do not
know if their advantage accumulated. No one would be surprised
if otherwise successful schools were successful in this as well, for
it is well established that science is characterized by such processes of "cumulative advantage."[58] In fact, some go so far as to
argue that cumulative advantage is proper and beneficial for science. But, the "strong manager" alternative, which would allow
the sponsor to choose both the equipment and the school to receive
it, would probably also widen the gap between "haves" and "have
nots." In this assessment of allocative mechanisms, Roy is implicitly arguing that the value of efficiency outweighs the value of
open competition (or fairness). Efficiency may be a more important value, but that argument must stand alone, in the clear and
on its own merits, not entangled with arguments about distributive justice.

Again and again Roy argues that basic research has been
overemphasized, at the expense of applied research and development. Underlying his argument is the assumption that applied research and development, which contribute directly and
measurably to the economic mission of the nation, have stronger
claims on federal support than does basic research. In one place,
for example, he argues that although "the government funded certain applied missions in defense, nuclear power, and space," the
U.S. science funding system drifted away from Vannevar Bush's
"sweeping vision" of the integration of science and technology for
economic and social good, taking instead as its mission "federal

support for that part of the profession who were believed to be at its apex—scientists, in universities, pursuing research having no application."[59]

So even Roy's extensive and, on the whole, salubrious critique of peer review is unsatisfactory in many respects. It is based on little evidence and is not closely reasoned, sometimes substituting hyperbole for argument and analysis. Furthermore, none of the criticisms reviewed above has attempted to take a comprehensive perspective on peer review. As a modest contribution to future deliberations, we will draw on the preceding discussion to propose a set of peer-review desiderata.

## CRITERIA FOR EVALUATING PEER REVIEW

To some degree the difficulties we have indicated in various criticisms of grants peer review arise because each critic has his or her own ordered list of desiderata, but neither the items on the list nor their order has been made explicit. We will offer our own list, drawing on the implicit lists of others and adding criteria of our own. Such a list has several uses. First, its comprehensiveness is an antidote to the common practice of promoting as universal standards those criteria that best satisfy one's own tastes and interests (e.g., a preference for efficiency over accountability). Second, conflicts and inconsistencies among criteria will become clearer, and conscious choices and preferences may be expressed. Third, results from studies of peer review may be used to evaluate current peer review systems against these standards.

Peer review should be an *effective* mechanism for allocating resources and communicating priorities to scientists. This means that peer review should succeed in supporting research in the areas intended, and the research should be of sufficient quality to advance scientific knowledge. Concern about the effective allocation of resources for science has been expressed often enough (e.g., NIH Grants Peer Review Study Team in 1976, Grace Carter in 1986, the NSF Merit Review Report of 1986). But no one has yet articulated the many facets of effectiveness and evaluated the role of peer review in promoting effective science.[60]

Some studies have identified exemplary innovations, and asked how basic research had contributed to the accomplishment (Comroe and Dripps's study of medical innovations in cardiovascular and pulmonary disease is an especially good example; see also the TRACES study and "Project Hindsight").[61] Others have looked generally at the "scientific impact" of research supported by a funding agency (e.g., the NIH "rainbow reports" produced by Francis Narin or Irvine and Martin's cost-benefit analyses).[62] But we know of no study that compares the scientific or practical effectiveness of research supported through peer review with research supported through *other* funding mechanisms.

To measure effectiveness correctly, one must consider the population of applications or awards, not merely the population of outcomes. And effectiveness must measure the frequency of "false positives," funded projects that ultimately yield little (the idea underlying Proxmire's "Golden Fleece" awards) as well as "false negatives," unfunded proposals that subsequently appear to have merit (the complaint of Richard Muller, Rosalyn Yalow, and others who contend that the funding system is risk-averse).

These criteria are similar to "sensitivity" and "selectivity" in testing jargon, terms that denote a test's ability to detect an attribute and its ability to discern one quality from another. It would be valuable to measure these properties of various allocation mechanisms so that a society could choose, at different times or for different areas of science, to accept the risk of rejecting good work or tolerating mediocrity. The U.S. probably has made such decisions, unwittingly and without examination, to wage war on cancer and AIDS, to pursue the Strategic Defense Initiative, and to populate the superconductivity and "cold fusion" bandwagons.

Such questions about the effectiveness of the peer review system, its ability to sponsor the research needed by science and society, are easily confused with questions of *efficiency,* or the costs in time, money, and moral energy of allocating resources through a peer-reviewed system. Roy's complaint about the competition among universities for equipment from the Defense Department has more to do with efficiency than effectiveness, as do many scientists' complaints about the amount of time they must devote to writing and reviewing proposals.[63] Great inefficiencies can reduce effectiveness, as Muller and Szilard have warned us, but for most purposes effectiveness and efficiency should be treated as separate issues.

Peer review should also promote *accountability* in science, insuring that funds have been expended appropriately, that laws and regulations governing human subjects, animal and lab safety, accessibility of raw data, and hiring practices have been observed, and that the proposed work has indeed been carried out. The first two forms of accountability have provoked complaints about paperwork, red tape, and the intrusion of political activists (animal rights groups, Science for the People) into the preserve of science. But accountability for scientific performance has potentially deeper consequences, for it limits the freedom of investigators to follow their scientific hunches. When the products of prior grants are examined to determine whether the work has been accomplished as proposed, and future funding depends in part on having established a record of performing the research as it was presented in the proposal, scientists will be more constrained by their work plans.

Peer review is also expected to be *responsive,* providing a mechanism for policymakers to direct scientific effort and for new science to shape future research. Concern about one aspect of responsiveness arises in policy debates about major initiatives, such as the AIDS health emergency or the war on cancer, where newly-allocated funds may be coopted for pre-existing purposes by the bureaucratic machinery, or new interests may be communicated only imperfectly to university scientists. Another form appears in the complaints of some scientists that entrenched scientific views stand in the way of their new ideas, and in the laments of other scientists that fads are rippling through modern science (driving out their mainstream work; this charge has been leveled against molecular biological approaches in the life sciences, for example).

In some instances peer review may seem an undesired drag on new initiatives, while in others its stability lends a beneficial *robustness* to modern science, preserving it from political, social, and scientific currents and encouraging continuity in research. Thus it is a flywheel, sustaining inertia.

Peer review should be *rational* in the sense that its inner workings should be knowable and seem reasonable to participants. This has been a central concern of agencies' self-assessments. For example, the Coles' study of NSF peer review asked whether "the procedure employed by NSF is an equitable and a rational one."[64] Conversely, one of the sharpest complaints about reviews is that they are incompetent and that the decisions based on them are mysterious or unreasonable. Such complaints are particularly stinging in science, for science is grounded in cognitive norms that abhor mystery and irrationality.

Peer review should also be *fair,* adhering to societal norms of equitable treatment as well as scientific norms of universalism and distinterestedness. (Fairness is different from rationality: something may be rational—that is, reasoned according to stated principles in a way that follows accepted logical conventions—but unfair, or entirely irrational but fair. Participants expect peer review to be both rational and fair.)

Finally, as peer review measures scientific performance, it should adhere to technical standards of good measurement: *validity* and *reliability*. A valid measure is one that measures the quality it is claimed to measure, not something else. Thus if peer review is to measure the scientific merit of a proposal, it should not instead measure the visibility of its author or the prestige of its institutional origins. A reliable measure is one that yields the same values on repeated measurements of the same object, with little random variation. In the case of peer review, this generally means limiting the role of chance in decisions.[65]

As these desiderata are not entirely consistent with one another, an optimal system would probably strike a compromise among them. For example, in an article about peer review of manuscripts submitted to journals, which applies to grants peer review as well, Stevan Harnad expressed the tension between reliability and validity in these terms:

> Without question, every effort should be made to strengthen peer review, not only in terms of its reliability (which, as has been suggested here, is only partly synonymous with low reviewer variance) but also in terms of its validity (which may well be improved by rational and creative disagreement).[66]

Similarly, accountability demands some sacrifice of efficiency, robustness reduces responsiveness, and fairness may cost some effectiveness. Yet many of peer review's critics do not recognize the full array of desirable properties of peer review, and so they treat one or another criterion as an absolute and, when the system does not meet *their* preferred standard, declare it malevolent or bankrupt.

Disputes about the proper role and operation of peer review may be divided into four categories. In the first category are differences of perspective, grounded in the divergent social roles that are appropriate, and perhaps even beneficial, for U.S. science. Chief among these is the tension between politicians' calls for greater regulation, oversight, accountability, and responsiveness from science, and scientists' pleas for freedom, autonomy, and the intrinsic benefits of scientific research. This difference in views is rooted in the social roles of politicians and scientists in the U.S. and is unlikely to change easily or rapidly. Without the extraordinary force of a lingering world war, or perhaps an equivalent mobilization for some peacetime crisis, scientists are unlikely to relinquish their claims to self-determination. Similarly, politicians would be remiss if they set aside their oversight responsibilities or ceased calling scientists to account for their research support in terms of societal benefits. In a sense, then, these are healthy tensions which need not be resolved, for they maintain a balance between freedom and accountability in science.

A second category of tensions includes value conflicts which may beneficially be resolved through negotiation, compromise, or analysis. Such resolutions need not be permanent, but may be bounded by certain historical conditions. For instance, today it may be most important to give science considerable autonomy, whereas at another time accountability may be essential. The attempt to resolve such value conflicts serves the important function of making us aware that our society must make some difficult choices between desirable courses of action. Thus we can acknowledge in principle the great benefits of risky, innovative research while acknowledging that, for a limited time in certain areas of science, this aspect of effectiveness must take second place to efficiency. (Alternatively, we might decide to accept less efficiency in exchange for the possibility of innovative, cutting-edge research.) Again, what most matters is that we confront the necessity of compromise or choice and attempt a resolution in principle which recognizes the merits of both values.

In a third category are disputes which can benefit from relatively straightforward data-gathering efforts. Issues of fairness are a prime example of this; ongoing data collection about proposals, proposers, reviewers and the content of their reviews would probably go far to insure fairness. Similarly, questions of distributive equity (e.g., success rates by race, sex, region, prestige, and so forth) can be addressed empirically. In addition, as the next chapter will show, surveys can provide insight into the attitudes and perceptions of a large cross section of scientists, to some extent counterbalancing our tendency to hear only a few loud voices.

The fourth and most important category comprises those aspects of peer review where theory-building and theory-based research might uncover important mechanisms. We would consider such issues apart from matters of value conflict, which may yield to philosophical analysis or political action, and from matters of fact, which require less theoretical framing to make sense. But these are among the most intricate questions, concerning (for example):

- the group dynamics of review panels, viewed as a problem in the social psychology of collective decision-making;

- the challenges posed by competition and resource scarcity to the communal character and normative structure of science;

- the consequences of age and prestige hierarchies in science for the allocation of research resources;

- the extent of universities' dependence on research resources (from government and industry), and its consequences for the university's place in society and for the work roles and research careers of academic scientists.

By posing and researching such questions, members of the science studies community move beyond the narrow, technocratic role of policy advisor, or the political role of advocate. It is dangerous terrain because the researcher becomes an unknown interloper in uncharted territory, not clearly affiliated with either party in the issues surrounding peer review.

## CONCLUSIONS

We have looked at peer review in theory and practice, recounting its origins and workings at NIH and NSF. We have seen, statistically, the pressures on the peer review system: a basic one-in-three chance of support at both NIH and NSF, with substantial differences by program and over time. We have also considered criticisms of the peer review system, from the perspective of politicians and administrators, on the one hand, and from scientists, on the other. Rustum Roy's extensive critique of peer review was singled out for special consideration. In general, no critique of peer review was found to be satisfactory, for all were flawed by the narrowness of their perspective or the soundness of their analysis and evidence. With these criticisms we proposed several more general and encompassing criteria for judging peer review, and we discussed four methods for resolving the value tensions inherent in those criteria.

The next chapter addresses the perils and pitfalls of studying the peer review system, summarizes what we know about grants peer review, and asks whether our knowledge base provides a useful foundation for making intelligent policy choices.

# 3

# *Funding Success*

## *and*

## *Failure*

One must never say anything new in a grant application.
Researcher funded by NIH

NIH is funding success and trying to avoid failure. That is not what medical research is really like and that is not what NCI is supposed to be doing.
Researcher declined funding by NIH

Success is counted sweetest by those who ne'er succeed. To comprehend a nectar requires sorest need.
Emily Dickinson

We have argued that the grants peer review system is pulled in several directions by the diverse values of those who have a stake in it. The clearest tension is between administrators or politicians, who wish for a system that maximizes efficiency and accountability, versus scientists, who prefer a system directed toward effectiveness and autonomy. Similarly, established scientists would argue for an inertial system that provides long-term, stable funding to investigators on the basis of their past accomplishments, while new scientists would prefer a more dynamic system that responds to novel ideas, findings, and methods, and that awards support mainly on the basis of a proposal, not career accomplishments. Other criteria are also, to a degree, incompatible with one another. For example, measures that guarantee fairness or rationality often reduce efficiency.

When we ask such questions as, How fair is the peer review system? How efficiently does it distribute resources? How effective is it in supporting innovative research? we are asking questions that should be answerable, at least to a first approximation, through research. Even when we ask more complicated questions about the compatibility between innovative research and accountability, or the career consequences of a declined grant application, we are again asking empirical questions. In this chapter the main findings of published research on grants peer review, in combination with some new data, will be used to address such science policy issues. In effect, we are asking how far empirical research can take us toward answering these politically charged questions.

At the outset we must acknowledge that these are difficult matters to study. Peer review is an intensely private process that originates within a scientist's mind, continues on paper as a bureaucratic procedure, and ends behind the closed doors of a funding agency. The process is at nearly all points inaccessible, opaque, and heavily infused with the values and interests of stakeholders. Peer review leaves few clues in the public domain, and many participants in the system insist upon minimizing public access to information. For example, the names of scientists who succeeded in their quest for support are accessible, but the names of those who did not succeed are generally unavailable to independent investigators. Thus, to preserve confidentiality, anonymity, and power the process remains shrouded in secrecy. Moreover, since the funding system occupies such an important place in the institution of modern science, it inspires unreasoning support among those who benefit from it and unreasoning criticism from those who feel wronged by it. Researchers approach such contentious topics at their peril. For that reason we will begin by considering the difficulties of studying the grants peer review system.

## ENTERING THE BLACK BOX

Peer review takes place within a black box, shielded from the public eye. But in the past dozen years or so, measures have been taken to reduce the shadows inside the black box and to illuminate some of the activity within. The Freedom of Information Act of 1974 (PL 93–502), for example, has provided leverage allowing scientists and the public to request access to verbatim copies of proposals that had been supported by federal agencies.[1] Studies of the grants peer review system have also become more frequent during this period, and they too inform us about what is going on within the peer review system. There are many different ways to categorize these studies. Some are chiefly concerned with fairness, while others examine efficiency or resource distribution; some survey scientists' attitudes and orientations, while others use experiments or archival analyses to examine social mechanisms. But more important than any of these approaches is the question of sponsorship: Under whose auspices is this research performed? We distinguish among (1) studies conducted under the auspices of a federal agency, either by its own staff or by scientists selected for the purpose; (2) studies conducted by independent scholars, with financial support—usually a research grant—from the agency under examination; and (3) studies conducted independently, without agency sponsorship or support.

## Agency-Sponsored Studies

Studies conducted under the auspices of the agency under study would include the NIH Grants Peer Review Study Team, Grace Carter's contracted studies for NIH, the various NSF "fairness" studies (including the Coles' work), NSF's 1976 and 1987 surveys of scientists' attitudes, and "insider" studies of panel operations by current or former agency staff (for example, Sigelman and Scioli, and Klahr).[2] Such studies are subject to intense political wrangling as the agency orchestrates a public performance to the greatest extent consistent with maintaining the appearance of objectivity and independence. Even after the work is done, the agency engages in a form of "spin control" by selectively highlighting and framing key issues in the prefaces and summaries of reports. (For example, the absurd conclusion in the preface to the NIH Grants Peer Review Study, quoted early in chapter 2, or the mismatch between objectives and findings apparent in the preface to the Coles' study, written by the chair of the National Academy of Sciences committee that was responsible for the study, which rightly irked Rustum Roy.[3] Of course, agency staff who write about their own agency's inner workings will be cautious for a variety of reasons, including informal expectations about their responsibilities, formal guidelines about confidentiality and conflicts of interest, personal commitment to the agency's mission, and sheer instinct for career survival. Stated in fewer words, insider studies have the best access to information about the peer review system but are constitutionally limited in their ability to use that information. Conflicts that may occur within such projects about analyses, interpretations, and recommendations are very likely to remain within the project, as hidden from view as the process under investigation.

A variety of methods have been used in such studies. For example, Phase I of the Coles' studies of peer review at NSF combined in-depth interviews with program managers and others involved in the review process, quantitative data about successful and unsuccessful applicants, and archival material gleaned from the files ("jackets") of successful and unsuccessful grant proposals. These diverse data were amassed to determine what role program managers play in the NSF peer review process and to assess how social characteristics of scientists (chiefly their "eminence") affect the fate of their proposals.[4] In Phase II of the Coles' study, an experimental design was used to evaluate the fairness and rationality of the NSF peer review system.[5] Other studies analyzed archival information, combined such records with interview material and citation data, or undertook large-scale sample surveys of scientists.[6]

Insider studies have enviably free access to data and substantial resources for their work. But they share the problems of the "court historian" who must please the king; thus their studies may be incomplete, self-serving, and incapable of penetrating the black box.

## Agency-Funded Studies

A further step removed are studies funded by a research grant, which typically afford the investigator fuller freedom of inquiry and expression, but limit his or her access to data. Thus Porter and Rossini's study of the review of interdisciplinary proposals at NSF is limited to "sanitized" *archival* information about *funded projects*; the decision processes at work within panels and the fate of unfunded proposals remained unseen and unknown.[7] This procedure is rather like trying to learn about a new disease from censored versions of survivors' medical charts. Hackett drew a sample of scientists who were awarded research support from published lists of grant recipients, but resorted to an indirect method of mail solicitation, with help from NSF, to sample unsuccessful applicants.[8] This gave him less than optimal control over the design of the sample, interfered with follow-up, and precluded analysis of nonrespondents. In both studies the compromise on methods somewhat distorted and complicated the investigation.

### Independent Studies

Studies of the third sort are conducted independently of the agency, and thus have the freedom of studies supported by grants without any of their financial and social resources. At the extreme are those studies, such as the one conducted by Chubin and Gillespie, which must struggle even to gain access to their study population.[9] In the following section we tell of litigation that compelled NIH to release the names of *applicants* for research grants (not merely grant *recipients*), thus permitting their views of peer review to be surveyed by independent social researchers. Chubin was involved in the litigation as an expert witness and subsequently conducted the survey. Before discussing the survey and its results as an example of independent research on grants peer review, consider the litigation necessary to obtain the list of applicants, that is, the context for conducting the study.

## LITIGATION AND SCIENCE: THE STORY OF A SOCIAL SURVEY

Studies of peer review which operate outside the auspices of a funding agency encounter a host of difficulties. We recount the story of one such study for two reasons: to show how difficult it is to examine the peer review system from the outside and to reveal the unusual logic which arises at the intersection of science and law.

### Obtaining the Sample of Scientists

The plaintiff, Dr. George Kurzon, originally brought suit against the U.S. Department of Health and Human Services in 1980. He took this action under the Freedom of Information Act (FOIA), 5 U.S.C. 522(b)(6), seeking disclosure of "the names of scientists who have made grant applications to the National Cancer Institute (NCI) and whose applications have been turned down."[10] The plaintiff argued that he needed these names to test his

theory that the peer review system . . . does not work well in
the case where the scientist is unconventional in his thinking. [Plaintiff] would like to test this theory by communication with the scientists who have been turned down [in their
proposals for grant support] by the National Cancer Institute.

For its part, the government argued that the names of scientists who have been denied grants are excluded from the provisions of the FOIA by the Act's Exemption 6, which exempts from
disclosure "personnel and medical files and similar files the disclosure of which would constitute a clearly unwarranted invasion of
personal privacy."

The crux of the initial suit was this: Dr. Kurzon alleged that
there is a public interest in the release of the names of applicants
whose grant proposals were not funded. To serve that public interest, he would use these names as part of a university study of the
peer review system. The purpose of the study would be to convince
NIH to redirect a small portion of the cancer research funds to
innovative, non-traditional projects, thereby improving the quality
of research supported by the taxpayer. At the time of the initial
suit, however, he had yet to find a university willing to undertake
such a study.

The government's response, sustained by the district court
which heard the initial case, was that the public interest in disclosing the names, alleged by the plaintiff, was not sufficient to
warrant the potential embarrassment and stigma that could
haunt unfunded investigators throughout their careers. A purpose
of Exemption 6, the government argued, is "to protect individuals
from a wide range of embarrassing disclosures." Admitting that
the public interest might be served by an inquiry into the nature
of peer review, the government proposed a solution that would not
require disclosure of unfunded investigators. The kernel of this
counterproposal is contained in the affidavit of Dr. Robert M. Berliner, Dean of the Yale University School of Medicine and former
Deputy Director of Science at NIH:

From my many years of experience with scientific journals, I
believe there are adequate alternative methods for plaintiff
(and any others similarly situated) to obtain the required information. There are a large number of scientific periodicals
which publish letters and advertisements. Often such letters
and advertisements contain attempts to contact other scien-

tists with similar concerns. This method would provide a relatively inexpensive way for the plaintiff to test his hypothesis without invading the privacy of unsuccessful applicants who wish to have the confidentiality of their records preserved.[11]

Two aspects of this proposal deserve comment. First, it is a woefully inadequate research design for measuring scientists' views of peer review. Such a survey would be tantamount to making projections about voting preferences from a tear-out ballot in a magazine, or studying the epidemiology of a disease by asking those who feel they might have appropriate symptoms to clip out and mail in a newspaper coupon. Such survey methods have been discredited for forty years. For Dr. Berliner to suggest such a research approach is powerful evidence of the emotional halo that surrounds peer review: even an absurd suggestion that would deflect scrutiny is preferable to direct examination of the system. Second, the reference to the "unsuccessful applicants who wish to have the confidentiality of their records preserved" is a bit strained. The federal government, not the applicants, is contesting this request for information. The unsuccessful applicants were not party to the suit and have not been heard. As we shall see from the survey evidence that follows, the government's interest may not have been benign, but may instead reflect an understandable but unacceptable desire to avoid criticism.

Our comments on Berliner's affidavit notwithstanding, his views, in combination with the district court's skepticism about the plaintiff's ability to conduct an appropriate study (even with the names in hand and a university researcher on board), led to a predictable conclusion. On August 21, 1980, the district court of Massachusetts denied disclosure of the names, holding that

> Those details [about unfunded applicants that were requested in the suit] would be a serious, unwarranted invasion of privacy and might reflect opinions about the competence of the applicant or his professional qualifications. Disclosure could substantially injure the professional reputation of the applicants.

> Even if we agreed that these suggestions [about research to be conducted on the population of applicants denied funding] possessed merit, there is little likelihood that the requested information would be helpful in devising ways to improve the peer review system approach. Rejected applicants would nat-

urally be inclined to possess subjective and possibly unreliable estimations of the worth of their ideas. The peer review system is designed to place those ideas before a panel of knowledgeable, dedicated, and objective experts. There is nothing in this record to show that the information will support [the plaintiff's] "theory." The potential benefit to the public is too remote. The objective of improving the system is too speculative and elusive . . .

## The Appeal

The plaintiff appealed the decision, contending that

he has sought information, solely for the public good, based on a theory which is well supported in the record, seeking to redirect a small proportion of the cancer research funds to non-traditional projects and so improve the use of taxpayer supported research against the leading cause of death in the United States.[12]

. . . and that, while the plaintiff's

accusation that the peer review system is structurally unable to cope with unusual but potentially promising new concepts is somewhat hard to comprehend for the lay person, a review of the record of supporting materials introduced by the plaintiff readily indicates a broad support for his concern.

. . . and that, furthermore,

the plaintiff has not sought to publicize the rejections nor is there anything in the record to support the assumption that the release of this unfunded list would then lead to its general publication. This is the real speculation and . . . it should be found that the court can and should fashion appropriate safeguards which will prevent unnecessary disclosure. The pressing need to locate a truly effective anti-cancer agent is too important a concern for the court to let the problem of limiting dissemination get in the way of a quest for a change in the way a small proportion of defendants' funds are disbursed that may result in a major leap forward in science's quest to control this dread disease.[13]

What shall we make of plaintiff's argument? Hyperbole aside, there is little here but an invitation to the court to impose "appropriate safeguards" on the dissemination of the list of names, and a reiteration that there must be a way to modify the peer review system in a way that would allow innovative work to be funded. (The claim that the theory is "well supported" in the literature is a bit too strong, and the reference to finding a cure for cancer through a small-scale innovation fund is a shameless emotional manipulation.) At this juncture in the appeals process, Chubin's affidavit of 5 February 1981 becomes relevant. In that affidavit he made two main points: that there was ample but unsystematic evidence that the peer review system at NIH tends to avoid innovative proposals and that the experience of having a grant proposal declined has become so commonplace in modern science that there could hardly be any stigma attached to it. Evidence that funding agencies tend to avoid risk was marshalled from diverse sources: a report produced by the National Commission on Research (a private, nonprofit organization that examines how the federal government supports scientific research and proposes improvements in the system), Congressional testimony of well-respected scientists and university administrators, scientists' published complaints, and an interview with the then-Director of the NCI, Vincent DeVita, conducted by Daniel S. Greenberg, a Washington correspondent of the *New England Journal of Medicine*.[14]

As to the stigma of having a proposal turned down, Chubin's affidavit reads in part:

> The stigma of being declined funding support, in this time of static or shrinking federal funding for research, has been, if not removed, then substantially diminished. The damage suffered by a rejected would-be principal investigator is offset by other proposals, often submitted to a variety of agencies, some of which are eventually supported. My own research on, and participation in, peer review systems convinces me that rejection is a fact of scientific life. One must risk rejection in the public process of competing for scarce resources, be they journal space for reporting research findings or federal funding that enables those researches to proceed (or proceed apace of one's peers, who are also direct competitors). If a scientist willingly competes in the research arena, he/she accepts the risk of failing as well as succeeding, persevering in the face of hardship and delay. No committed researcher abandons his/her investigations for fear that rejection will

bring stigmatization and do irreparable harm to future investigations.

Further, competition for funds is as much a part of Big Science as is team research. To claim, therefore, that disclosure of one's attempt to compete for those funds is an invasion of privacy seems inimical to the public interest—the same public whose tax dollars would subsidize the researcher's investigation were his/her proposal funded. Such a one-sided "disclosure of success" policy, as embodied in FOIA, and applied to the competition for public funding, is in principle unjustified.

My conjectures, however, and those of the scientists cited above, warrant systematic study. It is for this reason that I am interested in conducting research along the lines suggested by [the plaintiff] if and when the data sought in his Freedom of Information suit are released. Our need for research on peer review is, in my view, urgent. For as a Rand Corporation study prepared for the President's Biomedical Research Panel in 1976 concluded: "The peer review process is central to resource-allocation decisions at NIH and is viewed by many as the strength of the NIH system of research awards. Although no analysis to date has discredited peer review, there are many who question some aspects of its reliability and some who doubt its validity in general. . . ." What were legitimate questions in 1976 are urgent questions today. To answer them requires access to the kind of information [the plaintiff] seeks. Only if the experiences of would-be principal investigators whose proposals have been declined for support, or given too low a priority rating to receive support though approved by an NIH Study Section, are reconstructed can the effects of peer review be measured. Was the research declined for support by NCI pursued? Was non-NIH support subsequently secured? What was the would-be principal investigator's funding history prior to the declination in question? And on the review side, what were the grounds for declination? That is, what did Study Section members cite as reasons for recommending that the research not be supported? In short, are innovative approaches seen as wild speculations lacking any empirical support? Only research utilizing data heretofore not in the public domain could address questions such as these.

The appeal was successful, and on May 22, 1981, the First Circuit Court of Appeals directed the Department of Health and Human Services to release to Dr. Kurzon the names and addresses of applicants for NIH funding in fiscal year 1980. In the Spring of 1982, Chubin received a computer printout of the 7609 applicants for NIH support. Included were those who, during the period in question, had been declined support by NIH for at least one proposal. Thus *prospective* principal investigators could be systematically surveyed. It became possible to compare the perceptions of two categories of cancer researchers: those whose proposals were funded by the NCI and those whose proposals were not funded in the same fiscal year.

## Lessons from the Litigation

One perspective on peer review suggests that a scientist presented with a proposal or manuscript for review decides rather early on whether to support it or not. Once that has been decided, the task becomes one of marshalling arguments and evidence to persuade the editors or program managers that there are sound intellectual reasons for disposing of the case in the manner recommended by the referee. At these times the referee must become a rhetorician, for whatever the origin and basis of a judgment, the matter must be restated in compelling, logical prose with appropriate mention of substantive flaws and oversights.

The process of structuring arguments into a legal case is quite similar, and in that process errors of commission and omission occur. Courts rule not on the "merits of the case," but according to the evidence offered, admitted, and selectively employed. In related contexts, Gilbert has spoken of "referencing as persuasion" and Mulkay of "vocabularies of justification."[15] A judge also may be persuaded by the "missing" reference, the claim that evidence is lacking and uncertainty reigns. In the adversarial context of a legal appeal, vigor or logic may be inconsequential, for the merits of the case quickly become buried under layer upon layer of obfuscation and irrelevance.

The scientific ethos, as postulated by Robert Merton, provides little guidance to the academic scientist encountering the new rules and new roles which attend the exercise of "scientific expertise."[16] In court one's task soon becomes clear: within the broad bounds of honesty to offer a partisan judgment and influence a judicial audience to favor a position, means, or outcome to which you are committed. Participation in a legal proceeding thus makes explicit the kinds of behavior that many contend scientists routinely display, in a veiled form, in their interactions with fellow scientists: the promotion of their own interests.[17] The context and stakes may be different, but the process is fundamentally the same. Such tactics are fair, perhaps necessary, in a court of law (or at a Congressional hearing). But how well do they serve science and society?

## EMPIRICAL STUDIES OF GRANTS PEER REVIEW

What have we learned about grants peer review from empirical studies? We will begin with a discussion of survey studies, because these complement and respond to the issues raised in the ad hoc critiques presented in the preceding chapter. Then we will juxtapose these survey findings with the results of other studies to assess peer review on the dimensions of effectiveness, efficiency, responsiveness, and fairness that were developed in chapter 2.

### Surveys of Scientists

Empirical knowledge about grants peer review has been greatly advanced by two surveys of scientists: a survey of applicants to the National Cancer Institute (conducted in 1982–83) and made possible by the litigation discussed above), and a survey of NSF applicants (conducted in 1986 by the NSF's Program Evaluation Staff). Inasmuch as they differ in design and results, they are especially valuable to examine and compare in some detail.

The survey of NCI applicants, undertaken by Chubin and Gilbert Gillespie in 1982, was designed to provide basic information about scientists' experiences with the NIH funding system, to measure selected attitudes toward peer review, and to gauge scientists' reactions to proposed modifications in the system.[18] Beyond these basic measures, the survey also allows us to examine the proposition that current and prior success in the competition for research support will influence a scientist's behavior and attitudes toward the funding system. This proposition is grounded in a central tenet of the sociology of knowledge: "objects present themselves to the subject according to differences in social settings."[19] In other words, a person's thinking is substantially shaped by his or her position in society; more narrowly, one's views of peer review and science policy are influenced by one's experience with the system.

While this principle may seem intuitively true, its import is lost on many. For example, consider the Massachusetts court decision in the suit described above. In the decision, the judge noted that "rejected applicants would naturally be inclined to possess subjective and possibly unreliable estimations of the worth of their ideas." In other words, rejected scientists' would feel ill-used by the peer review system (because their valued ideas had been turned down) and therefore would be unduly critical of it. Of course this is perfectly true. But it is equally true that successful applicants will *also* form similarly subjective and unreliable estimations about *their* work. And, we would expect that both groups would have distinctive views of the machinery of science policy, and peer review in particular. Thus there is not a choice between the "biased" views of unsuccessful applicants and the "unbiased" views of successful ones; instead, there are two equally valid viewpoints that have been shaped by quite different experiences. Our job as observers and analysts is to hear both perspectives and through them to develop a rounded understanding of the phenomenon they experience.

To examine these ideas, Chubin and Gillespie drew a stratified random sample of 719 applicants from the population of 7609 provided by NIH. (See Appendix for details about the sampling procedure and response rate.) These applicants for what NIH calls "R01 project grants," or investigator-initiated research grants, were mailed a three-page questionnaire in the Fall of 1982. The cover letter accompanying it explained that the survey was intended to gather preliminary information about how participants in the NCI peer-review system assess its strengths and weaknesses. The questionnaire contained nineteen fixed-alternative questions and a request for additional, free-form comments. This open-ended request yielded a rich harvest: thirty percent of the respondents provided lengthy, often eloquent, remarks (some of which are quoted below).

The more recent NSF survey originated with the agency's interest in assessing scientists' perceptions of the peer review system and their reactions to changes in review practices. Some 14,000 surveys were sent to all who applied for individual research project support or research equipment in fiscal year 1985 (thus excluding applications for center support and facilities).[20] Over 9,500 responses were received, many containing extensive written remarks in addition to the questionnaire. (More details about the NSF survey may also be found in the Appendix.)

## Success in the Pursuit of Research Support

Success rates—the proportion of proposals that are funded—
may be the central obsession in scientists' and policy analysts'
thoughts about the funding system. When scientists talk about the
funding system, their discussion soon turns to success rates and
speculations about the reasons underlying them. They often suggest, for example, that cronyism or scientific feuds or the inner
workings of the science bureaucracy account for the relative success and failure of various scientists. Therefore we begin with scientists' experience as successful applicants (or "awardees") of
federal research funds.

On average, respondents to the 1982 survey were quite successful in their pursuit of research support from the NCI: 230
(68.5%) had at least one proposal funded in the period. Two hundred thirty-two respondents submitted a single proposal, of which
161 (69.4%) received support; 104 submitted two or more proposals, with 69 (66.3%) receiving support for at least one proposal. On
the other hand, 106 (31.5%) did not receive support for any of their
proposals. These results roughly parallel respondents' self-
reported career success in obtaining research support. More than
half characterized themselves generally as successful grant-
getters (more proposals funded than not), about a fifth termed
their success mixed (some proposals supported, but less than half),
and only 13% were unsuccessful in securing support for proposals
submitted to NIH. (Some 16% had never previously submitted a
proposal.)

In contrast, about 34% of all proposals submitted to NIH in
the mid-1980s were supported, and about 36% of first submittals
at NSF in fiscal year 1985 received funding (ultimately, about 48%
of all proposals to NSF in that year received some support).[21]

Many scientists' success in the competition for research support is due, in part, to the sheer volume of proposals they submit
and their persistence in revising them. (Recall that amended applications have increased as a proportion of all applications at
NIH, now accounting for about a quarter of the proposals reviewed
by that agency.) Half of the scientists surveyed in 1982 submit
about one proposal a year, on average, while the other half submit
from two to five proposals. Over the past three to five years, nearly
40% said they have been submitting more proposals to NCI; 47%
said they were submitting fewer. Thus, the number of proposals
written does not, by itself, account for increases in the self-
reported workload of scientists or the reviewing burden reported
in agency statistics. As one scientist noted,

The time involved in preparing grant applications, politically lobbying members of the study sections, administering and reporting on results of a grant if and when received along with all the other peripheral involvements that federal funding currently requires cuts the research time of principal investigators at least *50%* (that is the most conservative figure). Furthermore, the push to establish and maintain a good "track record" has caused good scientists to publish incomplete, inaccurate, and generally shoddy work. The NIH grant system is currently the major deterrent to advancement of science in the U.S.

This increase in proposal-writing activity parallels a longer trend: Wyngaarden notes that the proportion of applicants who submitted more than one application for funding to NIH rose from 10% in 1970 to 17% in 1986.[22] Thus growth in the number of proposals submitted to funding agencies is caused by increases in the number of working scientists and, independently, by their increasing propensity to submit (and resubmit) research proposals.

Scientists report that both the proposal-writing and the proposal-reviewing burdens are increasing, leaving them less time for research. In the period from March 1969 through October 1976, the average number of applications considered by an NIH IRG increased from about fifty-five to more than ninety.[23] These burdens appear less severe in the NSF survey data: about 10% of the NSF sample reported submitting six or more proposals in the preceding five years, and nearly half said they had reviewed seven or more proposals in that period (with 17% claiming to have reviewed twenty or more).[24]

## The Consequences of Failure

Two-thirds of those in the NCI survey whose proposals were not funded said they pursued the research anyway, with half seeking support from another source, including elsewhere within the federal government, and 85% reporting that the work was ultimately published. By comparison, in the recent NSF survey, 48% of those whose proposals were not supported said they stopped that line of research (25% were revising the proposal for resubmission to NSF, 11% planned to submitted it elsewhere, and the balance were accommodating in various other ways).[25] In her study of persons denied NIH support, Carter found that 37% of those whose proposals were not supported stopped the unfunded line of research, while 63% continued to seek support (of those, 80% eventually received support).[26] Thus the two NIH-related surveys indicate roughly similar proportions of persistent scientists, with quite comparable outcomes (the 85% of our survey's declinees who eventually publish is very near Carter's 80% who eventually find research support). However, both NIH-based figures are greater than the 52% of the NSF survey sample who persisted.

The burdens of a declined proposal are not shared equally by all scientists. For some it is possible to continue the work, at some level, without substantial support. Others are able to shift research interests. Still others may retreat into clinical practice or teaching. But there is also a sizable and growing minority of scientists whose livelihoods depend upon obtaining research support. For them a declined proposal may mean a job lost or a career ended. Some scientists mention this at second hand:

> This commentator has witnessed many cases in which established, good quality researchers who somehow happened to have remained in research positions rather than tenured positions, suddenly found themselves in a situation where they lost simultaneously their research support, salary and position. . . . The end result is that the sometimes casual pronouncements of peer reviewers have factually become life or death sentences for researchers.

. . . while others have experienced it themselves:

> I have discarded the proposal. The rejection cost me the opportunity to continue the research. I no longer prepare proposals since I am not employed at present in a research capacity. Without the support for innovative research, the teaching profession lost its appeal. . . . My current goals are a long way from the role of T cells in cancer research [the subject of her disapproved proposal].

Academic scientists who are not tenured and those in auxiliary or marginal positions within university institutes or research centers are especially vulnerable to failure. Such scientists must be prepared to redirect their research interests to accommodate isolated failures and long-term shifts in the funding environment. In contrast, tenured scientists, whose careers are more certain, may more readily persevere in the face of a rejected proposal.[27] Among those whose proposals are repeatedly rejected, some will turn away from research entirely, perhaps entering clinical practice or leaving science altogether. Others may persist in their pursuit of support, for reasons based in their social environments, such as organizational incentives to write proposals and rewards for receiving funds. Little more is known about such decisions as the science studies literature has hardly addressed these important issues.

## Attitudes toward Peer Review

The attitudes expressed in the NCI survey should be understood as the comments of active, resilient, generally successful researchers. Their views of the peer review system are intertwined with their perceptions of an environment of increasing resource scarcity, an environment that increases competition, weakens adherence to the norms and niceties of the scientific community, and threatens scientists' livelihoods. By and large, the critical comments do not come from unsuccessful outsiders striking out at a system that has excluded them. In fact, most respondents' personal experiences with the peer review system were generally favorable. Most thought their proposals were sent to the proper study section (80%), agreed with the assigned priority score (63%), and accepted their reviewers' comments (59%). About 40% rated the reviews they received to be "thoughtful, constructive, conscientious"; an additional 18% viewed them to be "sound but lacking detail." In contrast, 20% thought them "incomplete, inaccurate, and/or shoddy."

We asked whether these attitudes were influenced by respondent's success in securing support during fiscal year 1980. To address this, we compared the responses of two extreme categories of scientists: those who were uniformly successful, having gotten between one and four proposals funded during the period (235 respondents), and those who were uniformly unsuccessful, submitting between one and five proposals without receiving support for any (106 people). In effect, this excludes only twenty-five scientists who reported a mixture of success and failure during the year.

As predicted, there were strong, positive associations between success and agreement with the study section assignment (tau c = .276), priority score (tau c = .583), reviewers' comments (tau c = .549), and the quality of peer evaluations (tau c = .533). (See the note to table 3 for explanations of tau c and statistical significance.) Successful scientists think more highly of the system

**Table 3**

Attitudes toward the Peer Review System

| Statement | Agree | Neutral | Disagree | Association with success* |
|---|---|---|---|---|
| Reviewers are biased against women and/or minorities. | 4.9% | 29.6% | 65.4% | −.260 |
| Reviewers are biased against young researchers. | 16.6% | 20.0% | 63.3% | −.325 |
| Reviewers are biased against researchers at non-major universities or in certain regions of the U.S. | 33.7% | 35.0% | 31.3% | −.259 |
| Ideas are routinely pirated from research proposals by reviewers. | 32.1% | 32.7% | 35.2% | −.356 |
| "Old boys' networks" control the Study Sections [IRGs]. | 39.5% | 27.8% | 32.7% | −.418 |
| Reviewers are reluctant to support unorthodox or high-risk research. | 60.8% | 21.4% | 17.7% | −.205 |

* Tau c measures the strength of association between two ordinal variables (that is, variables whose categories reflect only the order of differences, not their magnitude). It is computed by the following formula:

$$\text{tau } c = \frac{2m \, (P-Q)}{N^2 \, (m-1)}$$

in which P is the number of concordant pairs, Q is the number of discordant pairs, N is the total number of pairs, and m is the lesser of the number of columns or the number of rows in the table. All the associations reported here are statistically significant at the .01 level, which means that among samples as large as ours, an association as strong as the one reported would be found purely by chance in only one sample in a hundred.

than do unsuccessful scientists. But these associations are far from perfect: while success predisposes one to approve of peer review practices, a large fraction of successful scientists were disapproving.

Despite respondents' generally favorable views of the reviews they had received, there were also some sharply worded comments from scientists dissatisfied with the quality of reviews and the qualifications of reviewers. Here is a sampling of such remarks.

My grant reviews gave worthless information about the problem.

Evaluations have varied. Some have contained inaccuracies, while being sound overall. Others were quite contentious. I have yet to find one that is constructive.

I have witnessed and experienced the peer review system since the early 50's. It was never ideal. But it appears to me that the reviewers have become less and less capable of judging proposals not exactly within their own spheres of interest. And there can be no doubt that the spheres of interest are becoming narrower and narrower.

If one looks at the composition of study sections published by the NIH and then matches the names of the members against their publications on a topic they may be reviewing, the results are often very disappointing. This leads one to a conclusion that many study section members are engaged in technical reviews of research grant applications without being qualified to do so.

The proportions expressing satisfaction and dissatisfaction in the NCI study are similar to those obtained from the NSF survey, which found 49% expressing some level of satisfaction with the review process, and 38% expressing dissatisfaction.[28] Success strongly influenced satisfaction: only 27% of those consistently declined funding were satisfied (57% were dissatisfied), whereas 83% of those consistently awarded support were satisfied (with 12% dissatisfied).[29] The quotations from NCI respondents closely resemble the "anomic" responses from scientists reported in Hackett's study.[30] Taken together, these results suggest that there is a significant minority of scientists who may be disengaging from the research system, who find its operation unfathomable and unendurable.

The NSF survey asked those who were dissatisfied to write their reasons for dissatisfaction, a procedure quite different from the NCI survey (which asked all respondents about a common set of potential sources of dissatisfaction). Thus the percentages in the two studies are not directly comparable, but it is nonetheless instructive to report some of the NSF survey results. The most frequently cited reasons for dissatisfaction had to do with the expertise and qualifications of reviewers and panelists, which was mentioned by 18% of those dissatisfied, followed closely by complaints about cursory or perfunctory reviews (17%) and conflicting reviews (12%). Cronyism, politics, and the operation of an "old boys' network" were mentioned by 12% of the dissatisfied respondents. Sexism, racism, and age discrimination were not mentioned at all, and regional or institutional bias was cited by only 4% of the dissatisfied respondents.[31]

The NCI survey did not rely on respondents to generate reasons for dissatisfaction, but asked whether they agreed or disagreed with seven charges frequently leveled against the peer review system (see table 3). The first three issues have to do with various direct biases in the peer review system. In this sample only a small proportion (about 5%) believed reviewers to be biased against women and minorities. About one respondent in six noted bias against young researchers, with one respondent in three noting bias by type of university or region.

More serious is the charge, made by one-third of the respondents, that ideas are "routinely pirated" from research proposals by reviewers. This is a grave and blatant violation of professional ethics, with potential legal ramifications. But such charges are exceedingly difficult to investigate and substantiate. Nonetheless, some respondents offered detailed accounts of what had been pirated and by whom.

Almost 40% asserted that NIH Study Sections are controlled by an "old boys' network," meaning a self-perpetuating group of scientists who conspire, perhaps indirectly and at arm's length, to insure that their own work and the work of like-minded scientists receive support, while other proposals go unfunded. Such charges are also hard to support, and empirical investigations have failed to turn up convincing corroborative evidence. Yet the proportion of scientists who noted cronyism of various sorts and the vivid detail of their accounts make it difficult to dismiss out of hand. For example, one respondent wrote in the survey:

> My grant was rejected outright. It was a renewal application. The original [proposal] had a score of less than 1.2 and was fully funded. The proposed "new" research was nearly completed. In the period covered by the original grant 4 or 5 papers were published—the renewal was written in the last of

the second year and there was one year more to go. All the evidence indicated we would succeed and would complete all aspects covered in the "Aims" section. At that time, in-house politics and the "Old Boy Club" exerted pressure in support of a group working in the same area but having no publications in support of the claims they made. Rather than a grant (which would not have been funded) a contract was arranged with the NCI—to do the same work as that proposed in [my] grant. . . . That contract was *fully funded*. At the same time, my renewal application was turned down *cold*! The results of the work have since been published in full . . . [and] I will no longer apply for grants from NIH. There is no peer review.

However, others see a positive role for an old boys' network:

The proposal was first assigned to Epidemiology and it belonged in Endocrinology. The second go-round it did go to Endocrinology, but two key members who know me and my work of 20+ years were absent. The study involves more than 20 years of experience in the *medical* treatment of goiter and thyroid nodules . . . and no one else in the world has equivalent data. . . . While I have been in academic medicine my entire career the proposal was the first one submitted and the last. The critique was an outrage and an insult.

In effect, this respondent is complaining that the review process was impaired because an old boys' network did *not* operate, so the true significance of the proposal was missed.

The most striking finding in this section of the NCI survey is that a substantial majority (60%) of scientists believe that reviewers are reluctant to support unorthodox or high-risk research, while only 18% disagreed with that assertion. This is a complaint frequently lodged against the peer review system. To accommodate it, scientists maintain a mix of more and less risky work, insuring that they will always have a stream of "bread and butter" papers while attempting to do "the breakthrough stuff." Some scientists are very cautious about proposing to do highly imaginative research because they believe that peer review panels are unlikely to approve such proposals.[32]

Respondents to the NCI survey wrote comments to the same effect:

It seems as though the desire is to get guaranteed results of small consequence rather than embarking on *new but risky* initiatives.

Often in the case of a truly innovative, pioneering approach in a frontier area there are no real peers. The reviewers are only marginally related to the area of the proposed investigation. It therefore does great injustice to the researcher to be evaluated by marginal reviewers who may elaborate on some minor points, but fail totally to grasp what is involved in the proposed research because they never had to go through the steps.

NCI is funding success, and trying to avoid failure. That is not what medical research is really like, and that is not what NCI is supposed to be doing.

[If the] primary reviewer is a square head, unconventional approaches do not score well.

Innovative research will *never* be funded by a management approach.

The proposals that get funded are generally the most boring and mundane. Reviewers seem to like a definite plan of attack, which they call "focused."

For three years study sections reviewing applications on chemical carcinogens were dominated by a few investigators who were unwilling to accept proposals which were directed to the study on "new" hypotheses that differed from their concepts.

One must never say anything new in a grant application.

Anything novel had to be bootlegged.

Paradoxically, nearly three-quarters of the respondents claimed that their proposals to NIH were "truly innovative," featuring "an unorthodox approach to the problem." Thus, despite the relatively low award rates of NIH, a substantial fraction of funded work is bound to be innovative, at least in the eyes of the researcher. Of course, this also suggests that innovativeness may be exceedingly difficult to detect and evaluate, and that it may not be such a powerful factor in reviewers' judgments.

Scientists' attitudes about peer review are significantly influenced by success in obtaining research support, as the rightmost column of table 3 indicates. For all items, success is negatively correlated with agreement: those who are rewarded by the system are less likely to criticize it than are those who go unrewarded. But these associations, while sizeable and statistically significant, are far from perfect. Successful scientists tend to be less critical, but they are *not* uniformly uncritical.

## COMPETITION FOR RESEARCH SUPPORT

Commentaries on first-person experiences with grants peer review provide a counterweight to federal agency defenses of their systems. Any agenda for studies of peer review must combine these perspectives, alternatively moving from the trenches to the command posts to develop a comprehensive perspective on the competitive environment for research funding.

James Wyngaarden, while director of the National Institutes of Health, began a recent article on the status of NIH in its centennial year by remarking that "the most satisfying aspect of my first 5 years as director of the National Institutes of Health has been the sustained growth of NIH funding." After considering various facets of NIH's 28% real growth in the period, he continued in these words:

> I have dwelt on the recent history of the NIH appropriation in order to gainsay the statements I hear on many university campuses, in many addresses of presidents of professional societies, and from leaders of voluntary health agencies that the NIH appropriation has been slashed, that the federal support of biomedical research is capricious, and that the future is uncertain. My experience convinces me that the opposite is true.[33]

Yet many scientists in our survey, and those interviewed in other studies, do not perceive this increase in research support, and instead experience disheartening competition for funds. One of the most convincing features of their comments is that the scientists see the problem from both sides of the funding decision, sometimes recounting their personal difficulties in obtaining funds, and other times lamenting the hard choices they must make as reviewers or members of panels and Study Sections. Comments such as these give a sense of their views:

It is unfortunately an inescapable fact (particularly in these days of scarce funds and low priority score funding cutoffs) that frequently reviewers are competing with the writer of the proposal under review for funds from the same decreasing money pool. Under these circumstances, it may be understandably difficult for even the fairest of reviewers to be completely objective, particularly since (1) there are many more proposals meriting funding than can be funded and, (2) it is not unusual these days for even well-established investigators to have funding difficulties. Therefore, I subscribe to the opinion that peer review does not produce the desired results when funds are as scarce as they are now. Unfortunately, a better alternative is difficult if not impossible to formulate.

Peer review is a workable and fair system as long as there is good balance between the number of new and competing proposals that can be funded and the number submitted. At present, many institutes at the NIH, such as NIAID [the National Institute for Allergic and Infectious Diseases] have so little money that the priority for cut-off in funding lies at the 1.5–1.7 level. This means that many excellent proposals will not be funded. I do not believe that there is a significant difference between a proposal receiving a 1.49 and one receiving a 1.89. The problem is not with the peer review system; the problem is with our national values and priorities.

When the research dollars are shrinking, the present system breaks down. When scores are assigned by individuals who are not familiar with the field, have not read the application, but assign a score based on the 2–3 sentence summary (or even the complete review), then the "review" process is nothing more than a lottery. Peer review is quite good at separating the scientifically qualified from the unqualified, but it is not capable of distinguishing between applications down to the third decimal, which is the present case.

In times of high competition the peer review system is inappropriate. It works to exclude poor research, but it cannot distinguish between competing high-quality research. It has become almost random.

I'm not sure what your point is, but I think you've overlooked the main problems in science funding: (1) lack of core, stable support for research; (2) faculty on soft money; (3) universities with an administrative financial interest in grants. These create the frantic atmosphere.

As a member of an ACS [American Cancer Society] study section, I am saddened by the decisions we must make. There are many fine proposals but funds are so scarce that we must eliminate two-thirds of the truly outstanding proposals. The survivors are just lucky. Often they have a convincing, respected reviewer on the study section.

We contend that many of the shortcomings of peer review result from intense competition for research resources. Several factors have made the competition more intense: (1) stable or declining allocations, in real dollars, for scientific research; (2) programmatic shifts from one area of science to another (e.g., the reductions in support for the social sciences in the early 80s and for the life sciences in the mid-1970s); (3) earmarking of funds for specific projects, which leaves a smaller pool from which to support proposals in open competition (discussed more fully in chapter 5); (4) increased costs of research, driven up by increases in salaries, equipment costs, animal care, supplies, and the complexity of research; (5) increased numbers of scientists; (6) organizational pressures exerted on scientists to obtain support, expressed in the creation of institutes, centers and the academic marginals who staff them (whose salaries are derived from research funds), graduate student and postdoctoral support (derived now more than ever from research grants), and the dependence of university budgets on external research funds (often to rebuild decaying infrastructure).

This intensified competition for resources has adverse consequences for the peer review system and for scientists. Peer review suffers because funding decisions must be made at a level of discernment that exceeds the "resolving power" of the evaluation instrument. In other words, a system that might be able to evaluate proposals within, say, a half-point average margin of error, is now forced to make funding decisions on proposals that differ by only a few hundredths of a point. (It is an interesting violation of good scientific practice: these decisions are being made using an indicator—the average priority score—that has more significant digits than its component scores, as well as a good dollop of measurement error.) This phenomenon and its causes are clearest in the experience of NIH.

Members of NIH IRGs are scientists who have had substantial experience with the federal funding system. Although they are instructed to evaluate proposal quality in the abstract, they do so in full knowledge that the ultimate decision will be to fund or not to fund. Knowing this, and knowing with substantial accuracy the "pay line" of the Institute likely to make the funding decision, they assign priority scores mindful of their judgments' effect on the proposal's ultimate prospects. (NSF panels function in much the same way, although the details of their operation are different.) Thus, despite the five-point scale, which has been graded in intervals of one-tenth of a point since 1980, IRG members are fully aware that they are deciding whether or not to support an application.

## Upward Creep and Resubmission: A Protracted Process

Amended applications, those that had failed to receive support and have been submitted in revised form, constitute a large and growing fraction of all NIH applications. In effect, an increasing portion of IRG members' time is spent reviewing again applications that were not supported on their first submission. This creates a fine engine for generating better and better priority scores, crowded ever more tightly into the top brackets of the scale. Not only are the applications likely to be materially improved by revision, but the IRG members, receiving for re-review an application they thought had received a "fundable" priority score, will understandably assign a better score to the amendment to be sure that it is awarded. While this formally violates the IRG's mandate—their task is to evaluate proposals in the abstract, without regard to funding status—it is nevertheless rational, even responsible, behavior. (In the less formal system at NSF such processes of collective judgment are even more likely, although the decision ultimately rests with the program manager.)

Priority score inflation compels judgments on ever-finer differences at the very top of the scale, which in turn: (1) weakens the *collective* power of scientists in the IRGs while increasing members' *individual* power; (2) decreases tolerance for speculation, intuition, or risk; and (3) disorients or discourages applicants.

To understand how recalibration of the evaluation scale can influence the distribution of decision-making power, we must first recall the special character of the NIH dual-review system: IRGs, representing fields of science, make scientific judgments about the technical merit of proposals whereas Advisory Councils make programmatic judgments about the value of proposals to an Institute's mission and national health. To be certified for funding by an Institute's Advisory Council, an application must first be approved by an IRG. Priority scores offer guidance to the Advisory Council, but they are not binding; in theory, the Council may choose to fund any subset of the approved applications. (In practice, a tiny fraction of all funded applications are chosen out of priority score order.)

As the proportion of approved applications increases, the funding latitude of the Councils increases, at least in principle, because the only definitive power of an IRG is negative: to disapprove an application and thus insure that it is not funded. Although there is no pressing reason to expect Advisory Councils to exercise this broader latitude, there is only tradition and the limits of members' interest and energies to prevent it. Thus, with the increasing proportion of approved applications, the power of an IRG, taken as a unit, has declined relative to that of an Advisory Council. And as the differences between approved applications grow narrower, it makes increasing sense for Councils to support proposals somewhat out of order (because, after all, an increasing share of the proposals they consider have been rated quite highly, with very small average differences between proposals).

Curiously, this crowding at the top of the scale also increases the individual power of IRG members, for a quite different reason. If Advisory Councils continue to support applications in priority score order, and if that order is based on smaller and smaller differences, any single scientist's rating can effectively blackball a proposal. A hypothetical example may clarify this point. Suppose an IRG of fifteen members reviews a proposal. Fourteen members regard it very highly and uniformly assign priority scores of 1.25, while the fifteenth person, for whatever reason, assigns a score of 5. (Scores are assigned by secret ballot, so IRG members are not formally accountable for their evaluations.) If the fourteen scores are accurate assessments of the proposal's quality, then we might say it is "really" a 1.25 proposal, and it will be among the top proposals at any Institute, virtually assured of support. When a single member assigns a score of 5, the proposal's overall priority becomes 1.5, which, today, approaches the boundary between funded and unfunded proposals at many Institutes. The principle is clear: as the payline creeps upward, the impact of a single poor evaluation increases. While in practice matters may not be as clear-cut as they are in the constructed example, it is plain that even a small number of poor scores will have an increased impact on the fate of a proposal. The lesson is clear, too: a proposal writer must please all of the reviewers all of the time, and be especially careful never to offend any of them.

And scientists in their comments make it clear that they perceive such powerful influences. Two instances will illustrate their perceptions.

> A vehement objection by one reviewer to even a minor part of a proposal can sway the objectivity of the entire peer review panel in a negative way (rarely is there a positive influence).

> I feel the major problem with peer review is the influence of the primary reviewer on the opinion of other people on study section who are unfamiliar with the field and who have had little or no time to consider the other proposals.

Under these conditions peer review will, over time, become increasingly ineffective as a method of evaluating proposals and allocating resources. The judgments required of the system will become too refined, and, among participants within the system, the critical decisions will more often rest on programmatic, not scientific, concerns. Such increased opportunities for partisanship, conflict of interest, and bias to determine a proposal's fate may corrupt the system from within by weakening scientists' faith in the "rightness" of the system (more about this below).

The upward creep of ratings will also influence IRG's ability to support risky or innovative work and, by extension, scientists' ability to perform such work. Two mechanisms account for this change. First, by definition, a risky project has a lower probability of success than a less risky one. Thus the evidence available to the reviewers, the proposal, will communicate this uncertainty. The proposal will appear "less perfect," and be less likely to yield results, than its safer competitors. And it will probably be rated accordingly. Second, prior performance has become increasingly important in the evaluation process at both NIH and NSF. Survey evidence from NIH applicants supports this point: scientists say that they have been held accountable to perform the experiments as proposed, and IRG members note that, when reviewing an application for a competitive renewal, they have looked for evidence that the workplan of the previous proposal had been completed successfully. At NSF, the evaluation of the products of earlier NSF grants has recently become an explicit criterion in decisions about a subsequent award. In consequence, not only is it less likely that a risky proposal will be chosen for funding, but it is also less likely that a scientist will pursue an innovative path that deviates from the proposed research plan. Hence one would predict that less innovative science will be performed under federal support.

The strains of the peer review system will afflict science and scientists in other ways as well. Consider, for example, the effect of the upward creep of priority scores and proposal ratings. As evaluations are recalibrated, the psychological effect will be similar to the effect of currency inflation or grade "inflation": it will become harder and harder to know, at a gut level, what the rating of a proposal means. Just as the grade "B" is no longer much of a reward for many able college students, despite its nominal significance of "good" performance, evaluations that average "2" on the 5-point scales used by NIH and NSF are less likely to lead to funding, and thus have lost their nominal meaning of "very good." After all, a scientist who has invested a month of effort in a proposal that is rated "very good" by her peers expects a more satisfying return than the opportunity to prepare an amended application for the next funding cycle. When this occurs, it signals to the scientist that something is out of balance in the world, that the accustomed standards of performance and rewards no longer apply. In sociological language, such conditions are termed "anomic," signifying that the rules or norms which regulate the social world are no longer working.

## Anomie and Reform

Scientists' great dependence upon external funding for research, coupled with their perceptions of the uncertainty and randomness of securing such support, have given rise to anomic conditions in science.[34] These conditions are reflected in scientists' statements of withdrawal and disengagement, for example:

> Because of the generally thoughtless and sometimes insulting comments of principal reviewers, and the fact that there is only one-way communication with no real possibility of exchanging views, I no longer request the pink sheets, nor do I read the letter sent. NCI funds by phone, so the mere receipt of a letter at the appropriate time is notification of "not funded."

> I have stopped submitting proposals to the NCI because I feel that it is a waste of time. Tumor antigen research . . . has fallen into what appears to be the "non-fundable" category. . . . reviewers appear to be very prejudiced and their re-

view comments summarily dismiss the project (at least mine) without thoughtful consideration of the merits of the particular study contemplated.

I have been reasonably successful in obtaining funding although I am quite young [six of fourteen proposals funded over a five-year period). Still I maintain the chances of any one proposal being funded are *purely statistical* at best. All one needs is one unsubstantiated or emotional comment by *one* reviewer to significantly lower one's chances. The philosophy of spending a great deal of time writing proposals which have 50% chance of being funded is appalling.

I regard the writing of unfunded proposals as a pure waste of time, irrespective of whether this is a failure on my part or on that of the review process. As a result, I have defected back to full-time clinical practice, where at least any contributions I make are largely real and unarguable.

These anomic conditions are also reflected in attitudes about reforming the peer review system. The NCI survey asked respondents to evaluate three proposed changes in the peer review process. The first, eliminating reviewer anonymity, would allow proposal writers to know who said what about their proposals. Reviewers would then become more accountable for their comments, possibly making reviews more thorough, conscientious, and helpful while reducing gratuitously cutting remarks. Respondents generally were not in favor of such a change: 27% favored it while 61% opposed it (12% were undecided or ambivalent).

Blind reviewing, the second change in procedure presented to respondents, met with a more ambivalent response. "Blinding" a proposal is accomplished by removing all evidence of the applicant's identity from the document, thus focusing the evaluator's attention on the proposal, not the proposer. Such a procedure might reduce the likelihood of feuds between scientists who have had a falling out of some sort, and it might also protect against regional and institutional biases. About 40% of the respondents favored blind reviewing, but 47% opposed it.

Finally, we asked whether an applicant's "track record" (or history of performance, chiefly publications) should be given more weight than it now has. Half thought it should be weighted as it is now, while 28% would give it more influence, 22% less influence.

Perhaps these survey respondents were equivocal because the survey questions failed to propose the best or most effective changes in the system. To be sure, the changes proposed are incremental in character, not particularly bold or sweeping. As noted in the preceding chapter, alternatives to peer review might include some form of two-stage funding, with direct support given to institutions for redistribution to scientists. Or funds might be allocated according to a formula that takes into account the scientist's career stage, track record, and other characteristics.

But we think the responses would have been equally ambivalent even if we had suggested more or different changes in the system. Scientists may be truly ambivalent about the peer review system, an ambivalence driven by equal parts of familiarity, commitment, and contempt. Their familiarity has grown out of long experience with the system, and is accompanied by apprehension that any replacement will only be worse. Their commitment has developed from participation as a reviewer or grant recipient, and from ideological justifications having to do with the importance of competition and the autonomy of science. Their contempt has been born of disappointment and failure, and causes a desire for almost any change. But it is an easy journey from contempt to despair and disengagement; scientists who make that trip do not much care how the system changes because they have no further use for it.

## INFERENCES: PEER REVIEW AND CONFLICTS OF INTEREST

Studies which examine peer review in isolation from the social, political, economic, historical, and cultural contexts of modern science are inadequate and misguided. Reductionism and the isolated study of components of a complex whole are worthy analytic strategies that have served science well. But lacking a comprehensive model of the entire phenomenon under investigation, such studies remain limited and incomplete. The essential issues of peer review are grounded in more general concerns about the allocation of scarce research resources, patterns of career development and mobility, the social organization of modern science, and the connection between science and society.

It is apparent that the quality of reviews and the appropriateness of reviewers greatly concern many scientists. In the statistical results of several surveys, respondents have pointed to the low quality of reviews and the apparently inadequate qualifications of reviewers as serious weaknesses in the peer review system. But on the other hand, qualified reviewers are also likely to be the proposer's acquaintances, colleagues, and competitors within the narrow research area. (Such research areas may be quite small: Price estimated that "invisible colleges" number about 100 members.) As research areas become more specialized (and perhaps narrower), particularly in relation to the size of the scientific labor force, the pool of qualified reviewers would be expected to shrink. Indeed, we might take the complaints of proposal writers as evidence that the pool *has* shrunk, that it is difficult to find reviewers who have the special combination of knowledge and skill needed to review a proposal. (Yet in their NSF-sponsored experiment, the Coles had no trouble locating a set of reviewers who did not overlap very much with the original set of NSF reviewers.)

The increasingly interdisciplinary character of science also contributes to the narrowing of the appropriate reviewer pool: while there may be ample reviewers available in each of the related fields, there may be few at the intersection. And those in the fields, too far from the intersection, may produce overly critical or otherwise inadequate reviews.[35]

In the worst case, the pool of appropriate reviewers may shrink to include only those likely to have a conflict of interest because they are so close to the proposer (as collaborators or colleagues). Selecting reviewers from outside this pool would invite an incompetent, incomplete, or inappropriate review, yet within the circle friendships, rivalries, and professional relations jeopardize the character and quality of reviews. Exacerbating these pressures is the shrinking pool of real dollars for research—that is, dollars adjusted for inflation in the cost of research, the increasing complexity of science, and the magnitude of competition for resources. The ethically difficult task of providing an objective, disinterested, reasoned review may soon become practically impossible.

## CONCLUSIONS

It is both difficult and dangerous for researchers to enter the black box of peer review, and what they find there is in significant measure colored by the sponsorship that allowed them to enter. Participants in the peer review system are strongly invested in it and may be reluctant to cooperate with researchers. Therefore, entry often must be sponsored by an agency—or the agency must study itself—and the mere fact of that sponsorship or the agency's choice of researcher to sponsor has some effect on the findings.

The intensity of competition for research support is high—absurdly high in some fields—and that competition brings with it a host of undesirable side effects. Among these are an unwillingness to take risks, priority score inflation, reported thefts of ideas, increasing possibilities for conflicts of interest, and bitterness over recurrent difficulties in securing support. A significant fraction of scientists surveyed were dissatisfied with the grants peer review system. While successful scientists tended to be more favorably disposed than unsuccessful ones, there was substantial discontent among scientists within the former group.

In sum, although there is no call for alarm about the grants peer review system, there is also little warrant for celebration or even contentment. While difficulties recounted in this chapter may seem a mandate for change, both scientists and policymakers are hesitant about reforming the system. Perhaps their reluctance is fueled by a greater willingness to confront a known obstacle rather than to face a new, unknown one. In part, too, it is grounded in the prior successes of many scientists. Whatever the basis for their stance, we must persuade them to set it aside and experiment with alternative funding mechanisms.

# 4

# *Peer Review*

## *and the*

# *Printed Word*

There's no glory, pay, or recognition in refereeing. It's done anony-
mously . . . and is presented as a good-citizen chore that comes with
membership in the scientific community.

Daniel S. Greenberg (1980)

Anonymity transforms the "peers" into a clique of censors and the
"reviews" into mandates of censorship.

Thomas J. Sernka (1978)

Publication is the lifeblood of science, conveying the symbolic nu-
trients of new theories, research findings, credit, and critical scrutiny. Journals and the articles they contain are so characteristic of
science and so firmly entrenched that today these regularly published collections of research results drive, and perhaps define, the
scientific enterprise. In the conventional view, scientific writings,
unlike fiction and poetry, purport to discuss objective, external
states of the natural and social world that are perceptible to all,
not limited only to those with special sensitivities or insights. Un-

83

like nonfiction books and articles, science is written for an audience of appreciative specialists, not for the educated general public. Unlike scholarly writing in the humanities, science strives to reveal and create enduring "truths" of a special sort: truths that are unbounded by historical events or prior assumptions and that can be demonstrated empirically as well as logically. While each of these characteristics helps to distinguish scientific publications from others, they are chiefly differences of degree and emphasis, not sharp boundaries that delineate science from nonscience. There are many enduring truths in poetry, and much art, intuition, and persuasive rhetoric in the best science.

Scientific writing is distinguished by the process and criteria that decide what is published, where, when, and in what form. "Journal peer review," the general term for the method commonly used to select scientific manuscripts for publication, establishes a communal interest in the publication decision by creating a unique, formal consultation among authors, editors, and reviewers (or "referees") about the merits, scope, style, methods, substance, and knowledge claims of a potential article. This method of selection, particularly its communal character and the formal and informal rules which govern its functioning, transforms a scientific manuscript into consensual "knowledge" and enduring testimony to the skills (or shortcomings) of its author.

The scientific journal has been a repository of research findings and a channel of communication for roughly 325 years. But most contemporary journals were founded very recently—a consequence of the rapid growth and differentiation of science. Despite this relative youth, the claims advanced in a scientific publication, especially a publication appearing in a prestigious, "peer-reviewed" journal, are given much credence by the public and have great evidentiary value among policymakers.[1] Through its roles in establishing priority and apportioning credit, publication has become central to the reward and resource allocation systems of science. Evaluations of publications (and, sometimes, simple tallies of the publications and others' references to them) today figure prominently in decisions to hire and promote scientists and to award them research support.[2]

In this chapter we will examine the scientific publication system and the role of peer review within it. To understand what goes on within *this* black box we must first consider the purposes and practices of peer review. Then we will review current studies of the organization and functioning of journal peer review, highlighting key findings and underscoring important areas of ignorance. Then, using illustrative case material, we will suggest what else might be going on within the black box, why it matters, and what might be done about it.

## THE PURPOSES OF SCIENTIFIC PUBLICATION AND JOURNAL PEER REVIEW

The practice of journal peer review began almost simultaneously with the founding of the first scientific journals, the *Journal des Sçavans* (January 1665) and the *Philosophical Transactions* of the Royal Society (March 1665). Before these journals appeared, scientists communicated through correspondence, exchange of personal reports of experiments and findings, and private printing (without editorial intervention) of scientific work. Publication in a journal, under the auspices of a scientific society and the guidance of an editor, replaced the haphazard circulation and content of letters with the generally available and more standardized journal article. It also solved the riddle of how to make new ideas and results available for general use while preserving a scientist's claim to priority and credit—in effect, creating communal recognition of private intellectual property. And, because publications carried the explicit approval of the scientific society that sponsored the journal, a measure of quality assurance emerged. In short, scientific publication facilitated communication, allocation of credit, and authentication of research results.[3]

A more elaborate list of functions, based on an analysis of historical material about the early years of the *Philosophical Transactions* of the Royal Society, has been offered by Harriet Zuckerman and Robert Merton.[4] Publication is first a method of *communication* that allows others to learn of a scientist's new theories, discoveries, and experiments, while establishing the scientist's claims to *priority* and *credit* for having been the first to discover a new fact or phenomenon or to advance a novel conjecture. Thus publications both then and now often bear the date on which the work was first received by the journal, establishing precisely when and by whom a set of claims were first made public, and journals that can provide rapid publication are especially valued by scientists eager to claim priority. Publication also bestows a modicum of *permanence* to a manuscript, entering both the work and its author into the archives of a discipline.

None of these functions involves peer review, but they instead exemplify the advantages of publication over private circulation.

Since journals are social entities, often published under the aegis of a scientific society, discipline, or specialty, they also bear the authority of that group, typically vested in the journal editor and, through the editor, in its reviewers. As the published manuscript will bear the imprimatur of the journal and its constituency, referees were called upon to *authenticate* the findings advanced in a manuscript. The importance and personal character of authentication is stated most plainly in this letter from Henry Oldenburg, the first editor of the *Philosophical Transactions,* to Robert Boyle:

> Before he will declare anything positively of the figure of these Glasses, [the president of the Royal Society] will by a gage measure them; and if the Invention bear his test, it will pass for currant, & be no discredit to the Society, that a member of theirs is the Author thereof.[5]

Underscoring the importance of this imprimatur, when the Society sometimes published work without such evaluation, it publicly diluted the authority of publication by invoking "the policy of 'sit penes authorem fides' [let the author take responsibility for it]: We only set it down, as it was related to us, without putting any great weight upon it.'"[6] Note also that the personal and almost leisurely character of authentication depicted in the preceding passage contrasts sharply with modern refereeing practice, in which replication and reexamination have virtually no place. Finally, referees not only authenticated a manuscript but also *evaluated* it, determining whether its results, however accurate, were important enough to deserve to be published in a particular journal.

Zuckerman and Merton summarize the institutionalization of refereeing and scientific publication in these words:

> Ingredients of the referee system were thus emerging in response to distinctive concerns of scientists taken distributively and collectively. In their capacity as producers of science, individual scientists were concerned with having their work recognized through publication in forms valued by other members in the emerging scientific community who were significant to them. In their capacity as consumers of science, they were concerned with having the work produced by others competently assessed so that they could count on its authenticity. In providing the organizational machinery to

meet these concerns, the Royal Society was concerned with having its authoritative status sustained by arranging for reliable and competent assessments.[7]

Implicit in this passage is the possibility that scientists' dual roles as producers and consumers of knowledge will not always be in harmony, and that the dual aspects of the institution of scientific publication—which both filters and distributes work—may be in tension. But Zuckerman and Merton do not pursue this duality and its inherent tensions. Perhaps because they were intent on analyzing the positive ("eufunctional") features of peer review, they chose not to delve into its darker aspects (or "dysfunctions").[8] In the pages below we will consider some of the contradictions, engendered by journal peer review, that arise within scientists and within science. Analysts of peer review at times are blinkered by the powerful values that make up the cultural context of science, hence are unable or unwilling to notice that science operates imperfectly. We will illustrate this phenomenon in our discussion of research on journal peer review.

### New Burdens

Peer review was part of the earliest practices of scientific journals and has made a unique contribution to the production and dissemination of new knowledge. Journal peer review has grown complex and taken on new functions and responsibilities appropriate for the social arrangements of contemporary science. For example, referees cannot guarantee the originality and accuracy of the manuscripts they review because replication (or even substantial recalculation or reanalysis) is hardly possible with the high cost of research, the intense pressures on scientists to produce new knowledge rapidly, and the dearth of necessary detail in the research report. To the contrary, the numbers of innocent oversights, sloppy errors, published retractions, and outright frauds, as well as evidence from studies of the review process, suggest that reviewers are incapable of authenticating results.[9] Often the question asked of referees is not merely whether the results presented appear to be correct and useful additions to the store of archival knowledge, but also whether they are sufficiently "spectacular" to warrant publication in a very visible journal. In consequence, referees' evaluations may make quite positive statements about the quality of the science presented in a paper, then suggest that the work be directed to a more specialized journal.[10]

The allocation of credit is also more complicated today than it was in the past. Referees insure that papers make an original contribution rather than repeating something that is already known (of which the author may be unaware), connect the current manuscript to prior work, and confirm that earlier work is appropriately considered and acknowledged.[11] Referees often accomplish this by suggesting that additional work be cited—sometimes their own work or that of their colleagues and associates. As citation counts become an increasingly important tool for science policy research and the evaluation of scientific work (see chapter 6), these subtler mechanisms of protecting others' credit grow in importance. In the seventeenth century, Robert Boyle worried that a "philosophicall robber," a highwayman of science, would purloin his discoveries; that robber's modern counterpart is a cryptomnesiac or plagiarist who uses others' work without attribution.

Today peer review has the character of an extended trilateral negotiation among authors, editors, and reviewers. Papers are rarely accepted at first sight, but instead undergo at least one and not uncommonly as many as five rounds of revision en route to publication.[12] In a close examination of the rhetoric of two scientific manuscripts and their associated revisions, correspondence, and referees' reports, Greg Myers has argued that peer review is a negotiation between author and journal about the scope of the knowledge claims that will ultimately appear in print.[13] Authors strive to make the most general knowledge claims possible, seeking the broadest feasible applicability and audience for their work, whereas reviewers evaluate and limit the claim. Thus the peer review process may be less concerned with authentication, narrowly construed, than it is with establishing the generality of the finding—the breadth or narrowness of its significance for other research. In this boundary negotiation journal peer review resembles the patent examination process, wherein the applicant lays claim to the largest plausible area of intellectual turf, while the patent examiner uses preexisting patents and other means to moderate and circumscribe the claim.[14]

### "Truth" as Consequence

The contemporary peer review system also has significant indirect consequences for the functioning of science. First, the anticipation of peer review may raise the general quality of scientific research because scientists may draw on their prior experience as reviewers and reviewees to *imagine* the criticisms that reviewers might make of their work and take measures to forestall or remedy them.[15] Second, peer reviewing increases the confidence with which nonspecialists, including laypersons, may use scientific results.[16] In one sense such "truth" is a direct consequence of the imprimatur of the journal and the scientists affiliated with it. But there is also a halo effect that lends credence to the whole of a journal's contents and, at a greater remove, to the entire corpus of peer-reviewed science. Third, peer review reinforces the stratification system of science by providing referees, who are more likely to be established, productive scientists, with a steady flow of privileged information about the work of others.[17] Although formally enjoined from using privileged information for personal gain by the ethical codes of professional societies and the specific provisions of conflict-of-interest policies, few scientists can resist making some use of the knowledge gained from reviewing. (At a minimum such information could be used preemptively to avoid unsuccessful approaches that others have tried.) Finally, peer review lubricates the process of selecting and reshaping manuscripts for publication. It does this by serving as a foil against which the editor can play during negotiations with authors. The shrewd editor need not overtly embrace the reviewers' criticisms and conditions. Indeed, an editor may deliberately distance himself or herself from the reviews, using them as an argumentative resource during negotiations. This distributes responsibility for the editorial decision into the scientific community, dissipating into a "sink" of anonymity much of the heat that the review process might generate.

Thus the scientific publication decision is overdetermined: there is often ample evidence for both publishing *and* not publishing a manuscript, so the editor is free to choose almost any action within the broad confines established by the reviews, using the arguments available in the referees' reports as justification. Similarly, straightforward as the purposes of publication may be, they too are imperfect guides to behavior: they are neither fully in harmony with one another nor always in agreement with the interests of all parties to the manuscript review system. The potential conflict between two scientists competing for priority in a research area is easily recognized but difficult to manage in the review process, for such scientists are also one another's most appropriate reviewers. Even more subtle are the inherent contradictions of interests and principles—the ambivalences—at work within scientists.

## PRINCIPLES AND PRACTICES: THE TENSIONS
## OF PEER REVIEW

Peer review is characterized by powerful tensions at virtually every level. Editors must both solicit and screen manuscripts. Referees may admire the insights of competitors' manuscripts, which they then may try to forestall or scuttle. Authors understand that a complete and lucid manuscript is more likely to be understood by reviewers, yet clarity would also make its failings obvious to critics and its innovations more accessible to competitors.

Journals serve science by publishing original research findings, but reviewers' standards often work against innovative ideas and novel results. Journals are instruments of communication, openly disseminating scientists' papers; yet the decision to publish is made in private and is based upon confidential reports of anonymous referees. Scientific research is putatively grounded in principles of free and open inquiry, yet journal peer review can create and reinforce scientific dogma.[18]

Innovativeness is widely accepted as a key to the advancement of science. But within existing peer review systems the premium on innovativeness is diluted. Nowhere is this more apparent than in scholarly journals that referee submissions and publish the products of research on a space-available basis, often charging for the privilege. But in other journals the negotiation about the knowledge claims asserted in a manuscript can be so intense that referees ultimately eviscerate the work, leaving little of importance available for publication (if they do not insist on outright rejection for the more innovative, risky work).

Trace the sequence of events in the research process that culminates in publication and you will find an accumulating investment in both the rhetoric of scientific progress and its affirmation in the printed word.[19] Once "peers" lend their judgment to manuscripts vying for space, they bestow the imprimatur of that journal on the knowledge claims it contains. This is a subtle and covert process of negotiation that often pits powerful egos and reputations against one another. The passing comfort of knowing more today than yesterday is accompanied by a tension over conveying that new knowledge to peers. Once persuaded, some defend the dogma, while others remain skeptical and chip away at it. The result is a fluid, fragile, ephemeral consensus about what is "known" and what is "good" science.

Journal peer review comprises a major part of this ongoing psychological, political, and intellectual jockeying.[20] Since publication is the return on the investments made in the research funding process, we often hear the formula "money in, papers out." But the process is not quite so simple; problems abound in the conversion process that operates within the black box of peer review.

As societies demand more of science (in the service of national defense, economic competitiveness, or some fleeting new priority), and as the resources available for science are spread more thinly, pressures toward increased efficiency, accountability, and responsiveness will multiply the wrenching forces already at work and further jeopardize an already fragile arrangement. Whatever the difficulties and dangers, journal peer review must be better understood as an enabling mechanism and its principles and operating practices reconsidered.

### Journal Practices

As a counterweight to the idealized purposes of journal peer review that abound in public testimonials to its virtues, consider these operating principles:[21]

1. The advice embodied in a referee's report is usually solicited in confidence and the referee's anonymity is preserved. Without this guarantee, the candor of referees and the relationship among peers are purportedly compromised. Yet this also means that the author has little recourse against a malicious or shoddy review: without knowing the reviewer's identity, it is hard to judge the reviewer's competence, biases, and professional interests. While reviewer anonymity reduces the likelihood of reprisals and open feuding, it may also foster suspicion and stifle legitimate concerns about reviewers' qualifications and predilections.

2. Even in so-called double-blind reviewing, the identity of authors often may be deduced from the manuscript's bibliography (since authors are incurable self-citers), its research focus, language, logic, or the materials and methods employed. Thus "blind" reviewing may be less blind than participants imagine. Moreover, both the reviewer and the author may benefit from opening the blind a bit: the reviewer who learns the identity of an author now has a fuller interpretive context within which to evaluate a text ("I wouldn't have said that if I had known it was *your* paper"), while the author who lets slip

his or her identity is letting the reviewer know the cali-
bre and power of the scientist whose work is being
judged. This may explain why manuscripts submitted by
eminent physicists to *Physical Review* were disproportionately likely to be reviewed by the editors alone.[22] To send
such work out for anonymous review, assuming that anonymity could be preserved, would risk embarrassing and
inconvenient criticisms that could not be readily handled
in the editorial office.

Correct guesses of identities in this masquerade, if
acted upon, become moderately serious breaches of professional conduct; incorrect guesses may lead to the identity confusions of a Molière comedy. And incorrect
guesses seem more likely than correct ones: Michael Mahoney asked a sample of journal editors (who are presum-
ably more knowledgeable than the average reviewer) to
identify the authors of a set of manuscripts. The editors
predicted that they would guess correctly 72 percent of
the time; in fact they were right in only 36 percent of the
cases.[23]

3.  The journal editor occupies a delicate position between
    the author and reviewers, alternating among the roles of
    wordsmith and gatekeeper, caretaker and networker, lit-
    erary agent and judge. When caustic reviews scald an au-
    thor, the editor applies salve. When reviewers fail to
    detect flawed or fraudulent work, the editor takes the
    blame. While editors have the power to allocate scarce re-
    sources of journal space, recognition, and legitimacy, they
    depend upon authors to supply workable manuscripts
    and rely upon reviewers for accurate and thorough as-
    sessments. However formalized, open, and principled the
    review process may be, much that determines the fate of
    a manuscript takes place within an editor's mind and
    within his or her range of discretionary behavior.

    Editors are beholden to their journal's readership in
    surprising ways. When an author complained about the
    rejection (without review) of his manuscript, Libbie Hen-
    rietta Hyman, editor of *Systematic Zoology,* replied

    Inquiries among subscribers indicate that the jour-
    nal has had enough for the present of articles about
    numerical taxonomy. However, further opinions on
    this matter are desired. An article of this nature is

scheduled for the March, 1962, issue, but that will
be the last of this nature for the present.[24]

4. Many subtle devices are available to referees who find a
manuscript objectionable for one reason or another. One
may ask for further evidence, more detailed analyses, a
fuller description of methods; call attention to neglected
literature, or in ways bold and subtle impugn the value of
a manuscript and the integrity of its author. Expressed in
telephone conversations, private languages (in which
terms may not carry their usual meanings), and privileged communications between editor and reviewer (such
as portions of review forms *not* intended for the author's
eyes), such fugitive criticisms are seldom read by outsiders, let alone analyzed systematically, and their sources
are rarely held accountable for their remarks. Referees
also need not discharge their responsibility expeditiously,
as time is on their side. Sometimes delay affords a competitive advantage, allowing the reviewer to use information contained in a manuscript to professional advantage.

5. The inequality in the author-referee relationship overwhelmingly favors the referee. The referee is a surrogate
for the research community, as constituted and "licensed"
by the editor, and acts as a gatekeeper whose judgment
affects whether, when, and in what form knowledge
claims will be disseminated. Editors may vary in their
dependence on reviewers, attenuating the association between reviewers' recommendations and the ultimate disposition of a manuscript. Some review forms explicitly
solicit comments for the editor's eyes only, allowing the
reviewer to make comments that will not be passed along
to the author. In other instances, the amount of journal
space available is so small in comparison with the number of manuscripts submitted that it is impossible to publish even those manuscripts unanimously approved by
reviewers. In such circumstances the editor may ask for
additional advice from one or more trusted reviewers, or
may choose to make the decision alone.[25]

6. Editors have almost unbridled freedom in their choice of
referees and in the number of referees they consult. Some
journals with high acceptance rates apparently assume a
manuscript to be publishable unless there is forceful evi-

dence to the contrary; editors use the review process to
screen out only the most obviously misguided efforts, and
therefore only consult with one or two referees.[26] At the
other extreme, controversial articles in contentious areas
of science may receive as many as two dozen reviews offering the full range of recommended dispositions.[27]

The upshot of these operating principles is that the peer-
reviewed printed word is subject to secrecy, caprice, delay, rejection, and premature disclosure. It is not difficult for any of these to
occur; in many instances reviewers need only act in their rational
self-interest, disregarding formal (but unenforceable) rules and informal guidelines for good conduct. Thus motives other than the
extension of certified knowledge may influence editorial decisions,
although such actions betray the community's trust in the gatekeepers. But the community is kept outside the circle of confidentiality and anonymity drawn by the journal, and measures to
insure accountability are time-consuming and distastefully intrusive. Members of the community cannot be informed of the worka-
day history of manuscript processing and are probably disinclined
to receive such detailed information anyway.

This is the paradox of journal peer review: the open sharing
of knowledge through publication is preceded by secret deliberations among a few scientists acting with calculatedly restricted information, vague and unenforceable guidelines, and little
accountability to authors. Scientists (as well as outsiders such as
the public) are told that this system of evaluation and resource
allocation is good for all concerned, that it allows the community
to cohere, to sustain and reproduce itself. Moreover, peer review is
often presented as a fragile and sacred thing that could not bear
scrutiny, and thus has been sheltered from systematic inquiry. But
we must ask, has peer review been working well, and is it the best
method for choosing publishable manuscripts? Or, on the contrary,
does it destroy or subvert social arrangements that are essential
to the production of new knowledge?

One way of appraising a system is to examine not its products but its processes. Editors' correspondence with authors and
referees, however, is not in the public domain, and referees' evaluations typically are not available for public examination. These
writings are private and unadulterated communications among
authors, editors, and evaluators. ("Open peer commentary" in *The
Behavioral and Brain Sciences,* which allows critical commentary
to be published alongside a paper, seems to be an exception. This

is not as open as it may seem, however, for the journal does not publish unexpurgated reviewer comments but solicits comments from a carefully chosen collection of peers in a format governed by fairly strict "rules of engagement.")

It is important to ask how authors, editors, and reviewers together transform the raw material of manuscripts into the finished product of validated knowledge claims, that is, how they convert research resources into new knowledge. Some ingenious studies have provided indirect illumination of the process by constructing experiments, analytical models, and other means for revealing the shaded operations of journal peer review. Sometimes it is also possible to view portions of the process more directly, through analysis of journal review files or examination of correspondence.

## Studies of Journal Peer Review

Journal peer review has both practical and ceremonial (or symbolic) aspects, which can be distinguished in principle but become entangled in concrete cases. In the practical sense peer review provides technical assessments that assist editors in selecting manuscripts and authors in revising them. Entwined with the practical purposes of peer review are its ceremonial meanings as an enactment (or celebration) of the normative principles that guide science. Peer review as ceremony reaffirms scientists' commitment to the core values and rules of science, and displays these for outsiders to see and acknowledge.

Studies concerned with the practical side of peer review often focus on the accuracy of manuscript assessments or the reliability and validity of reviewers' comments. Such studies might ask, for example, to what extent do referees' judgments tend to converge? Are editors' decisions consistent across (surreptitious) resubmissions of an already-published manuscript? By comparison, studies in the cultural genre view peer review as a window on the soul of science, an opportunity to observe ideals in action. Such studies decry bias and the intrusion of favoritism, preferences, and other forms of prejudice into an (ideally) universalistic world. To do this, they may contrive a manuscript with certain of its key characteristics (for example, conclusions or authors' affiliations) systematically manipulated, then submit it to several journals and compare the results. Other studies use material from a journal's archives to ask whether characteristics of the author, the manuscript, or the editors are associated with different outcomes. Such studies ex-

pose some of the workings of the black box, but at a risk few editors or analysts are willing to take.

## The Dangers of Studying Journal Practices

It is ironic that journal editors, who are "the arbiters of rigor,
quality, and innovation in scientific reports submitted for publication do not apply to their own work the standards they use in
judging the work of others."[28] The journal peer review system, no
less than the proposal peer review system, serves the competing
and inconsistent purposes of powerful actors and factions. As in
the case of proposal peer review, journal peer review shows the
strains and tears of persistent cross-pressure. And, like proposal
peer review, the journal peer review system is difficult to study,
both because it is inherently hard to observe and because its members actively resist investigation.

So active is the resistance that one researcher, William Epstein, recently faced censure by his professional society, the National Association of Social Workers, for submitting a fictitious
manuscript to journal editors for review as part of a study of peer
review practices.[29] While this story is not unique, it is recent and
has been reported widely and in some detail, affording us a
glimpse of the logic and mechanics of resistance. A panel found
Epstein in violation of two ethical precepts: deceiving journal editors by submitting a contrived manuscript and failing to obtain
the informed consent of his research subjects, the journal editors.
While we are not privy to the ethics committee's deliberations on
the matter, and lack an ethicist's or lawyer's fine eye for formal
transgressions of principle, as a practical matter these charges
strike us as excessively harsh, obdurate, and obstructive.

On the first charge, submitting a mock manuscript, the most
serious ethical violations would arise if (1) the author intended to
publish contrived work or (2) the already-overburdened review system could not bear the weight of another manuscript. Neither aspect of this violation seems at all likely. The first dissolves when
one notes that an author would hardly attempt to commit publication fraud by *simultaneously* submitting a manuscript to several
journals. Could the committee seriously believe that Epstein intended to publish an identical article simultaneously in perhaps a
dozen journals? Even the wildest frauds in the annals of science
fail to approach that level of audacity. Instead, Epstein's behavior
is far more consistent with his stated purpose of studying review
practices. The possibility of overburdening the editorial system

also seems unlikely, for one mock manuscript could add little to the huge volume of manuscripts already under review and re-review, many of which are undoubtedly mediocre or worse and have no stronger claim to the journal's attention than a study of reviewing practices. Even supposing that many such studies were undertaken each year, together they would add a trivial amount—certainly less than one percent—to the thousands of manuscripts already under review. That seems a small price for the virtues of self-study. Perhaps Epstein's accusers fear that the circulation of such mock manuscripts would make editors and reviewers more wary, and would somehow erode the moral climate of peer review. It seems to us more likely that the increased alertness and reflection generated by such studies would have an altogether wholesome effect on review practices.

The second charge, that informed consent was not obtained, is more difficult to dismiss, as that charge may be leveled against any study employing deception of any sort. A few social researchers contend that deception in research can never be justified, although the majority will probably permit deception provided that the deception is necessary, harmless, and fully explained when the study is completed. The study of review practices could easily satisfy these requirements. Unless one is categorically opposed to deception in research it is hard to find this deception problematic, and any Institutional Review Board known to us would probably find the "human subjects" of Epstein's study—the editors and reviewers—sufficiently well protected as to be at no discernible risk.

Oddly, whereas such review boards were created to protect relatively powerless research subjects from relatively powerful investigators, Epstein's problems stem from the substantial power of the groups he tried to study. In this case, principles promulgated to protect weak subjects from unscrupulous or inept investigators have been coopted by powerful interests and applied to their own ends. It is always very dangerous to study powerful individuals and groups which, when annoyed, can readily mobilize social and cultural resources to thwart the intruding researcher. That is why we know so much more about the poor, weak, downtrodden, and deviant than we do about the wealthy and powerful in society. The severity and baselessness of the charges leveled against Epstein testify to the power of the groups offended, the magnitude of the threat they felt, and the relative powerlessness of the intruder (Epstein is reported to be "a consultant on social programs," hardly a position of much institutional power).

Epstein's experience echoes those of other students of journal peer review. Mahoney, a pioneer in the use of quasi-experimental techniques in the study of journal peer review, was attacked when the deception of his studies was made know. Douglas Peters and Stephen Ceci were similarly harassed. These events bring to mind J. R. R. Tolkien's warning: "Do not meddle in the affairs of wizards for they are subtle and quick to anger." So too are journal editors (and their sponsors, publishers, and professional societies), and for that reason the ambitious agenda of necessary research about journal peer review may remain largely unexplored.

## What the Studies Tell Us

Dangers and difficulties aside, there is a large and growing (though still insufficient) body of research on journal peer review. The studies are quite varied in their research approaches. Some propose formal analytic models of the review process, comparing the models' predictions against data drawn from one or more journals. Some studies, concerned with the normative features of peer review, survey scientists about the principles that guide, or should guide, the review process. Other studies analyze statistics about the fates of manuscripts from one or more selected journals, asking how attributes of the author, manuscript, reviewers, editorial board, and journal or field of science influence a manuscript's evaluation and probability of success. Yet other studies are quasi-experimental in character, contriving a manuscript with certain characteristics and submitting it to journals for review. Such studies enjoy many of the beneficial design characteristics of experiments, but lack some crucial ability to exclude competing explanations (because they are conducted in the "real world," not the laboratory). Finally, case studies and content analyses of documents from journal archives, including reviews, editors' files, and correspondence among editors, authors, and reviewers, are sometimes used to look, unobtrusively and retrospectively, at the inner workings of peer review.

Each method focuses on some aspect of peer review, and each has its own strengths and weaknesses. For example, normative studies are susceptible to respondents' providing socially desirable responses which may not reflect the principles that guide their actions. Formal models do not necessarily uncover causal processes, for the mere coincidence of an ideal mathematical pattern with an actual pattern tells nothing of the *social* mechanisms at work within science. Studies of the agreement between referees' evaluations of a manuscript are similarly silent about the reasons for such agreement or disagreement and often place unduly high value on agreement among referees. Experimental studies are quite narrow in scope, typically confined to a single stimulus in one area of science with a small sample of respondents. Case studies and content analyses are also sharply limited, telling us a great deal about a manuscript or two, a scientist, or a journal: such studies yield suggestive insights, but nothing generalizable in the strict sense.[30] With these general limitations in mind, let us turn to studies of journal peer review which, taken together, are our best guide to the works within the black box.

The first notable finding is that editors and reviewers agree about the criteria that *should* be most important in determining whether a manuscript deserves to be published.[31] According to studies of several research areas, scientists generally agree that such properties of the manuscript as "contribution to the field" and "adequacy of research design" should have greatest weight in determining whether a manuscript should be published, whereas such author characteristics as reputation, seniority or institutional affiliation should have very little weight. Thus scientists align themselves in principle with universalistic indicators of the quality of a manuscript, not particularistic attributes of a scientist. Agreement in principle notwithstanding, in practice pairs of referees tend not to agree in their judgments about manuscripts. As Cicchetti wryly observes, "reviewers are in considerable agreement about the relative weighting of scientific attributes. They just cannot seem to agree on which high and low scores should be paired with which manuscripts."[32] The low correlation between referees' judgments is astonishing: based on a range of studies of different areas of science, with different (and, unfortunately, sometimes flawed) designs and measures of association, the average association between two referees' ratings (or the inter-reviewer reliability) is about .25 (on a scale that ranges from -1 for perfect *dis*agreement to +1 for perfect agreement). If the reliability of a single referees' judgment is .25, then the reliability of a *composite* based on two referees' ratings would be .40.[33] While knowing one reviewer's rating of a paper provides very little help in predicting another's rating, two or more such ratings, taken together, provide a sounder basis for decision.

Reliability is not merely a technical issue but has consequences for a manuscript's chances of acceptance for publication and for the quality of published work in a field, as Lowell Hargens and Jerald Herting demonstrate. Suppose that there is space to publish the top sixteen percent of all manuscripts in a field, and that we are certain which manuscripts are the best. If we then submit one hundred manuscripts for review to a journal with a .40 composite reliability, we would expect about half of the sixteen best papers to be accepted. Of course, this means that half of the "best" papers would be rejected and that other manuscripts, of lesser "true" quality, would also be published.[34] Fallibility of judgment alone, without appeal to bias or venality, can generate a significant number of mistaken judgments.

No one disputes the fact that referees disagree in their ratings of manuscripts, but there is a sharp debate about the underlying causes and significance of low agreement. Social characteristics of referees may account for some of the difference. There is evidence, for example, that higher-status referees produce less thorough reviews than lower-status referees, which may cause them to miss aspects of the manuscripts that others will notice.[35] Referees from higher-status institutions review manuscripts from similar institutions more favorably than manuscripts from lesser institutions, according to some studies, but there is conflicting evidence on this effect.[36] And reviewers may notice the same strengths and weaknesses in a manuscript but judge their importance differently: a revisable manuscript, in one reviewer's judgment, may be fatally flawed to another.[37]

Contextual variables may matter, too. Fields of science may differ in their level of consensus about the relative importance of research problems and the relative merits of methodologies and techniques.[38] Reviewers in low-consensus fields will not share such criteria to the same degree as reviewers in high-consensus fields, thus contributing to differences in the evaluation of manuscripts.[39] Similarly, shortages of available journal space may condition referees to search for flaws, thereby insuring that a sufficient number of manuscripts are rejected. Thus, for such journals, referees would be encouraged to focus divergently on flaws at the periphery (flaws which they alone may perceive) and to over-emphasize the magnitude of the flaws detected, rather than excusing such small weaknesses to focus convergently on the central merits of a manuscript.[40] There is a sharp debate about whether differences in manuscript acceptance rates among the physical, social, and biological sciences may be attributed to underlying differences in consensus or differences in resources. For our purposes, however, these may be treated as complementary explanations.[41]

In one very well-known field experiment, Mahoney suggests that referees' judgments about a manuscript may be conditioned by the certainty of the conclusions presented and by whether the reviewer agrees with those conclusions.[42] Mahoney sent various versions of a contrived manuscript to a group of psychologists whose theoretical perspective was inferred from their association with a journal that had actively advanced a particular research agenda. Five versions of the fictitious (and incomplete) manuscript were prepared:

1. Positive results (purportedly in agreement with the reviewer's inferred perspective) and no discussion of them.
2. Negative results and no discussion.
3. No results and no discussion.
4. Mixed (inconclusive) results and a positive discussion.
5. Mixed (inconclusive) results and a negative discussion.[43]

The main finding of this study, which has been widely cited, is that "referee evaluations may be dramatically influenced by such factors as experimental outcome."[44] Mahoney calls this "confirmatory bias," by which he means that referees are favorably influenced by results that concur with their views of what is true. This conclusion is based chiefly on the significantly more favorable rating given to manuscripts presenting positive rather than negative results on such dimensions as methodology, data presentation, scientific contribution, and summary recommendation (on the manuscript's publishability). Mahoney mentions but makes little of the fact that manuscripts presenting *no* results at all were rated slightly *more* favorably than those presenting positive results. Perhaps reviewers projected their preferred conclusions onto those manuscripts—for one could hardly find confirmation in a *missing* results section—but it does seem an inconvenient outcome for the "confirmatory bias" argument. Similarly, there was no appreciable difference between mixed results manuscripts that offered a positive versus a negative discussion—further evidence that weakens the confirmatory bias argument. Finally, as Hargens has pointed out, there is a weakness in the contrived manuscripts Mahoney used.[45] The only difference between the conditions of positive results and negative results is the labeling of two curves, called "A" (treatment) and "C" (exposure), which lie, respectively, above and below the control group curve ("B"). In the positive condition, curve A (treatment) is substantially above curve B (control), while curve C (exposure) is only somewhat below curve B. Unfortunately, when the labels are reversed for manuscripts with a negative outcome, the exposure curve lies significantly above the control curve, but the treatment curve is probably not significantly lower than the control curve. Since the positive manuscripts present a conclusive experiment whereas the negative manuscripts present an inconclusive experiment, it is unclear whether reviewers are responding to the *direction* of results or to their *clarity* and decisiveness.

Flaws aside, Mahoney's ingenious field experiment offers suggestive evidence that a manuscript's results may interact with a reviewer's substantive preferences to influence his or her evaluation. But these results are far from conclusive. To the contrary, there are also compelling reasons for confirmatory bias to work in reverse: Reviewers who share an author's substantive outlook may judge the manuscript *more* harshly because they do not wish to allow weak arguments into print (for these present easy targets to scientists of opposing views). For that reason material with which the reviewer *disagrees* may be judged *less* harshly, thus allowing an embarrassment or an inviting target into print. As David Hull recounts in his discussion of the journal *Systematic Zoology*,

> In fact, deviance is more serious when it comes from an ally. If, for instance, a pheneticist writes a stupid paper, it only helps the enemies of phenetic taxonomy. . . . When someone in your own research program writes a stupid paper, it damages everyone else working in that program. That is why cladists were so willing to recommend rejection for manuscripts submitted by their fellow cladists.[46]

While most studies treat low referee agreement as damning evidence that peer review is not working properly, others have noted that diversity of opinion among referees may be desirable and beneficial, bringing new and broader perspectives to the review process.[47] This difference is hard to resolve, for it rests upon a fundamental position about the inherent value of consensus in science as well as a practical judgment about the merits and consequences of disagreement. If it can be argued from first principles that good science requires consensus, or if it can be shown empirically that disagreement is confusing or demoralizing to scientists, that the diversity of opinion gives editors unhealthy latitude in their decisions (rather than a healthy broadening of perspective), or that intolerable outcomes result, then the issue can be resolved. Lacking such arguments and analyses, the (de)merits of inter-referee (dis)agreement remain matters of taste and conjecture, with plausible arguments on both sides.

There is a small amount of evidence, derived from a field experiment, that journal peer review may be quite reliable (in the sense that reviewers agree in their ratings) but not valid (in the sense that their judgments disagree with an external criterion of quality). Peters and Ceci resubmitted one article to each of the twelve "highly regarded and widely read American psychology journals" which had published it one and one-half to three years earlier.[48] The manuscripts were altered in only one significant way: fictitious names and institutional affiliations were substituted for the original authors (who were located in "prestigious and highly productive American psychology departments.") Only three of the thirty-eight editors and reviewers who examined the manuscripts noticed the resubmission (each catching a different manuscript), so nine manuscripts continued through the entire review process. Of these nine, only one was accepted for publication.

Reviewers mainly cited two sorts of reasons for rejecting the manuscripts: methodological flaws (that is, errors in design and analysis) and weaknesses in the exposition and argument.[49] These criticisms are especially puzzling, for one would expect a published article to be firmer in argument, crisper in presentation, sharper in supporting detail, and freer of methodological errors and oversights than the typical submitted manuscript. Moreover, inter-referee disagreement is not an issue in this study: for every manuscript, all reviewers were in complete agreement about their decision to reject or accept the manuscript in question. Instead, this research raises questions about the validity of journal peer review, for publication is a generally accepted criterion of scientific quality which offers a good standard for judging peer review. It is indeed troubling to learn that previously published manuscripts are judged inadequate in method and presentation (not, however, "freshness" of topic or plausibility of conclusions).

Peters and Ceci conclude that "response bias," the preference of reviewers for manuscripts written by scientists from prestigious institutions, is the most plausible explanation for the results obtained.[50] As authors' names and affiliations appeared on the manuscripts sent to referees (that is, none of the journals "blinded" material sent out for review), it is likely that the high rejection rate and high level of inter-referee agreement both arise from reviewers' shared skepticism about work produced by an unknown scientist from an unknown institution. Of course, this sharply contradicts general principles of universalistic evaluation in science and the specific assertions of scientists (cited above) that the quality of a manuscript was the foremost matter in their decision-making, while author's reputation and affiliation were among the very least important.

Other research confirms the effect of authors' characteristics on the outcomes of journal peer review. The strongest and yet most puzzling evidence is found in a recent study by Von Bakanic, Clark McPhail, and Rita Simon of 755 manuscripts submitted to the *American Sociological Review* between 1977 and 1981.[51] The researchers were concerned with several outcomes of the review process, including the average recommendation of the (blind) journal referees (scored on a four-point scale) and the final editorial decision (a seven-point scale). The predictor variables included *author characteristics* (such as rank, gender, professional age, and prestige of doctoral institution and employing institution), *manuscript characteristics* (such as the type of data used and the number of authors), *editorial characteristics* (such as which editor handled the manuscript, how many reviewers were consulted, how long it took to reach a decision, and the number of revisions requested).

For our purposes, the most important findings are that (1) authors' characteristics did not significantly affect *reviewers'* ratings, but that (2) even when the effect of reviewers' ratings is statistically controlled, authors' academic rank, professional age, and prestige of employing institution significantly affected *editors'* decisions.[52] Higher rank and greater institutional prestige increased the likelihood of a favorable editorial decision; increasing professional age decreased the likelihood of a favorable rating. We view these results as strongly suggestive evidence of particularistic decision-making—favoritism, in plain language—in the editorial decision process. The evidence is striking, we think, because the ratings of *blinded* referees are not affected by authors' characteristics, whereas those of "sighted" editors are influenced *even when the "quality" of a manuscript, as reflected in referees' ratings, has been statistically controlled.*[53] In other words, manuscripts with the same average referees' ratings submitted by authors of different academic rank, located in institutions of different prestige, will be treated differently by the editors—behavior that virtually defines particularism.

More notable than the evidentiary value of this study for our argument is the Herculean effort of its authors to *avoid* concluding that particularism may have been at work. In their initial presentation of the results discussed above, the authors note the findings and the fact that referees were blinded while editors were knowing, and then argue:

> Thus, it is conceivable (although, we think, unlikely) that assigning editors might defer to the prestige of the institution (or affiliated author) when assigning the manuscript to referees. It is also conceivable (and, we think, more likely) that prestigious institutions provide better environments and more resources for scholarly work, encourage publication, and provide more released time for its accomplishment, all of which increase the likelihood that more and higher quality manuscripts will be generated and submitted for prepublication review.[54]

They return to this inconvenient result in the discussion section of their article, concluding that

> Authors at prestigious universities were more likely to have their manuscripts published. This may result from the expectation at such institutions that faculty will publish, the provision of released time and extraordinary resources to facilitate research leading to publication, and the recruitment and retention of older faculty with established records of scholarly productivity and younger faculty with great promise.[55]

None of these explanations seems plausible to us, and no evidence was presented to support any of them. Pressures to publish and resources for research may very well differ by prestige of employing institution and academic rank, and resources may in turn affect the number and quality of manuscripts submitted, as Bakanic, McPhail, and Simon argue. But the *number* of manuscripts will have no effect on referees' and editors' ratings, which are *averages*. Moreover, the quality of manuscripts should be substantially reflected in the referees' evaluations. Once those blind evaluations are taken into account, remaining differences in outcomes are more likely to reflect particularistic favoritism than universalistic assessment of quality. (True, one might argue that indicators of quality remained in the manuscript but were not detected by the reviewers, and were perceptible only to the more discerning eyes of the editors. But this is not an entirely plausible position, we think, because it implies that editors have certain gifts of perception that others lack. After all, reviewers for one journal may have editorial responsibility for another journal, and today's reviewers become tomorrow's editors.) Furthermore, any differences in the abilities of younger and older faculty located at more and less prestigious universities could be detected by including appropriate interaction terms in the equations. That is, following the explanation of Bakanic et al., advanced professional age has a negative effect on the publication decision. But advanced professional age *in conjunction with* employment at a prestigious university would have a positive effect. Even if these interaction terms were significant, referees' recommendations should reflect much of the difference in manuscript quality, so the remaining influence of editors may very well reflect favoritism.

Stephen Lock makes an argument similar to that of Bakanic and his coauthors but uses more straightforward language. He argues that editors are justified in applying institutional prestige as a selection criterion because papers from more prestigious universities are subsequently cited more frequently than papers from less prestigious universities.[56] Of course, this assumes that citation counts are a valid measure of quality—that they are not yet another correlate of prestige—an assumption which should not be granted lightly.

Perhaps Bakanic et al. felt compelled to offer their tortuous defense of universalism because they published their article in the very journal whose review process they studied and because two of the authors (Simon and McPhail), were editor and deputy editor, respectively, *during* the period from which the data were drawn. Not only would it be impolitic to accuse one's publication outlet of inappropriate behavior, but it would be silly to indict oneself of particularism. These matters pose serious questions about the conflicts of interest inherent in research on the journal peer review system. "Outsiders" may have difficulty gaining access to such sensitive data, yet "insiders" cannot be trusted—perhaps cannot even trust *themselves*—to approach those data with the required degree of intellectual openness.

## AN ANALYSIS OF REFEREE COMMENTARY

How do referees convince editors that a manuscript should or should not be published? Of course, journals establish review criteria to guide referee reports, and referees usually invoke these when justifying their decisions. Manuscript reviewing is typically discussed in somber tones of impartiality: How important is the topic to theory in the area? Are the hypotheses logically derived from theory? Are the research methods and subjects appropriate? Are the conclusions warranted? Ultimately, the editor must decide whether the manuscript's strengths outweigh its deficiencies and whether a revised version of the paper deserves to appear in print. Yet the criteria presented to reviewers typically describe a minimally competent manuscript; much like the stripped-down version of an automobile, they offer a vision of an adequate vehicle (for knowledge, in this instance), one that would provide little security, pleasure, or pride. Just as the prospective purchaser of an automobile expects (and usually buys) more than basic transportation, journal referees expect, and usually demand, something better than a stripped-down manuscript.

Reviewers must decide whether to "buy" the ideas in a manuscript, and, having made their decision, must in turn "sell" it to the editor and author. Reviewers try to make a case; they attempt in their reviews to persuade a decision maker to commit space or forestall publication, to convince an author to undertake revisions or abandon hope of publishing *this* paper in *this* journal. Referees surely make their cases in idiosyncratic ways, and the referee's reputation shapes how a review is received and read by an editor. Manuscripts also vary in many ways, which forces reviewers and editors to adopt suitable strategies. But there are also likely to be regularities of argument and expression which hold across reviewers, manuscripts, journals, and perhaps fields of science.

These regularities might be termed the "idiom of refereeing," the language through which editors and referees communicate. For example, when a scientist describes another scientist's theoretical ideas as "interesting," it may, when decoded, mean that the writer finds the author's position flawed in some way. Similarly, to say that someone "claims" something to be true may in fact mean that the writer is about to express reservations.[57] Or, for an example of idiomatic expression from another context, consider the language of referees' reports ("rapports sur les travaux") on candidates for admission to the French Academie des Sciences.[58] In evaluations of candidates for membership in this select body, longer and more detailed reports generally signaled a more favorable evaluation; comments about a candidate's youth or the conclusion that "he was worthy of being considered" for membership meant, paradoxically, that the scientist was not yet worthy of *receiving* that honor. In the following section we examine the decisions of referees and the language of editors in search of similar idioms.

## A Sample of Referee-Editor Discourse

In 1982, G. Nigel Gilbert and Daryl E. Chubin undertook an analysis of manuscripts *rejected* for publication by the quarterly *Social Studies of Science* (*SSS*). Established in 1971 (under the title *Science Studies*), this journal is a major outlet for research in the international and multidisciplinary specialty of its name-sake. Historians, philosophers, and sociologists of science dominate the pages of *SSS*, but psychologists, economists, information scientists, and natural scientists are also represented—if not in the printed pages, then certainly in the unpublished referee reports.

As former "collaborating editors" of *SSS* and contributors to it, Gilbert and Chubin requested of its co-editor, David Edge, access to a sample of manuscripts rejected through the review process. For the period 1971–81, there were 131 such manuscripts. (Another sixty-four were "disqualified"—rejected by the editors alone or withdrawn by the authors.)

Of the 131 reviewed and rejected manuscripts, twenty-nine were selected in a sample (roughly stratified by year) and the sixty-two referee reports for them were obtained. Referees' reasons for recommending rejection were organized into ten general categories, as presented in table 4. More than one reason for rejection can be offered by a referee. For this sample, each paper was reviewed by a mean of 2.1 referees, and 4.4 reasons, on average, were assigned to each paper, or slightly more than two per referee.

Referees most often criticized authors for "poor argumentation," that is, failing to make a convincing case. In recommending that a manuscript be rejected, referees also cited the author's writing style, ignorance of the literature, and incorrect claims about the originality of findings. (Unfortunately, we don't know how often such flaws were identified in manuscripts ultimately *accepted* for publication, nor do we have an independent standard against which to judge the accuracy of these criticisms.)

Of course, we do not know how the editor weighed these criticisms in deciding not to publish the manuscript, which underscores a critical factor in the review equation: what does the editor make of the information provided by referees? And on what basis does the editor choose referees in the first place? (It most assuredly is *not* by random selection from a rolodex.) Such private decisions will not be documented in editors' files or referees' reports.

## Table 4

Reasons for Rejection of a Sample of SSS Manuscripts

| Reason | Number | Percent |
|---|---|---|
| A. Defective methodology: sampling, generalizability, measurement errors | 11 | 8.6% |
| B. Writing style: incoherent, obscure, jargon, cluttered, bad tone | 16 | 12.5 |
| C. Ignorance of relevant literature | 15 | 11.7 |
| D. Poor argumentation: superficial analysis, opinion only, polemical, atheoretical, unscholarly | 31 | 24.2 |
| E. Misunderstanding/misapplication of data and/or literature; referee incredulity | 16 | 12.5 |
| F. Lacks novelty/redundant or obsolete findings | 15 | 11.7 |
| G. Disciplinary hubris/program differences | 6 | 4.7 |
| H. Inappropriate for *SSS* | 2 | 1.6 |
| I. Length of manuscript | 2 | 1.6 |
| J. Substantive omissions/naivete | 14 | 10.9 |
| Total | 128 | 100.0% |

Note: Based on sixty-two reviews of twenty-nine papers submitted to *SSS* between 1971 and 1981 for which "rejection" was recommended.

This content analysis suggests that the manuscript review process, even in an "interdisciplinary" specialty journal whose "cited research and objects of investigation reveal an overwhelmingly Anglo-American bias," involves some "universals" of scholarship.[59] Referees for *Social Studies of Science* are not likely to invoke programmatic differences or methodological proclivities as grounds for rejection in their reports.[60] Perhaps these criteria are masked by invoking universalistic standards or conveyed in discreet notes or calls to editors. Perhaps such criteria are concealed by the personal characteristics that qualify or disqualify a scientist as a suitable reviewer for a manuscript.

Evidence from a study of numerical taxonomy, a field of evolutionary biology, suggests that such programmatic differences may work in opposite ways. As mentioned above, in some instances referees who *shared* the bias of a manuscript were also its sternest critics, as they were loath to allow into print a weak exponent of their views. In contrast, opponents of the perspective of a manuscript may be willing to publish it, flaws and all, then take the opportunity to attack it in print. Moreover, a scientist's attitude toward a manuscript may not be readily predicted from his or her theoretical orientation, but may instead depend upon the state of substantive dispute in the field, the usual patterns of argument, the resources available, and so forth. Similarly, a referee's judgment to publish a manuscript may not always signal approval or endorsement.

The referee report, though more candid than a published article, still reflects an etiquette seasoned by life in a research community. Though "damning by faint praise" and ad hominem attack are as much part of the referee's arsenal as the "reasons" presented in the preceding typology, such comments are unacceptable in the universalistic rhetoric of science. So scientists often appeal to "rigor," "clarity," and "objectivity" because the image of scientific inquiry demands it. Just as Peter Medawar once asked, "Is the scientific paper a fraud?" we are led to wonder, "Is the referee report also a fraud?" In both cases authors are reconstructing a process to convince a decision-maker to act in a certain way. And each is deceptive.

Science, embodied in a manuscript submitted for publication, is a bag of particulars for referees: who is writing, from what theoretical perspective, institution, or country of origin, supporting or refuting which hypothesis with what method? The rejection rate in *Social Studies of Science*—60 percent (and 80–90 percent in most single-discipline social science journals)—indicates that referees find fault. Do they seek it? Do they sense it even when it is not there? Do they address it in their commentaries or merely vote by checking the summary statement "requires major revision"? These are part of the process that also eludes analysis—an analysis of confessions perhaps, or reconstruction of the sequence that leads peers to pass favorably or not on one another. This is a formidable agenda that demands the attention of researchers.[61]

## The Rhetoric of Referees

Just as would-be authors employ an "implicit theory of citing" in determining which documents deserve inclusion in the bibliography of their manuscripts, referees employ an implicit theory of reviewing when confronted by a manuscript.[62] How do referees approach their task? Do they assume publishable quality and look for evidence to the contrary, as in the years of *Physical Review* examined by Zuckerman and Merton?[63] Or do they grant no benefit of the doubt and require that the author's text, in content and style, earn the journal space? To what extent is this influenced by the overall acceptance rate of the journal? As Thomas Stossel points out, the prestigious, high-circulation, interdisciplinary journals (such as *Science* and *Nature*) have very high rejection rates and demand "spectacular" science.[64] For these outlets the default decision is to reject a manuscript unless there is compelling reason to accept it. Is the referee's decision reached gradually? Does he or she keep a mental tally of points pro and con as the text is read? Or is the decision made virtually at the outset, with the text supplying ammunition to marshall and invoke in support of the decision?

## Toward a Theory of Refereeing

Let us suggest some principles that might contribute to a theory of refereeing. Manuscripts are issued periodically from scientists' laboratories and offices, providing a highly stylized snapshot of the workings within. In other words, manuscripts "freeze" for viewing and evaluation the ongoing flow of a research enterprise and career of a scientist. Once published, a scientist becomes a bibliographic entity that lives in the literature and bears certain intellectual interests and competences. A "good" paper reflects positively on its author, and successive papers are expected to be similar in quality. Similarly, publication gives enduring life to a research enterprise, stating openly not only a set of findings but also a theoretical perspective, a method, a research site, and a likely path for future investigation. Thus, when a manuscript arrives for evaluation it carries *encoded* information about the author and the research enterprise which produced it, information which creates a context for assessing the work. Referees grope for clues about the origins of a manuscript (if they are not provided openly on the title page), for such information greatly simplifies the reviewing task. If the author is accomplished, or perhaps eminent, then the reviewer may be reassured about the significance of the problem addressed and the technical quality of the research. If the author is unknown, the reviewer may be less willing to grant even small assumptions or forgive peccadillos. Moreover, the knowing reviewer will then be aware of whom he or she is taking on in a highly critical review, and may choose battles accordingly.

Much of this deduction occurs before the referee has grappled with the substance of the paper. Call it introspection or intuition, but some of this attribution will affect the referee's decision.[65] Whether it is, or can be, expressed in the referee's report is unknown. How the etiquette of journal refereeing is transmitted, learned, and practiced is altogether mysterious. To some, it gives the appearance of nothing less than conspiracy.[66] The confidentiality of reviews makes for sizzling conversations and correspondence among editors, authors, and referees. But the written reports are often plain vanilla; for the record scientists often censor themselves or cloak their misgivings in the language of editorial "criteria for publication."[67]

One innovation for forcing the "creative disagreement" of refereeing into the published domain is "open peer commentary".[68] Although the reviews are edited for public consumption, they testify to the convictions that separate specialists in a research area. Such commentary supersedes even the pursuit of priority and the pettiness surrounding rules for its establishment and disclosure.[69] Open peer commentary shares a version of the referee's private assessments with a reading audience that must discern the intellectual contribution of the refereed and now published paper. The commentary moves us nearer to a referee's implicit theory of refereeing, telling us not only about the disposition of the paper, but also about the reasons for such a disposition—or, in keeping with the argument above, the *rhetoric* of such reasons. Taken in the aggregate, peer commentary reveals the implicit principles of evaluation and the main lines of intellectual cleavage for an entire research area.

Publication allows readers to place an article's knowledge claims in the context of the author's prior work. Open peer commentary adds another dimension, juxtaposing the author's claims with the views of referees. In effect, this is a Rorschach test: both the article and the referee's interpretation are the readers' to weigh or discard as they see fit. Layer upon layer, paper upon paper, science grows as careers unfold. Bibliography endows biography by projecting order, reputation, and intellectual locale, while biography endows bibliography by providing continuity, intellectual context, and the authority of past accomplishments. Peer review sanctions both processes.

## VIGNETTE: THE SANCTITY OF JOURNAL PEER REVIEW AND A CONSPIRACY OF IGNORANCE

The insights that accrue from an analysis of aggregate patterns in the rhetoric of referee reports can be augmented by the experiences of individual authors who find themselves caught in an assault on their life's work. We learned of the case recounted below through the author's reaction to our ongoing research and publications; thus we felt obligated to listen. Because the author dutifully compiled and catalogued his personal correspondence, we were afforded an off-the-record look at "negotiations" that are sometimes forced on authors and seldom available for study. Yes, we present only one side of this story, and it is an individual instance that cannot claim to be representative of broader trends in science. Yet it raises issues so troublesome and antithetical to the ideals of scientific publication that they demand attention.

On balance, the case of University of Florida entomologist James Lloyd shifts sympathy away from referees and back to the author. But there are no sharply-drawn heroes or villains in this story. Rather, the case as a whole offends our sensibilities about the scientific publication system. The "system," driven by peer review, pretends to depersonalize what is so frustratingly personal, yet compartmentalizes differences of opinion in ways that make full communication difficult and resolution of differences impossible. Blame for contentious exchanges within the journal system is usually heaped on the only person who wields formal power— the editor. The Lloyd case stands alone here, but it is no isolated incident. It is the stuff that scientists admit in casual conversation with one another and sometimes to outsiders like ourselves.

We present the chronology of events as a vignette, a glimpse into exchanges between author and editor and, "silently" lurking in the background, referees. The science that sparked the exchange, while published in *Science,* a prestigious journal, is quite unexceptional by most external standards. A count of citation records to the original article from literature published in the following seven years yields a total seven citations: three by the author himself, two by Carlson, one by Huber, and one by Copeland, whose criticism fueled the exchange on which we report. By this standard the original work, whatever its intrinsic qualities, hardly bestirred the scientific community. The sharp exchange between Copeland and Lloyd, published in *Science* in July 1983, is subsequently cited three times by Lloyd and once by Carlson. In other words, read this not as an epic struggle in science, nor as a case to be decided by apportioning blame and assessing penalties. Instead, attend to the discourse that divides the principals and the resources they draw on to substantiate their positions.

In November 1980, *Science* published a three-page paper by James E. Lloyd reporting a breakthrough after thirteen years of field studies. As stated in the abstract.

Since *Photuris* females prey on males of other firefly species by mimicking their females' flashes, the *Photuris* males may be using their [own] mimicry to locate and seduce their own hunting females. This mimicry is without known parallel in other animal communicative systems. It explains why the genus *Photuris* has been a frustrating mystery to taxonomists, who have long used flash patterns to distinguish sibling species in other genera.[70]

A year later, Senior Editor Eleanor Butz informed Lloyd that

We have received [a comment] on your recent paper in *Science*. Please let me know your opinion of it before we send it out to be reviewed. It has not been accepted for publication. If it is accepted, you will be given an opportunity to reply.

The purpose of this communication, at least as Lloyd apparently interpreted it, was to solicit his views informally, perhaps off the record (notice that Butz requested Lloyd's "opinion," not his "review" of the piece). The letter allows the inference that Lloyd's critique would somehow decide the fate of the comment (the comment had not been sent out for review and had not been accepted).

Lloyd's response two weeks later (30 December 1981) is unequivocal:

I have read the manuscript by Copeland, "Do Male Fireflies Mimic Sexual Signals of Their Female's Prey," that has been submitted as a criticism of my 1980 Photuris male mimicry paper. I find it difficult to respond to because it is completely off base. It completely misunderstands the information and concepts presented, and overlooks the data base for concluding that it is a case of mimicry. It misunderstands some and ignores other of the possible explanations for the mimicry that I suggested. It reveals a lack of understanding of insect biology in general, and of the limitations of the critic's own research because of their limited scope (performed only on one species, and the individuals were laboratory captives). It is difficult to believe that he had access to my paper when he wrote.

Lloyd continues for four more pages, supplying an elaboration of the phenomenon he describes, tracing its intellectual history, and advancing a nine-point refutation of Copeland's critique. Lloyd concludes his letter:

Copeland is so completely wrong. I can't understand what motivated this business. And really, I hope it never sees the pages of *Science,* because it is absurd, really stupid, and I have a hundred other things I'd rather do than write a formal and concise rebuttal. The original paper says it all. Thanks for sending the letter to me. Please understand that my comments are not politically motivated, and I am not trying to manipulate you. I sure hope that Copeland, with his lack of knowledge of biology, fireflies, and logic, isn't the ref eree of my recently submitted paper to *Science.*

Lloyd's disclaimer to the contrary notwithstanding, his comments were indeed "politically motivated" and he was indeed trying to "manipulate" Butz. There is no question that he was attempting to exert the power of expertise and persuasion to prevent *Science* from publishing the comment. But this does not weaken his criticisms or impugn his conduct as a scientist. More properly, those are not for us to judge. His response to Butz was prompt, lengthy, and detailed. Perhaps he thought his criticisms would prevent publication and perhaps even preempt formal review of the piece. As there were no further communications for months, Lloyd might have thought the matter settled. But nine months later (August 1982), Lloyd writes to Editor Butz:

In our recent phone conversation regarding the Copeland letter . . . you indicated that the editors had decided to have the letter refereed, even though I had written a very comprehensive letter regarding its failings. You indicated that my "informal" response to your first letter had been included as a "referee comment" and sent to Copeland along with the others, and that his letter had been approved for publication. . . .

I would like to see the referee's comments. Please send them to me.

By this account it appears that Lloyd's informal reply to the comment has attained the more formal status of a "referee comment," without any further action on his part. One reasonable and ironic construction of subsequent events is that Lloyd's conscientious reply worked at cross-purposes to his interests in the matter: by offering a speedy, detailed, substantive, and somewhat heated critique of the comment Lloyd inadvertently legitimated the comment, signalled the editors that there was indeed a hot issue here, and alerted his critic (Copeland) to the line of counterargument he would choose.

On the surface this seems a sensible and decent course of action by Lloyd, but (as the story will show) it appears not to have been in his best interests. By comparison, Hull describes how a younger author (who was perhaps less idealistic and more politically savvy than Lloyd) chose a different strategy when presented with a comment on her published work.

Now that Rohlf and Sokal were no longer members of Mickevich's dissertation committee, they felt free to rebut Mickevich's published work. They submitted a joint manuscript to Fitch as the appropriate associate editor [of *Systematic Zoology*]. Fitch sent a copy of this manuscript to Mickevich in order for her to write a preliminary response for Rohlf and Sokal to see. That way unnecessary confusions and disagreements could be eliminated prior to publication. Although this process can work when the authors involved are not too strongly divided, Mickevich did not like the idea at all. She preferred to have Rohlf and Sokal publish their piece without any help from her. She would then respond to them in her own good time. . . . [Thus] Rohlf and Sokal would have to publish without any advance notice of the faults that Mickevich was likely to find with their paper.[71]

The field in which Mickevich was working, numerical taxonomy, was at the time quite confrontational: the journal in which she had published (*Systematic Zoology*) had recently been characterized by sharp exchanges, and she was married to one of its more fractious members. Thus she was better prepared for the verbal battle, more fully *en garde,* than an entomologist might be.

One month later, Lloyd writes to Butz again:

I wrote you several weeks ago but received no reply. . . . Since I indicated in my (requested) comments to you that the Copeland paper was without merit, in fact completely invalid and in error, it naturally is of some concern to me that your expert referees would find it worthy of publication. Please send the comments to me so that I may study them.

Two weeks later (September 1981), Butz replies:

> We do not usually send reviews of papers to anyone except the author of the paper. I am sorry but I cannot comply with your request.

Thus Butz used the privileged character of author-editor-referee communication to exclude Lloyd. Nonetheless, Lloyd countered by writing:

> I don't understand. Why is [it] not "usual" to send such comments to the person whose paper is being questioned by these same reviewers? After all, in this case *Science* sent my comments on the original criticism that were made to *Science,* to the author of the criticism. I can understand this, though perhaps bending the rules of etiquette would be for the advancement of science. Why not then wouldn't my seeing the reviewers' comments, or even knowing when you sent my comments to the author, be done in the same vein? I am extremely disappointed in this matter, and probably, rather than fight with big science, after I have answered the final, formal ms of Copeland, will quit the AAAS. It is clear, and I will put it in a nonpublished ms I will circulate, that your referees were not behavioral ecologists and had no experience in the matter being challenged. They were perhaps neurobiologists, completely out of their element. The facts speak for themselves. It is as though geologists had been asked to referee a paper on brain function. I have better things to do than try to reform systems. This is not one of science's or *Science*'s prouder moments.

A reply of ill-controlled fury, most clearly evidenced by the petulant threat to quit the AAAS, testifies to the intense frustration and threat engendered by the exchange. Another six months passes—not all science is a priority race—and Butz informs Lloyd:

> We have accepted for publication the enclosed technical comment on your recent [that is, 2.5-year-old] paper.

> You may prepare a reply for simultaneous publication if you wish to do so. Your reply should be no longer than, and preferably shorter than, the comment.

A month later (May 1983), Lloyd submits his reply for simultaneous publication. He remarks:

> The long delay between our last correspondence and your letter led me to believe that the editorial staff at *Science* had become aware of the nature of the "science" of Copeland and his peers. I am surprised and disappointed that you decided to publish his critique.

As was the case with Lloyd's remarks of the original comment, the passage of time seems to signal rejection (in this case, a favorable outcome for Lloyd). After another six weeks Lloyd writes to Butz again, this time with an allegation and a query:

> I am very happy that we had a chance to speak on the phone a week ago, and to discuss the Copeland letter and my response. I am sure that there is a great deal to this matter that I am unaware of, and there is a great deal to the "science" that *Science* doesn't know about. . . .
>
> . . . I hope that *Science* might consider examining the case somewhat closely after the critique is published, because there seems to me to be much more than a reasonable error or misunderstanding—I personally believe the evidence indicates just plain unethical conduct was involved. . . . I would like to help *Science* investigate this business. . . . Is there any interest in this at your end? Believe me, the scientific aspects of Copeland's letter . . . are at odds with 70 years of research in this field. The fact that referees could recommend publication indicates at least a conspiracy of ignorance.

Two aspects of this communication deserve comment. First, it highlights the power of informal, off-the-record telephone communication to calm an unsettled author. In this context, the conversation appears to be an instance of "cooling out the mark," a practice originated by con artists (and adopted as an analytic construct by sociologists) whereby measures would be taken to render the victim of a swindle more accepting of the deed, to restore a measure of lost dignity. Second, it accuses Copeland of a most serious breach of scientific ethics—research fraud—and invites (even urges) *Science* to undertake an investigation. There is no evidence that the accusation was examined or the invitation accepted—a not unusual response to allegations of misconduct at the time. The Copeland comment and the Lloyd reply appeared in the 29 July 1983 issue of *Science* under the title "Male Firefly Mimicry," and the alleged "conspiracy of ignorance" reappeared almost two years later. As Lloyd puts it in a May 1985 letter to Eleanor Butz,

> The Copeland-Lloyd-Firefly incidence of a couple of years ago . . . unfortunately will not go away. Recent events, and the appearance of new evidence in the latter, require that it be looked into again. The recent events are that Copeland and his former doctoral chairman submitted a more extensive paper (subsequently withdrawn) dealing with the same and related subjects, and like the one Copeland published in *Science,* it again misrepresents the published record. The new evidence is that the single valid point that Copeland's "Comment" in *Science* made was not valid after all—it had already been disproved by research done in the same (Carlson, Stony Brook) lab and published in 1978.[72] Though I had seen a manuscript of this paper at some time prior to 1978, I had forgotten it. Thus Copeland used information he certainly had to know was false and Carlson failed to stop him or to report this after publication. . . .

> While it is expected that in courtroom legal proceedings information may be withheld, not brought forward, this is not acceptable in science. I believe Copeland used *Science* to get a publication, and thus unfairly treated science. He and Carlson cited the *Science* "Comment" as though it were legitimate, and thus they used the prestige of *Science,* its credibility and authority, against me and my work. . . .

> . . . I believe that you can only confirm that Copeland misrepresented published literature of which he was surely aware. If you confirm this, then his comments involved fraud, and *Science* should so notify its readers. . . . For more than three years I have had my research and my life disrupted by this incident. The disruption would have ceased in 1981 had referees or editors acted responsibly. . . .

James Lloyd has not heard again from Eleanor Butz. (Perhaps he is now, finally, "old business.") A few interested readers have sent him notes of encouragement. But they, too, are encircled by the "conspiracy of ignorance" which the review process of a prestigious journal has sanctified. In a personal communication (July 1985), Lloyd remarked,

> It is clear that no one really gives a damn. Everyone is out after another publication, even though they know that all are made less valuable by the occurrence of slop and dishonest papers.

Elsewhere, however, Lloyd has written a public postscript that shows fury over "the pernicious aspects of peer review" without ever mentioning his private war with *Science*:

> But does the review system work? We have no formal or objective way to tell, for it is all left to chance. There is no systematic way to see if manuscripts have been improved, or comments relevant; no provisions for discovery of potential or even actual misbehavior, nor for handling complaints or suspicions of incompetence, impropriety, or fraud. On the contrary, there are subtle and powerful constraints and pressures that promote silent submission to the system.[73]

The Lloyd vignette is a kind of "reality test" for the general principles advanced at the outset of this chapter. The vignette shows:

1. How the confidentiality and anonymity of blind reviewing may facilitate editorial indecisiveness and ad hoc decision making, while not necessarily causing such behavior, by concealing certain arguments and voices in a dispute.

2. How unsuspecting authors may be held hostage by the system, as there is no statute of limitations to commentary on one's published work except the editor's evaluation of the attempted commentary.

3. The terse and noncommittal character of editorial written communication, which may leave the door open to a range of subsequent actions and interpretations, in contrast to a willingness to converse by phone (in a sense "off the record," as it would be hard, without a tape recording, to present solid evidence of what was said and agreed in such conversations).

4. In contrast to the putative importance of candor by all parties throughout the process, in practice such candor may be one-sided or merely another rhetorical device.

The protracted flurry of behind-the-scenes correspondence has no public face. The rhetoric of editors, referees, and authors is shielded, in large measure, from one another. Suspicion and inference fill the gaps in the narrative. Melodramatic as it may sound, scientists' careers do hang on the words exchanged. And there is very little recourse.

## SOBER CONSIDERATIONS

This chapter began with a discussion of how journal peer review practices arose and how they contribute to the goals of science. The chapter ends with more sober considerations: Is journal peer review, as currently practiced, consistent with the production of high-quality scientific knowledge? What is "proper" referee behavior? How are an editor's expectations of that behavior conveyed and reinforced? What are the rights and responsibilities of authors who enter the review process by submitting a manuscript for publication? How can these rights be preserved? These fundamental questions are seldom studied.

What lies behind the printed word is a question of ethics, of the ways peers relate as they switch from the role of "author" to "editor" to "referee." In the next chapter, the focus shifts from the words that peers use when discharging their various roles to the deeds themselves. By now, peer review should be seen as a political process regulated by gatekeepers who invoke the peer "community" selectively as a mechanism of social control. Sometimes this tactic exposes the "research malpractice" that journals, federal agencies, and other evaluative institutions unintentionally foster, and perhaps even warrant, in science.[74]

Journal peer review is not benign. Its force reverberates from the printed word through the careers of scientists and is felt well beyond the scientific community. Journal peer review may not be efficacious. It does not dependably authenticate research results, and some of its functions and objectives are in conflict with one another. Above all, journal review is not well understood. Available studies are few, flawed, and perhaps misdirected, squelched or led into unproductive channels by self-censorship, by powerful editors and other scientists, by the force of scientific ideals, and by practical opportunities and obstacles.

A central theme of this book is that peer review in science is subject to wrenching contradictory forces. Peer review serves the practical ends of allocating rewards and resources at the same time that it embodies and enacts the most cherished values of science—values that are essential to the very definition of science. Outside of science, peer review serves society in a practical way by encapsulating scientific judgment. To know that a paper, a proposal, or a course of action has been "peer reviewed" by a board of competent scientists is reassuring to many of us, for it signifies that impartial expertise has entered into a decision.[75]

Peer review is difficult to reconcile with democratic values, as it is shamelessly secretive, elitist, and oligarchic—as is science itself. Yet our society makes this uneasy exception from democratic principles as an act of faith in the knowledge, wisdom and impartiality of those oligarchs, the expert scientists.[76]

## CONCLUSIONS

Today peer review is besieged on both practical and symbolic grounds. In their complaints, critics point to the operating characteristics of peer review: low levels of consensus among reviewers, inconsistencies of judgment, errors of omission (when a flawed or fraudulent manuscript slips through) and commission (when a competitor's manuscript is blocked or delayed, or its results or argument are stolen), the partisan flavor of reviewer comments (which seemingly violates principles of impartiality), and the unsettling influence of authors' characteristics on the fate of their manuscripts. These are neither a blueprint for selecting the best science nor an enactment of the values we hope science will honor.

How did peer review come to this sorry state? The problems of peer review do not arise from a population of "bad scientists" and need not originate with flaws unique to modern science. Instead, they may be understood as specific instances of the decoupling of symbolic and practical ends which plagues highly institutionalized organizations (that is, organizations deeply infused with values and about which members of society have broadly shared and reciprocated expectations).

Science in the twentieth century is heavily steeped in social values: we believe in science, put faith in science, and expect science to deliver much in exchange. The magnitude and freedom of support for basic scientific research in the U.S. since about 1950 testifies to the strength of this belief: to date few explicit, enforceable, and reciprocated expectations have been directly attached to the billions of dollars spent. Of course, there are powerful *general* expectations about science, captured in our expectation of "progress" and our faith that progress will be "good" for us. And funding agencies certainly justify their budget requests in practical terms. But until recently these expectations have not been explicit; the investment character of funding for scientific research has been unstated.[77] When these new pressures for performance and efficiency are heaped onto the existing internal tensions between the practical and symbolic functions of peer review, the mechanism strains and sputters.

# 5

# Scientific Malpractice

## and the

# Politics of Knowledge

Do scientists think they are writing too many grant proposals? Of course not. Do university presidents think they are asking for too much overhead? Of course not. Do editors think they are requiring too much data for an acceptable article? Of course not. It follows as the night the day that peer reviewers are at fault.

Daniel E. Koshland, Jr. (1985)

Few precepts of laboratory ethics seem more straightforward than the notion that a scientist should take responsibility for his research, accepting both praise and blame.

William J. Broad (1981)

To this point we have been concerned with the technical shortcomings of peer review. We have shown that peer review seldom operates according to strictly meritocratic criteria, that it is frequently unreliable (in that reviewers, quite predictably, disagree about the merits of the work under review), and that it may be sensitive to influences other than "true" scientific quality (such as the prestige or past performance of the scientist whose work is under review).

In this chapter we look beyond the technical properties of peer review to examine two challenges to peer control of science: misconduct in scientific research and political earmarking (or, less charitably, pork-barreling) of support for science.

## MALPRACTICE DEFINED

Although they pose unique problems for scientists, misconduct and earmarking have similar origins in the massive resource needs and sharp competitive pressures of modern science, and each poses a challenge to scientific self-management. Research misconduct demonstrates that science may not be the disinterested, self-regulating enterprise it claims to be. This recognition weakens the public's trust in and commitment to science and gives rise to new mechanisms of oversight and control. Earmarking shifts certain resource allocation decisions from the scientific community to the political arena, thus challenging science's ability to direct and govern itself.

Consider misconduct. Good statistics about the prevalence and distribution of fraud and misconduct do not exist for a variety of reasons: definitions are fuzzy, the behaviors are fastidiously concealed from public view (although that is changing as funding agencies insist upon full and open investigations), and it is difficult to establish the appropriate basis for calculating a rate or proportion of misconduct.[1] (A recent proposal to conduct an audit of research papers, using a probability sample of published articles to estimate the prevalence of error, misconduct, [perhaps] fraud, and the generally growing amount of basic information about such matters, promise to advance dramatically our knowledge about misconduct.[2]) Despite the dearth of data and the fugitive character of the events themselves, volumes have been written, commissions empaneled, policies formulated, and bureaus created to analyze, examine, remedy and regulate scientific misconduct. Why?

To some extent scientific misconduct has become a national concern because of the practical importance of research for science and science for society. For example, Mark Spector's fabrications about the "kinase cascade" attracted great attention among the cancer research community; Cyril Burt's false claims about the heritability of intelligence formed the basis of a heated policy dispute; and Stephen Breuning's pseudo-psychopharmacology influenced patients' treatment plans. Beyond such practical consequences of misconduct lie important moral and symbolic issues. Science holds a privileged position in modern society—it is almost a public trust, although intensifying commercial pressures on university campuses are transforming it—and episodes of misconduct are powerful violations of that trust. They profoundly offend us, and thus draw our attention.

Consider earmarking. Federal support for basic academic science is disproportionately awarded to the top graduate universities, and thus is concentrated in the few states that are home to the most prestigious universities.[3] Many have asked if this concentration is proper and effective, and answers have varied. Some argue that all universities and scientists contribute to the body of scientific knowledge and therefore should be supported to perform research. Others assert that all institutions are not equally able to advance knowledge but that research activity at second-tier institutions is valuable and deserves support because it improves the quality of teaching and learning. Still others have argued for a division of labor, contending that basic research should be the province of the top scientists at the best universities, while lesser scientists should spend their time in applied research or teaching. Underlying this policy debate is a political issue: are resources for science best distributed by scientific criteria alone, or should additional geographic, institutional, political, or strategic criteria be applied in making awards?

Scientific misconduct and pork-barrel support for research have several characteristics in common. As science becomes more closely identified with public health, national pride, economic performance, and military security, and as scientific research becomes more expensive, scientists are drawn into the public eye and pressed to produce or called to account for their failure to do so. Such high performance standards, coupled with resource scarcity, give rise to intense competition for material and symbolic resources and set the stage for improper conduct or political maneuvering. In addition, science has become more bureaucratized as increases in the scale and cost of research activity have been accompanied by larger and more diverse research teams and by more intrusive (and demanding) sponsors, universities, and local communities. These changes in the social organization of academic science create organizational pressures which may work against the communal and professional standards of scientific disciplines. Finally, scientific misconduct and pork-barrel allocations can be construed as failures of the peer review system, for they are both instances in which the state and other organizations have stepped in to manage some important aspect of science that formerly had been the preserve of scientists alone. In this way misconduct and earmarking pose direct challenges to the autonomy of science.

## Can Peer Review Help?

As currently organized and practiced, peer review can do little to prevent or remedy scientific misconduct because review bodies lack the authority, information, and energy to detect and act on improprieties. Unless a committee has been formed to investigate alleged misconduct, peer reviewers ordinarily do not examine the sorts of records that may reveal fraud or misconduct (or exonerate a scientist from accusations). Even when such records are examined by experts, it is not always possible to ascertain whether or not fraud occurred. Moreover, journal or proposal peer review panels are sufficiently far removed from the scientist's employing institution that they are unable to impose sanctions for improprieties. Reviewers are attuned to ferreting out *honest* error; they seldom suspect deliberate deception.[4]

Peer review panels also lack the political and institutional base to resist earmarking. Generally constituted as ad hoc committees of scientists, gathered for the occasion by an editor or program manager, such panels are not stable enough to counteract the political will of career administrators or elected officials. Moreover, scientists' allegiances are torn between their employing institutions, which may have reason to seek earmarked funds, and the invisible colleges of their research activities, which transcend institutions and represent the collective interests of scientists. This divided loyalty further confounds scientists' ability to act effectively on earmarking. In brief, peer-review bodies are well qualified and well situated to participate in technical decisions within a narrowly circumscribed context (such as a journal or a funding program), blemished by all the imperfections recounted in the preceding chapters, but they lack the legitimacy essential to exert leverage in the wider world.

These shortcomings of peer review have created a vacuum, eliciting institutional responses (in the form of regulations, policies, Congressional hearings, review bodies, self-studies, and the like) which themselves pose a further threat to the self-governance of science. And misconduct and pork-barreling have eaten into the moral capital of science, degrading it in the public's estimation, "leveling" science to the moral status of any other profession or interest group. A certain amount of leveling may be necessary and even salutary, but the sudden shift can be disorienting and disruptive.

## THE EMERGENCE OF PUBLIC SCIENCE

Once science is understood as a variety of instrumental craft work that is valued both within the institution of science and also by the broader society that supports and sanctions the institution, stereotypes about the "scientific method" and its role in producing certified knowledge are replaced by public understanding of other dimensions of scientific practice.[5] Foremost among these are the strategies and practices scientists use to make their work appear sound and "accountable," that is, responsive to the expectations of other scientists and to the society as a whole.

The rhetoric of scientific practice will differ when the scientist is justifying his or her behavior to fellow scientists rather than to "interlopers" from other institutional spheres (such as journalists or politicians). While it may be politically advantageous, even necessary, to mythologize science to the "laity" in the interest of retaining autonomy or securing resources, the internal practices of the community will reflect its socialization and habits of discourse.[6]

The science that philosophers, historians, sociologists, and others make "public" through their studies of scientists' behavior also reveals a Public Science in which society invests substantial amounts of money and moral capital and from which it anticipates measurable returns of productivity, health, defense, and pride. As science becomes Public Science, scientific practice assumes new proportions and responsibilities. Criteria for creating and validating theories, choosing and employing research techniques, and mapping out fruitful research programs are displaced by concerns about trust, secrecy, research probity, science policy, and national priorities. The principles and customs of science may define acceptable practice, but public pressures will shape scientists' *descriptions* and *interpretations* of practice as more or less virtuous, valuable, and shrewd.[7]

The (arguably) narrower task of producing and certifying knowledge has been augmented by other roles that cast the scientist alternately as entrepreneur, bookkeeper, soothsayer, soldier, and priest. Public science (little "p" and "s") has become the Public Science of press conferences, television, Nobel Prize races, bestsellers, and Congressional testimony. As we write, the international competition and curiosity surrounding superconductivity and cold fusion have brought the activities of leading laboratories and the personalities of their inhabitants to the pages of the *New York Times, Boston Globe,* and *Wall Street Journal* even before their latest results have appeared in the journals of physics or materials science. Not just the scientific community but the whole world is watching and weighing this research.[8] (Ironically, fear of prematurely disclosing a patentable idea has recently dampened scientists' enthusiasm for reporting results through the media. Thus, another form of publication and the intrusion of another "public"—the business community—has revised the character of Public Science.)

Federally financed, nationally monitored Public Science is inherently problematic.[9] Combining elements of public policy with lay translations of scientific concepts, Public Science is the forum in which the scientist employs political rhetoric and the politician discusses scientific results and prospects. This interpenetration of cultural realms reveals tensions deeply embedded within the ethos of science, tensions that were ignored in the earliest formulations of the norms of science and only glimpsed in later reformulations.[10] These tensions are most clearly seen by studying events at the interface of economics, politics, and traditional scientific practices, where powerful forces cause dislocations in traditional scientific practice, such as research misconduct and pork-barreling, and give rise to revealing debate within the scientific and policy communities.

Inasmuch as research misconduct and pork-barrel allocations are perceived by scientists to threaten their enterprise, scientists will justify their actions by invoking the most powerful and persuasive arguments available to them. These "vocabularies of justification" typically make use of idealizations of scientific practice—its openness, objectivity, independence, and effectiveness—to persuade the public that, appearances to the contrary notwithstanding, all is well with science.[11] Such idealizations are commonplace in Public Science.

We would expect differences between the rhetoric of scientists formulated for public consumption and scientific assessments internal to the community; for example, testimony before a Congressional committee is likely to use a rhetoric different from that of comments on a manuscript offered to a journal editor in a referee's report. And just as referees cite such qualities as originality and rigor to justify their judgments about a manuscript, scientists provide rationalizations for excusing incidents of research misconduct (as innocent sloppiness, inadvertent misstatement, or idiosyncratic interpretation) and for seeking pork-barrel funds (as an undesirable necessity, a political expedient, or a remedy for past inequities). Through such instances we learn about scientists' images of their craft and discover the limits of acceptable practice.

## Malpractice as a Grappling with Norms

If pressures from funding sources, commercial interests, research facility and equipment costs, and public demands for greater accountability are changing the social context of science, then we should expect scientific practice and the definition of malpractice also to change. We expect the institution of science to insist upon greater autonomy, to underscore in public statements that it is critically important for *scientists* to determine what is, and what is not, acceptable scientific practice. In this way, science attempts to preserve for itself the right to muddle through these changes in relative privacy, with little systematic outside interference. Unfortunately, such efforts to preserve professional autonomy may, for the public, be as unsettling as the initial instances of questionable conduct. And as interested and powerful parties— such as universities, funding agencies, and the Congress—insist upon more openness and accountability, scientists are increasingly unable to keep matters among themselves.

To express the reluctance of the scientific community in individual terms, scientists seek praise and avoid criticism or blame. But the tactics scientists use to win public accolades or support, and to evade public criticism or blame, may be termed "almost wrongs" for they depart from generally accepted, appropriate behavior yet fall short of clear-cut misconduct.[12] We hear about such actions only infrequently, and we seldom observe them directly. Some occur when a spectacular scientific result (for example, high-temperature superconductivity, "cold" fusion, and the artificial heart) or an acrimonious dispute (the "Baltimore affair," discussed below) is brought to the public's attention. These almost-wrongs violate widely held principles of scientific conduct: they might preempt publication in the scientific literature or circumvent peer review and replication; they might entail dubious procedures at the laboratory bench, in the "inscription" and storage of data, in relations with colleagues (such as allocation of credit or sharing of tacit knowledge about research procedures and materials). But without access to researchers' motives and daily behavior, they are difficult to substantiate.

We subsume these almost-wrong behaviors under the terms "malpractice" or "misconduct" because their definitions, while clear-cut in the abstract, are fuzzy in application, and because the exact nature and seriousness of the violation, even in the presence of clear facts and definitions, are hard to establish. Members of the same laboratory, let alone the same research community, might differ in their appraisals of proper and improper behavior: they share the ambiguity of "misconduct" rather than the certainty of "fraud." For example, "data trimming" is a time-honored (mal)practice of selecting data points for publication from a larger series, discarding those that inconveniently fail to support one's hypothesis.[13] At times a scientist is justified in discarding data that are tainted in some way, yet selective reporting, if admitted openly, would probably be sharply censured. But the historical record suggests that Mendel's peas had some assistance in sorting themselves in a theoretically agreeable fashion, and Millikan's measurements of the electron's charge benefited from judicious rounding and pruning to obtain values that agreed with calculated expectations. Even today, some neuroscientists say that data plots published in U.S. journals have enjoyed a bit of smoothing and shaping, attentions that their counterparts published in other nations' literatures were spared. Although the practice of scientists is subtle and the boundary between exemplary technique and misconduct is fluid, the "certified" instances of fraud and their reception in the scientific community guide us to the boundaries.

### Fraud in Research: The Social Structure of Scapegoating

Incidents of scientific misconduct have been in the public eye for over a decade. The cavalcade begins with William Summerlin's mouse-painting incident at the Sloan-Kettering Institute (1974) and continues along to the 1987 disclosure of Stephen Breuning's experiments at Illinois and Pittsburgh on psychotropic drugs to control the behavior of mentally retarded persons in institutions.[14] Pillars of the scientific community who are called before Congressional committees and sought after by the media for statements of accountability routinely try to dismiss these cases as "overblown" and "atypical." Why dwell on them? And why attend to the "sensationalizing" by reporters who have neither a comprehension of science nor a commitment to the production of "truth"—scientific or otherwise?

In the era of Public Science it is naive and indefensible to regard research misconduct as an anomaly that arises haphazardly, through individual weakness or venality, and poses no threat to the inner working or public perception of science. Science is in the public mind and on the national agenda, and it will not do to view science incompletely, inaccurately, without skepticism. Even a single incisive account of scientific misconduct, typically produced by a so-called "muckraking" journalist reputedly lacking insight into the "real" world of science, can underscore how arrogant and ultimately ineffectual it is for science to hide behind the laboratory door. The high esteem and munificent support bestowed upon science entails an obligation to keep the citizenry informed. Attempts to deflect or preempt discussions of misconduct cannot make the events disappear. Feeble efforts to ascribe incidents of misconduct to deviant scientists whose fatally flawed characters were doubtless formed *before* they ever entered the laboratory cannot deter those seeking systematic explanations. No longer will it do to maintain that scientific misconduct results from the isolated actions of a few wrong-headed individuals. But it would also be incorrect to castigate the "science system." Instead, we must recognize that incidents of misconduct and their aftermaths vividly illustrate how ill-defined are notions of intellectual property, due process, full disclosure, collegial responsibility, and appropriate laboratory technique and conduct. Such "value" issues remain unresolved, and their resolutions shift with the changing conditions of research.[15]

Institutions with a stake in research, including federal agencies, universities, professional societies, and journals, are only now devising procedures for detering and investigating misconduct. As one academic administrator has put it:

> Like so many other institutions, we have been tardy in setting up official mechanisms for handling this problem because of what might be called a form of psychic numbing. It never occurred to us that it could happen to us.[16]

And these policies must resolve complex issues. For example, when should a university announce that a researcher is under investigation for misconduct? At what point should the sponsor be informed? Anonymity and confidentiality are essential to protect the accused's character and reputation. Yet due process also demands openness, so that evidence may be freely obtained, presented, and evaluated.

And what of the accuser? In a court of law one has the right to confront one's accuser. In cases of misconduct, should accusers' identities be concealed and, if so, until what stage in the proceeding? Or should they stand in the open from the outset? Like other whistleblowers, accusers become the pariahs of the profession: no longer peers but sanctimonious "persecutors" rocking the research boat as well as endangering reputations and careers.[17] In the absence of certainty about accusations and misdeeds, it is difficult to tell who is victimized in these disputes—the suspected perpetrator or the one who calls attention to the behavior. There is ambivalence here as well: within the collective ethic of science is a countermanding individualistic ethic. Peers are quick to celebrate the brilliance in their midst, but hasten to shun those who, through their misdeeds or vigilance to expose misdeeds, open the profession to scrutiny that both challenges and embarrasses.

Without procedures in place, investigations may also assume an ad hoc and ad hominem quality. Yet should the procedures be modeled on law, science, or some other canon? Rules of procedure, standards of proof, timetables for investigation and hearing, and even costs would be very different under legalistic principles.

It is thus at once interesting, sobering, and alarming to learn, according to a recent survey of policies for responding to alleged fraud in research, that there is "a continued widespread belief in the reliability of routine processes of self-correction in science." As a result, one quarter of the 493 academic institutions and hospitals participating in the survey have no guidelines or plans for dealing with fraud. Instead, they rely on the "peer review process of journals and the regular representation of research to peers."[18] There has been some change in this regard since late 1987, when NIH announced that it would soon require grantee institutions to have in place procedures for investigating incidents of misconduct and that these procedures would have to meet NIH's standards of openness, timeliness, and the like.[19]

Is this procedural vacuum (or impasse) an invitation for congressional action? Congressional hearings conducted during 1988 and 1989 would suggest so. While reluctant to insist upon federal intervention in scientific disputes, these hearings highlighted Congress's concern that neither funding agencies nor universities appeared to be fair and expeditious inquirers into allegations of wrongdoing, for both were hamstrung by obvious conflicts of interest. The issue then became how to translate policies into procedures and regulations that would lessen the effects of conflicts of interest, insure accountability for expenditures of public funds, and preserve the integrity of scientific research. No firm solution arose, but proposals ranged from the drastic (creating an independent "quality assurance" agency) through the pragmatic (requiring fuller disclosure of ongoing proceedings and the presence of outside experts), to the ineffectual (insist upon research ethics courses in graduate science education).[20]

The fallibility of informal and ad hoc procedures, as we have seen, is compounded by the ambiguous definition of research malpractice. On the one hand, plagiarism, fabrication, falsification, and misrepresentation of data are apparent wrongs; on the other, careless record-keeping, unconscious bias ("experimenter effects" in the argot of psychology), and unwillingness to share data are almost-wrongs. A 1985 editorial states, "Desire to protect one's data from criticism or predatory use often prevails over the scholar's duty. . . . A scientist who denies legitimate inquirers access to the data frustrates the validation process of science."[21] But, as we shall see, this matter is far murkier in practice.

Table 5 summarizes the "normal" and "deviant" behaviors associated with the research process. Clearly, the determination of impropriety is relative to prevailing customs (they are hardly explicit "definitions") within a research community and particular production sites. Viewing the research process as four sequential stages removes the onus from individuals per se and places the burden for misconduct on the peer collectivity (local and distant). Deviant behavior thus becomes one portion of a range of responses to the research environment, a matter of interpersonal relations and definitions of appropriate conduct, not the expression of individual psychopathology. This does not excuse the behavior, but locates it in social space: deviance is recognized as a consequence of time and place, of expectations and pressures, of shared perceptions that, at some point, behavior that is eccentric or bizarre becomes offensive, morally wrong, and intolerable to the community. This insight, derived from labeling theory in sociology, warns us that the same behaviors will be assigned different meanings according to who performs them in which circumstances.

To reduce ambiguity, tension, and embarrassment, the researcher who commits an almost-wrong is likely to be labeled unequivocally wrong or unequivocally right. Dismissal of the wrongdoer is the easiest way to "correct" the problem and, indeed, had been the norm in misconduct cases. (For example, William Summerlin was dispatched from Sloan-Kettering with a year's medical leave, to allow him to get the "professional treatment" he apparently needed. This was a clear effort to treat the *social* problem of research misconduct as an isolated instance of *individual* illness.) At the other extreme, powerful administrators and lab

**Table 5**

"Normal" and "Deviant" Behavior in the Research Process

| "Normal" | "Deviant" |
|---|---|
| **PRODUCTION** | |
| Idea generation | Plagiarism/appropriation |
| Data collection (including record-keeping) | Fabrication ("dry labbing") |
| Analysis (bench procedures and coding) | "Trimming" |
| Internal cross-checking (of data, analysis, interpretation) | Self deception |
| **REPORTING** | |
| Information selection and presentation (including "dry run" seminars in own lab) | Misrepresentation and nonrepresentation (omission, e.g., "cooking," lack of citation, and hyperbole in knowledge claims) |
| **DISSEMINATION** | |
| Preprint distribution beyond own lab (including correspondence, phone conversation, and invited colloquia) | Unacknowledged or misattributed collaborators |
| Submission for publication | Author deceit in simultaneous multiple submission to journals and reviewer "pirating" of data |
| Manuscript processing | Citation fabrication or embellishment and foot-dragging in supplying editor with raw data |
| Publication (including revision as condition for publication) | Lack of acknowledgement of preprint readers, data sources, anonymous reviewer comments, and funding support |
| **EVALUATION** | |
| Replication/refutation | Author claim of raw data unavailability and peer silence despite suspicion over reported method or interpretation |
| Application/education | Reader negligence or misrepresentation of reported contents of scientific paper |

Source: Chubin, 1985, note 1.

chiefs cannot be dealt with in such cavalier fashion, for their accumulated reputations and considerable power make such disciplinary action both awkward and newsworthy. This was amply demonstrated by the reverberations of the John Darsee affair, in which Walter Stewart and Ned Feder assessed a portion of Darsee's blame to his coauthors at Emory and Harvard and to the editors and referees of the journals that published the fabricated results. In another form, similar aftershocks affected Yale Medical School Professor Philip Felig, whose handling of accusations against Vijay Soman was deemed so inadequate that he abandoned plans to take on a new post as a chaired professor and chair of the department of medicine at the Columbia Medical School.[22]

Universities and other research institutions can ill afford such strife and notoriety. They, too, have a community of faculty and students to maintain and a status in the wider world to cultivate. So their most expeditious response is to excise the embodiment of misbehavior, hoping to leave the body robust. Revising customs, monitoring routines, and codifying definitions of wrong and right are expensive, time-consuming, and insulting to professionals. Therefore, such reforms are difficult or impossible to carry out.

From the perspective of the community, especially its gatekeepers, what is at stake here? The editor of the *Annals of Internal Medicine*, Edward Huth, refers to "ethical offenses."[23] Perhaps they are little more than bad form or breaches of etiquette, but no one is quite sure what to make of such episodes—unless one is caught up in the swirl of events, charges, and counter-charges. False authorship or redundant publication is no solitary act. It occurs in an organizational setting that either induces such behavior or does nothing to prevent it. Such a setting creates a climate for malpractice, a climate characterized by vague and inconsistent rules, weak mechanisms for oversight and correction, and general agreement that infractions are best met with silence.

After an incident of misconduct has been recognized, blame is typically heaped upon those low in the hierarchy. Lesser scientists, such as William Summerlin, Vijay Soman, John Darsee, and Mark Spector, are publicly excoriated while their superiors (Robert Good, Philip Felig, Eugene Braunwald, and Ephraim Racker, respectively) are initially judged blameless or even pitied as victims. Individual scientists are under intense pressures to publish, to compete, to excel in research and thereby distinguish themselves in the eyes of federal program managers, journal editors, and their academic overlords: the lab chiefs, department chairs, and deans.

In this way tension arises between the individual scientist and the communal organizations that distribute honor and other rewards. Few in positions of power are willing to acknowledge that the causes of misconduct are built into the social fabric of modern science, especially its forms of social organization and standards of achievement, performance, and conduct.

Editor Arnold Relman, writing after two articles coauthored by cardiologist Darsee were retracted from the *New England Journal of Medicine,* expresses the sense of helplessness scientists feel in the face of research misconduct:

> What kind of protection against fraud does peer review offer? The Darsee affair gives a clear answer: Little or none. Most of Darsee's fraudulent work was published in peer-reviewed journals, some with very exacting standards, and yet in none of the reviews was enough suspicion to warrant rejection.
>
> There is no practical alternative to this presumption of honesty in research, because it would be impossible to verify every primary datum and every descriptive statement in a research report.[24]

The problem of scientific misconduct is systemic. It has grown as professional science has grown; it has also reinforced the autocracy of science. The profession of science is no longer the privileged domain of "great men," but it is still controlled by them, so "currying favor" remains a valuable skill in career mobility.

## MISCONDUCT AND PUBLIC SCIENCE

A recent controversial case illustrates the intensely public character of modern science (and some scientists' efforts to keep it private), underscores the difficulty of sharply demarcating "bad" science from "good," and offers a glimpse of the powerful but clumsy intervention of large institutions into such disputes. The controversy surrounds a paper published in *Cell* by six scientists, including (as fifth author) Nobel laureate David Baltimore. (The paper is Weaver, D., Reis, M., Albanese, C., Constantini, F., Baltimore, D., and T. Imanishi-Kari, "Altered Repertoire of Endogenous Immunoglobulin Gene Expression in Transgenic Mice Containing a Rearranged Mu Heavy Chain Gene," *Cell* 45 [April 25, 1986]:

247–259.) The central claim of this paper is that a gene from one strain of mouse, when transferred to another strain, can influence the recipient mouse's immune system. Important science, perhaps, but hardly the earth-shaking stuff of pitched scientific battle. Yet this article

> has been investigated by scientists at the Massachusetts Institute of Technology, where some of the research was done . . . evaluated by a trio of experts at Tufts, where some of the coauthors are working . . . analyzed in 37-page detail by Walter Stewart and Ned Feder of NIH. . . . It has been the subject of hearings by two committees of the U.S. Congress. It has been investigated by a special three-person panel of experts convened by the NIH. And it has been studied by at least ten NIH officials who evaluated the investigation by its own panel of experts.
>
> Altogether, hundreds of thousands of taxpayers' dollars have been spent investigating the data and circumstances surrounding publication of this paper which, even after all this attention, remains difficult for nearly all researchers to fully understand.[25]

We might add that the paper has also been discussed in *Science* on at least six occasions, *The Chronicle of Higher Education* twice (once in a "Point of View" piece by the whistleblower), appeared in untold newspaper stories nationwide, and was the subject of two published articles and a nine-page "Dear Colleague" letter, written by David Baltimore in order to

> set the record straight, not just to clear my own name and the names of the other authors who have been compromised by this attack, but for another, more compelling reason: A small group of outsiders, in the name of redressing an imagined wrong, would use this once-small, normal scientific dispute to catalyze the introduction of new laws and regulations that I believe could cripple American science.[26]

And the story is not over yet. We will first recount the events, then analyze the matters at issue.

While this initially appears not to be a case of scientific misconduct, narrowly construed, it shares one odd trait with many misconduct cases: the initiating events seem thoroughly mundane, but the reactions of scientists, university officials, and policymakers draw our attention. Indeed, the "Baltimore affair" has become a cause célèbre, mobilizing friends, foes, observers, and constituencies everywhere. The controversy began, in the words of Margot O'Toole, one of the principals, in this way:

> While working as a postdoctoral fellow at the Massachusetts Institute of Technology in 1986, I discovered serious misstatements in a paper published by my supervisor [Dr. Imanishi-Kari] and five others. A series of experiments were not done as stated. I brought the misstatements to the attention of the three principal authors, all scientists at MIT. Although they acknowledged that the published article contained misstatements, they refused to submit a correction because, they said, the misstatements were the result of inadvertent errors. Published inaccuracies of this type were common, they said, and only false claims made with fraudulent intent required correction.
>
> I informed university administrators of the misstatements. Professors at MIT and Tufts University, where the principal author [Imanishi-Kari] and I were about to move, investigated informally, agreed with the authors that inadvertent misstatements need not be disclosed, and reported to the administrators that my assertions had not been substantiated. They told me the corrections I proposed were "out of the question" because they could adversely affect the authors' careers and financial support. Since other researchers were relying on the published paper, I asked the professors to reconsider. They responded that my persistence indicated a vindictive motive. No faculty member supported me, and since my appointment depended on a faculty sponsor, I was left without a job.[27]

Much of the preceding story is unexceptional: A postdoc takes issue with the evidence presented in one of her sponsor's papers but is told that the errors that she finds so upsetting are not particularly important in the larger scheme of things scientific. Indeed, one might even consider it a bit of professional socialization, with the more experienced researchers teaching the neophyte what matters and what does not. It is also important to notice that while O'Toole writes of "misstatements," she does not (yet) allege fraud, despite the rather serious charge that "a series of experiments were not done as stated."

But the attribution of vindictive motivation, and the consequent "branding and banishment" of the writer, give one pause, for now it seems that a conscientious young scientist who properly called her superiors to account for shortcomings in a manuscript has improperly suffered for her efforts. Furthermore, those who believe in the purity of scientific knowledge will find it unusual that scientists are so tolerant of published error and so strongly influenced in their judgments by the material necessities of modern experimental biology.

## The Mainstreaming of Dispute

Had the tale ended here, we might feel some passing sympathy for O'Toole and some discomfiture about the contemporary scientist's attitude toward truth. But matters soon became more convoluted. David Baltimore's letter provides details about the next events in the story.

Dr. O'Toole's criticisms, as described by her, were based on certain experimental attempts of hers involving some of the reagents used in the study described in *Cell*. A part of her criticism was based on 17 pages of selected laboratory notes, a small fraction of the notes compiled during this project....

Basically, Dr. O'Toole is arguing that an alternative interpretation of the data is possible that postulates a series of low level events that together bring about the results.... Reviews by Dr. [Herman] Eisen [of MIT] and by a panel formed by Dr. Henry Wortis, an immunologist at Tufts... concluded separately that, although alternative explanations are possible for most data, there was no compelling reason to believe that any one of Dr. O'Toole's four points [about why the published interpretation was in error] represented a serious misinterpretation. Only further experimentation, the reviewers said, could properly resolve the differences between Dr. O'Toole's and others' interpretations.[28]

The curtain fell on the first act of this drama in June 1986, when in Baltimore's words,

Drs. Eisen, Imanishi-Kari, O'Toole, Weaver, and I sat down and went over in detail the questions raised by Dr. O'Toole. At the conclusion of that meeting, Dr. Eisen wrote a memo that includes the following sentences:

I do not think that I or anyone else present at the meeting felt that Margot O'Toole's disagreements were frivolous. They are indeed based on pretty carefully thought out ideas of the literature of the analytical methods. On the other hand, it is difficult to see that even with these shortcomings [Dr. O'Toole's substantive criticisms could be valid].

These kinds of disagreements are, of course, not uncommon in science and they are certainly plentiful in Immunology. The way they are resolved, traditionally, and effectively, is by publishing the results and having other laboratories repeat and evaluate them. . . . If they are incorrect and require revision, then so be it. This is the way science operates; and in fact it is the kind of contentiousness seen in this dispute that helps drive the science "engine." Therefore, it appears to me that the entire exercise is not an unusual one, except for the intensity of the feelings generated and the circumstances concerning Dr. Imanishi-Kari's pending appointment at Tufts.[29]

And in his formal report, Dr. Eisen concluded

that Dr. O'Toole is correct in claiming that there is an error in the paper; but it is not a flagrant error. . . .

The other issues raised by O'Toole, which are largely matters of interpretation and judgement, are best dealt with by allowing the scientific process to take its course. Other laboratories are trying to extend the findings. In this way we will know if the findings are right or wrong.[30]

The dispute has become more public as two universities undertook independent, informal investigations. O'Toole's motives and qualifications as a scientist have been acknowledged, at least by Eisen in his memo, for he found that her disagreements were "not frivolous" (indeed, they turned up an error) and that there are grounds for her interpretation of the published data. But most importantly, the dispute has been "mainstreamed" or normalized, recast as a "not unusual" and even healthy airing of diverse views about scientific evidence, something that "helps drive the science 'engine.'"

Eisen's is certainly a plausible explanation and one may be well justified in accepting it (with the caution, raised by Eisen, that a lot of ill will has been generated by this dispute). But one can also put a less charitable interpretation on these events by wondering if the senior scientists in this case, as in many cases of outright fraud, have disingenuously rephrased the disagreement in terms they can manage. By framing it as a matter of data interpretation, the reader is invited to decide whether to give more weight to the judgment of a Nobel laureate and several accomplished scientists or to a postdoc. By mainstreaming the dispute— that is, by explaining that this sort of thing is "normal" and might happen every day in even the best worlds of science—the reader is invited to pass over the event, defer to the collective expertise of science and trust its self-correcting character to settle matters in time.

But would self-correction ever occur? We doubt it. It is very unlikely that a person with O'Toole's perspective on the science at stake here—a perspective at odds with a prominent publication of prominent scientists—would be awarded a research grant to develop and explore her ideas. (After all, she is a long-term postdoc now lacking that most basic emblem of academic credibility: an academic or research appointment.) Thus, in this less charitable construction, the outcome of these informal investigations is not very satisfactory. And matters soon took a turn for the worse, as the scientific dispute went public and became entangled in the national political machinery. In Dr. O'Toole's words,

> Although I was not aware of it at the time, another researcher from my laboratory [Dr. Charles Maplethorpe] had not assumed that the universities' investigations would be fair or thorough. As a safeguard, he kept two uninvolved scientists from the National Institutes of Health informed of events while the investigations were under way. The two scientists, Walter Stewart and Ned Feder, are known for their study of the integrity of scientific literature. After the universities had closed the case, they decided to do a scientific analysis themselves. They compared data, which I had sent at their request, with the published presentation of those same data. They concluded that the central claim of the paper was erroneous.[31]

Baltimore's view of these events is somewhat different:

> ... Mr. Stewart and Dr. Feder produced a written manuscript that critiqued the paper on the basis of a review of the

17 pages of laboratory notes that had been made available to them by Dr. O'Toole. They circulated the manuscript widely within the scientific community, seeking comments. I have never seen the full range of comments, but a number of scientists have sent me copies of their comments and all rejected the contentions of the Stewart-Feder manuscript. This is not surprising; a critique of a paper based on a selected, random set of data is extremely unlikely to be accurate. Dr. Feder and Mr. Stewart then attempted to publish the manuscript. *Cell* and *Science* rejected it. I do not know if they sent it elsewhere. In April, 1988, I learned that they were visiting college campuses and discussing the issue in very explicit and unflattering terms. At this point I realized that I might have to take some action to preserve my own reputation.[32]

The wide circulation and repeated submission of Stewart and Feder's manuscript was nearly as good as publication, for it put the issue before many key scientists. (In passing, we wonder how many referees committed the "almost-wrong" of discussing—perhaps even circulating—the manuscript they were sent for review?) Then they took their issue before another part of the public, discussing the case at colleges. This is the scientific analogue to "trying a case in the media"—presenting the matter and one's interpretation of it to a general audience. It is a form of public science akin to the revelation of research findings, such as cold fusion, in the media before publication in the scientific literature. There are few legal protections and no scientific ones to prevent or remedy this use of the media. It is simply seen by most scientists as bad form or poor taste: audacious, amateurish, and a circumvention of review by peers.

One might ask why the Stewart-Feder manuscript was based on such a poor selection of data from the original paper? Why not reanalyze the entire data base of the study? Baltimore's letter provides the answer:

[Stewart and Feder] wrote formal letters to all of the authors of the paper asking for all of the laboratory data so that they could compare them to the published data. We discussed this proposal and declined for the following reasons:

1. Dr. Feder and Mr. Stewart are not immunologists and from the types of questions they raised clearly showed a lack of understanding of the complex serology involved.

2. The two were self-appointed and had no right to the data. . . . For random people, scientists or not, to investigate scientific papers would severely disrupt ongoing scientific activities. On the other hand, duly constituted investigative bodies or colleagues in the same field should be provided the data for investigative purposes without question. . . . Dr. Feder and Mr. Stewart persisted with letters and phone calls, and finally I decided simply to stop responding.[33]

Consider first the issue of access to data. In Baltimore's view, not all scientists have the technical competence and "standing" (in the legal sense of a stake in the matter at issue) to participate in a scientific dispute; some simply lack the expertise to examine certain data and have no business doing so. Of course, this assertion begs the questions of how an investigative body is "duly constituted" and of who passes judgment on a scientist's credentials and standing to participate. Must all parties to the dispute agree about the expertise and interest of others? Why was it not sufficient that O'Toole had invited Feder and Stewart into the fray? Feder and Stewart are hardly "random people" but were drawn in by O'Toole, one of the principals. Indeed, the fact that they are not "random people" but have developed a reputation as scientific gadflies and troubleshooters in matters of misconduct may account for some of Baltimore's uneasiness.

Next, notice the irony in the case to this point. Eisen's report called for science to correct itself, for subsequent research to determine which interpretation has greater merit. But in many sciences a secondary analysis of data, such as Feder and Stewart proposed to undertake, is a perfectly acceptable (and very economical) procedure for resolving differences of interpretation. Yet the authors' unwillingness to provide the data forestalled this self-correcting mechanism. On what grounds would an independent replication, involving fresh data, be superior to an independent reanalysis of these data, for the purpose of settling the interpretive issue at stake? Moreover, the difficulty Feder and Stewart encountered in trying to publish their manuscript mocked Eisen's view of scientific publication as an instrument of self-correction: their systematic critique, even crippled as it is by their inability to obtain all the relevant data, might have stimulated and shaped the further research that Eisen thought necessary to resolve the issue. And if Stewart and Feder's views were in error, their work could be overlooked or corrected by subsequent research. Is that not also a part of the "engine" of science?

Finally, notice that by April 1988 this "once-small, normal scientific dispute" had become Public Science, and the initial almost-wrong had been overshadowed by subsequent almost-wrongs. Each side contributed to the publicity: Feder and Stewart by openly criticizing the *Cell* article (in a way, incidentally, that got back to Baltimore, as did some scientists' comments on the manuscript and its fate at two journals) and Baltimore by choosing to respond with his "Dear Colleague" letter. But the public would soon see much more of this dispute.

### Out of the Nursery, Into the Night

The dispute became much more public when the Oversight and Investigations Subcommittee of the House Committee on Energy and Commerce, chaired by Representative John Dingell (D, Mich.), took up the general issue of NIH handling of misconduct allegations, and the specific matter of the disputed *Cell* paper. Asserting that reported cases of fraud and misconduct in science are but the "tip of an iceberg," and avowing a "special affection" for whistleblowers, the Committee charged that the NIH had done little to protect whistleblowers—indeed, it may have engaged in harassment and "carefully programmed ignorance"; thus its investigation procedures are "hopelessly inadequate." In this hearing NIH and universities were portrayed as reluctant to investigate alleged misconduct. Since universities could not be trusted to investigate themselves, since NIH seemed incapable of doing so, and since scientists individually or collectively (in their professional societies) were caught in a web of entangling allegiances, then it became incumbent upon Congress to provide new "quality assurance" mechanisms. One representative proposed that an independent agency for quality assurance be established. In the interim, perhaps as a fact-finding venture or a demonstration of how to conduct an investigation, the subcommittee itself got into the business of reviewing scientists' behavior by taking a look at events surrounding the *Cell* article. In David Baltimore's words,

Two Congressional subcommittees became interested in the issue [the Dingell subcommittee and a House Government Operations subcommittee chaired by Ted Weiss, D, N.Y.]. One of the subcommittees . . . held a hearing at which the witnesses included Mr. Stewart and Dr. Feder, Dr. O'Toole and Dr. Maplethorpe and certain NIH officials. The authors of the paper were not invited to testify, nor were we even informed that an investigation was underway.[34]

Once the investigation was underway, it developed a voracious appetite for evidence, as Baltimore recounts:

> The Dingell subcommittee . . . has asked, through NIH, for MIT and Tufts to literally empty their files of everything pertaining to the situation. A letter was sent by the subcommittee counsel, Mr. Michael F. Barrett, Jr., to NIH on May 4, 1988, and demanded that all of the data be supplied the next day.

> The subcommittee's chief investigator, Mr. Peter Stockton, who was quoted in the *Boston Globe* making highly inflammatory and condemnatory statements about the authors of the *Cell* paper, has been aggressively attempting to schedule interviews with some of the authors [but] I have never [as of 17 May 1988] been contacted by him or any other member of the subcommittee or its staff on this matter.[35]

These events raise questions about due process or, less formally, basic principles of fair play, and underscore how underdeveloped are the procedures for handling scientific misconduct. District attorneys generally do not make "inflammatory and condemnatory" statements in the press, at least as long as a case is pending, yet there are no firm rules governing the behavior of Congressional investigators. Indeed, the media are essential for the public and political character of their work.

Of course, where congressional subcommittees go, newspapers often follow—or are led. In Baltimore's account:

> Prior to the [subcommittee's] meeting, Mr. Stewart and Dr. Feder called up certain newspaper reporters and briefed them. They refused to talk to other reporters (from whom we first heard about the hearing), saying that they were "already working with other reporters."

> Thus, in the few days before the hearing there were newspaper articles about the O'Toole-Imanishi-Kari dispute throughout the country, including all of the major newspapers. Although we offered to as many reporters as would listen as complete an explanation as we could, our story was not as "flashy" as that profferred by Mr. Stewart and Dr. Feder. With the exception of the *Washington Post* and the *Los*

*Angeles Times,* we fared badly. The most damaging article to me personally was in the *Boston Globe,* one from which I have not yet recovered.[36]

With powerful politicians and influential newspapers now involved the dispute has taken on a new timbre, with overtones of public accountability, due process, and preservation of scientific autonomy and integrity. For us, the principal image evoked by the subcommittee's intervention is drawn from the classic cartoon, "Bambi Meets Godzilla," in which the fawn stands briefly in the meadow, then disappears beneath the lizard's crushing foot. Whatever weight the scientists may have thrown about to influence the informal, internal investigations conducted by MIT and Tufts— and they may not have thrown about any weight, but merely benefited from others' deference to their standing and accomplishments—that unequal confrontation is dwarfed by the intervention of these congressional subcommittees. And the participants are blinded by the glaring light of the national media. As Benjamin Barber reminds us, to claim that knowledge is power is an act of hubris—we offend the gods when we equate our limited understandings with their (comparatively) limitless power. The *Cell* dispute elicited the wrath of our secular gods and exposed the broad expanse that separates knowledge from power, reminding us that *power* is power.

What is the subcommittee up to? In Baltimore's words, "They appear to plan to judge the science through the hearing process, a totally inappropriate forum for deciding scientific questions."[37] But if a congressional subcommittee is not the most appropriate forum, what is? If fellow scientists (such as Feder and Stewart) lack the qualifications and standing to take part in the debate, who is qualified? Baltimore had suggested that NIH assemble a group of immunologists to review the paper, confident that

> this panel—or any other qualified scientists—who look dispassionately at all of the records and experiments will conclude that the published paper appropriately reflected the state of the science at the time it was written.

> Whether this point will ever come across to the Congressional subcommittee, or to the public at large, is problematic. But I take solace in the knowledge that the scientific community will know and understand.[38]

David Baltimore got his wish. NIH formed an investigatory panel, though with some difficulty, according to O'Toole: two of the three members of the initial panel had ties to Baltimore, which might have presented conflicts of interest. NIH did not replace these members until Representative Dingell "scheduled a hearing to air his concerns about the adequacy of university procedures for handling allegations of scientific misconduct."[39] The panel conducted its business under very unusual circumstances: apart from the inherent discomforts of examining allegations of professional misconduct that concern such prominent scientists and have attracted such general interest, the panel also had a group of NIH staffers looking over its shoulder, just as NIH had a Congressional subcommittee overseeing its oversight.[40]

The panel's official findings, which provide small comfort to either party, were made public in early 1989. The ambiguity of the panel's central finding and the intensely public character of the scientific dispute are apparent in the headlines and leads of stories about the report that appeared in *Science* and *The Chronicle of Higher Education. Science*'s headline proclaimed, "Baltimore Cleared of All Fraud Charges" and the story began by noting that the panel "found no evidence of (quoting the panel's report) 'fraud, misconduct, manipulation of data, or serious conceptual errors.' "[41] For the *Chronicle,* the news was "Nobelist Found Guilty of Errors in Paper, but Innocent of Fraud," and that the panel found (again quoting its report), " 'significant errors of misstatement and omission, as well as lapses in scientific judgment and interlaboratory communication.' "[42] The good news is that the authors of the *Cell* paper were not intentionally deceptive; the bad news is that their basic craft skills were found deficient.

Acting on the panel's report, James B. Wyngaarden, director of NIH, asked the authors to prepare a more complete correction of their *Cell* paper and to send it to him for review prior to publication. (One correction, which acknowledged three "misstatements" had been published in *Cell* on November 18, 1988, but that was judged inadequate.)[43] In a statement to *Science,* Baltimore said " 'If further clarification of the paper seems warranted, we will respond appropriately. . . . However, we do not see that [either the panel or its reviewers] have identified such questions.' "[44] This exchange is at odds with Baltimore's earlier statements that a panel of scientists would find the paper acceptable and that he would willingly abide by the judgment of duly appointed and qualified peers.

For her part, O'Toole also found little satisfaction in the report's conclusions. Commenting on a draft of the report, she told NIH that it was a " 'wholly inadequate scientific analysis' that fails to answer specific allegations—namely, that 'the report draws important conclusions from experiments that Dr. Imanishi-Kari stated had not been done.' "[45] On the other hand, "Imanishi-Kari, and three Tufts scientists who have seen the data, all told NIH in writing that O'Toole is simply wrong."[46] Thus O'Toole is continuing to allege that data were fabricated, but she has been contradicted by the testimony of other scientists. Most surprising,

> The panel also found that a series of tests had not been performed, even though the text accompanying a table in the paper said that they had been. Panel members said that, after separate follow-up interviews with Mr. Baltimore and his two main co-authors, the panel had decided that the misrepresentation was unintentional, the result of "poor interlaboratory communication."[47]

Serious as the consequences may be for the parties involved (and they are serious, as careers and reputations have suffered irreparably), the consequences for science and its connection to politics are more serious, even dire. Ironically, this is a matter of agreement among all parties, although the threats they perceive and the remedies they propose are quite different.

For O'Toole, this case illustrates weaknesses in the conduct of science and in its ancillary mechanisms of self-correction. Of current practice in biology she writes,

> It is clear that the current standards of the profession do not even require that published claims accurately represent the data.... If this case is a manifestation of acceptable practices of biologists, neither researchers themselves, nor the public paying for research, can rely on published claims.[48]

Beyond scientific practice, science's self-correcting mechanisms are flawed because

> instead of confronting the problem of eroding professional standards and trying to solve it, many scientists maintain that the delicate endeavor of research can only be damaged by those who seek reform.[49]

She goes on to note the dangers of relying on individuals to point out errors and demand their correction, thereby putting their careers in jeopardy, and relying on universities, which have an interest in the reputations of the scientists they employ, to investigate incidents of misconduct. O'Toole does not prescribe a solution, but we can infer that it would involve some form of collective, independent oversight, stronger protections for individual whistleblowers, and a change in the guiding principles and incentives of science to reward accurate results and to allow sufficient time to produce such results.

O'Toole's remarks take no account of the financial circumstances of science today and the economics of higher education, forces which have shaped the conduct of science.[50] Nor does she consider the threats to scientists' independence that an oversight agency would pose. Finally, normative change is exceedingly difficult to effect, as the recent history of race and gender relations in the U.S. shows us. One cannot simply erect new standards of conduct, legislate new attitudes and values, and expect instant conformity.

For Baltimore,

> What we are undergoing is a harbinger of threats to scientific communication and scientific freedom. The halls of Congress are not the place to determine scientific truth or falsity. NIH must put in place procedures that will protect us [scientists] from such investigations and that will neutralize the activities of such as Mr. Stewart and Dr. Feder by quickly responding to charges of fraud and misconduct. [Formally, however, neither charge was initially levelled against the *Cell* paper.] Several scientific societies have begun to take the issue of scientific misconduct and fraud more seriously; they will perhaps encourage more rigorous NIH procedures. As long as such procedures are effective against fraud and do not impede scientific progress, I would support them. The pressure to deal with fraud directly is too great to resist, but I worry that over-regulation might impede scientific progress or scare off younger scientists, especially those with controversial or progressive ideas. These are difficult times for those of us who pursue knowledge in the biological sciences. I see this affair as symptomatic, warning us to be vigilant to such threats, because our research community is fragile, easily attacked, difficult to defend, easily undermined. What is now my problem could become anyone else's if circumstances present themselves.[51]

There is much to consider in Baltimore's warning. For example, some might think that the activities of "such as Mr. Stewart and Dr. Feder" are exactly what science needs "to determine scientific truth or falsity," so their activities need to be encouraged, even institutionalized, not "neutralized." Based on the account presented above, without Feder and Stewart's intervention, even agitation, and their success in drawing the eye of one or two members of Congress, it is very likely (1) that O'Toole and Maplethorpe would have been relegated to the "scrap-heap" of bioscientists whose "difficult personalities" stand in the way of academic success; (2) that even the modest correction of the original *Cell* paper, published in November 1988, would not have appeared, and (granting that the NIH panel and its overseers are correct) the other necessary corrections would also have gone unwritten; and (3) that the entire incident, handled informally and quietly, would have remained unseen, thus depriving the scientific community of the important cautionary lessons about the dangers of carelessness in the age of Public Science and the vulnerability, born of hubris, of even a Nobel laureate.

And there is more to consider in Baltimore's words. He is willing to accept "more rigorous NIH procedures" as long as they "do not impede scientific progress." But others may wonder in what sense a seriously flawed paper represents "progress," and, more generally, whether the public may be better served by impeding "scientific progress" in the interests of improved quality and accountability. Moreover, Baltimore's concern that over-regulation might frighten away "younger scientists . . . with controversial or progressive ideas" is ironic, perhaps even fatuous. O'Toole's ideas were controversial, uncomfortably so: had the inquiry ended with the informal investigations at MIT and Tufts, would she be any less "scared off" than she was by the actual course of events? We doubt it. We can think of little more discouraging to a young scientist with new ideas than to see another young scientist speak out and be crushed by the weighty reputations and formidable institutional interests of modern science.

Baltimore is exactly right in saying that this affair is "symptomatic," that "vigilance" is necessary, and that the research community is "fragile." But we find it symptomatic of the performance pressures that impede good science, the entrenched interests that impair fair hearing, the social entanglements that preclude scientific self-regulation, the painful unwieldiness of federal responses to local problems, the unmodulated amplification (even distortion) of media accounts, and the terrifying likelihood that science will soon reside in the stifling iron cage of bureaucracy. The problem is emphatically not whether Baltimore or Stewart and Feder,

Imanishi-Kari or O'Toole, NIH or Congress will ultimately "win" the tussle; it is that the tussle itself has the potential to yield a stronger, healthier science or a disfigured, constrained science; and, at this time, the latter seems more likely.

## EARMARKING AND THE PORK BARREL

Seventy years ago, in a classic essay entitled "Science as a Vocation," Max Weber warned:

> Only where parliaments, as in some countries, or monarchs, as in Germany thus far (both work out in the same way), or revolutionary power-holders, as in Germany now, intervene for political reasons in academic selections, can one be certain that convenient mediocrities or strainers will have the opportunities all to themselves.[52]

If we substitute the adjective "scientific" for "academic" in Weber's comment, it may well serve as a contemporary caution about the dangers science faces when Congress allocates funds for specific facilities or projects at particular institutions. When politicians directly allocate resources for science, some would argue, and use extra-scientific criteria to guide their judgments, the quality of work and the orderliness of the scientific enterprise are endangered. But on the other hand, if scientists' allocative mechanisms are ill suited to expressing social priorities in the scientific arena, then direct political involvement is needed.

Unlike misconduct, earmarking in itself is neither dangerous nor wrong. But it is symptomatic of underlying flaws in the allocative system and it poses a challenge to scientific autonomy in the future. Thus it merits attention, alongside misconduct, as a strategic site at which to examine the limits of peer review and scientific self-governance. It may also be the first wave of a deeper integration of science with the traditional economic and political institutions of the U.S., bringing to a close the postwar era of relative freedom of scientific inquiry.

The pork barrel is a time-honored institution of U.S. politics. Dams, roads, military bases, and other worthy projects are routinely sited in one or another district through such exchanges. As scientific endeavors become larger, more visible, and more expensive, they too become fair game for legislative politics. The most effective brake on legislators' willingness to treat funds for science in the same way as other allocations has been the perception that science is a unique enterprise that requires special treatment.

Over the past forty years the policy debate about the special character of scientific allocations has been framed as a choice between using excellence as the primary criterion in allocation decisions versus insisting upon principles of geographic or institutional equity to insure that support for science does not become unduly concentrated. The issue appeared most plainly in the congressional debate that preceded passage of the National Science Foundation Act of 1950.[53] In brief, some Senators believed that scientific talent was distributed nationwide, that participation in basic research was an integral part of science education, and that concentration of research funds would lead to an undesirable concentration of talented faculty.[54] Others countered that

> we would obtain second- or third-rate results if we simply scattered our money, when it ought to be concentrated to get first-rate results. . . . Some of the very best men will be gotten in the smallest institutions in the country. We know them and can find them. But that does not mean that in order to get those few stars we have to subsidize every state and every institution in the country. We cannot afford to do it. It is not sound Federal policy. The thing to do is to be discriminative.[55]

Thus the lines of debate were drawn, with those arguing for broad dispersion of support elaborating their position by invoking considerations of equity, economic development, impact of scientific fields, and the like, while their opponents held that the scientific excellence of research was the paramount concern, with all other considerations distantly secondary.[56] The matter was eventually resolved by incorporating the following language into the National Science Foundation Act of 1950:

> It shall be an objective of the Foundation to strengthen research and education in the sciences, including independent research by individuals, throughout the United States, and *to avoid undue concentration of such research and education.*[57]

The issue of equitable geographic distribution emerged again in the "Seaborg Report" of 1960 (entitled *Scientific Progress, the Universities, and the Federal Government*), which argued in part that "The growth of science requires more places with superior faculties and outstanding groups of students. Existing strong institutions cannot fully meet the nation's future needs."[58] Thus the nation must "increase support for rising centers of science. Over the next fifteen years the United States should seek to double the number of universities doing generally excellent work in basic research and graduate education."[59] There followed a succession of programs designed to increase the scientific activity of "second-tier" universities and four-year colleges: Science Development, College Science Improvement Program, and the Experimental Program to Stimulate Competitive Research were among those initiated by NSF.[60]

Most recently the issue has moved from the realm of policy initiatives, Presidential Commissions, and programs to the political arena, with universities taking direct political action, in the form of lobbying, to secure funds for laboratory space, equipment, and research. For example, *The Chronicle of Higher Education,* a weekly "trade paper" of higher education, reported that $289 million worth of such allocations were made by the 100th Congress.[61] These funds supported activities at ninety campuses, including, for example, $20 million to the Florida State University system for work on advanced semiconductor materials, $14 million to the University of Hawaii at Manoa for a strategic-materials research facility, and $10 million to build the Barry Goldwater Center for Science and Technology at Arizona State University.

Many institutions that obtain funds in this way do not get a large share of peer-reviewed research support, although there are leading research universities among the beneficiaries of the pork barrel.[62] Institutions that receive the lion's share of peer-reviewed support justify their position in one language, while those who support earmarking as an allocative mechanism use quite different arguments.

Some supporters of earmarking are unvarnished pragmatists. For example, Charles E. Backus, assistant dean for research at Arizona State University's College of Engineering and Applied Sciences, said simply:

> My need is to have a building. I don't really care if it's state funds or federal funds or private funds, as long as we get the money.[63]

But scarcely beneath the pragmatic surface is a principled argument, based on his intuition about the distribution of scientific talent:

The more gardens there are out there, the greater the probability that that unique flower is going to bloom someplace.[64]

Soon Arizona State willl have its own garden and "that unique flower," the important scientific discovery, may bloom there.

Others offer more pointed arguments, contending that direct allocations are necessary to overcome the old boys' biases of peer review and the cumulative disadvantage such biases have created. Boston University President John Silber has been particularly outspoken on the subject, saying:

> the real pork barrel in scientific research is the system that benefits the very research universities that have been loudest in claiming the purity of peer review.[65]

Appearing at a House hearing on 26 June 1985, Silber asserted that

> universities . . . not among the top twenty in federal research support are forced to seek direct congressional funding for facilities in order to compete "on an equal footing" for the limited federal research funds dispensed by peer review.[66]

Silber is joined by Richard Rose, President of the Rochester Institute of Technology, who observes that the "first tier" of thirty elite East and West Coast institutions receive roughly half of all federal R&D funds, while the 500 schools in the second tier share the remaining half.

In contrast, the sharpest critics of earmarking are universities that generally do quite well in the contest for research funds. They reply that earmarking circumvents the collective judgments of scientists, thereby weakening the influence of the scientific community and allocating resources inefficiently. Attempts to circumvent peer review have been deplored by such influential organizations as the National Academy of Sciences, the Association of American Universities, and the National Science Board.

Others reply that "when the level of inequity is so high, it actually builds inefficiency," thus creating a need for earmarking and other mechanisms for building scientific capacity.[67]

But the efforts continue and the rhetoric has escalated. A milestone in the debate came in a May 1987 (non-binding) vote by the heads of those fifty-five of the nation's leading research universities which make up the AAU. By a margin of forty-three to ten, with two abstentions, members resolved "to observe a moratorium on seeking pork barrel funds from Congress to build facilities."[68] Soon thereafter a blunt editorial in the *Washington Post* pinpointed the dilemma:

The AAU group says this practice [earmarking] could threaten American research by undermining the principle of money for merit in science—"merit" being defined, as it traditionally has been in the sciences, by a group of other scientists in the field.

But this is a fight between institutions of higher learning [not scientists]. The universities that have turned to earmarking retort that these "merit reviews" are an elitist charade in which a small group of wealthy, well-known, and well-equipped institutions keeps getting more and more money, while the small and obscure universities fall further and further behind. In addition, these same universities that get the money are in many cases—by virtue of name, history and steadily improving research facilities—the ones most likely to have other sources of money besides the government to fall back on, sources such as an endowment fund or a large group of well-heeled alumni. This description of the "haves" comes uncomfortably close to being a description of the AAU membership and makes their "moratorium" on seeking earmarked funds a dubious gesture. If everyone could get funds through "merit review" as easily as they can, earmarking would be far less prevalent.[69]

The media are not the only third party observing this dispute, nor are they the most powerful. Congress controls the federal budget and has asserted unequivocally its intention to continue earmarking funds for specific projects. The rationales are varied. Senator Russell Long (D, La.) asked incredulously, "when did we agree that the peers would cut the melon or decide who would get this money?"[70] From the other house, Representative Manuel Lujan, Jr., (R, N.M.) the former ranking minority member of the House Science, Space, and Technology Committee, declared that, in view of the concentration of federal R&D funds, "Congress has a role to play in redressing this imbalance."[71] If this perception endures, the scientific pork barrel will long be with us.

But table manners at the pork barrel are changing. Senator Robert C. Byrd (D, W.V.), nettled by the University of West Virgin-

ia's decision to retain Cassidy and Associates (a Washington lobbying firm) to help them obtain funding for a materials research
center, has introduced legislation that would forbid the use of federal funds to pay for such lobbying.[72] Byrd's irritation arises in
part from his desire to maintain direct contact with his constituency—and thus to reap the full benefit of any favors rendered. But
it also stems from a deep-rooted ambivalence about the place of
academic science in society. Should science receive special consideration, based on past performance or future promise, or is it just
another interest group? On what grounds does science justify its
claims on public resources, and how should those claims be evaluated? Lobbyists use persuasion, influence, and exchange to obtain
resources for their clients. Are these the appropriate terms of debate for scientific allocations, or should other considerations come
into play?

Beneath earmarking is a far larger issue which has roots in
the founding years of the U.S. science establishment: To what extent should science justify its federal support by producing useful
results, such as cures for diseases, economically valuable innovations, and weapons systems? The answer in many of the founding
documents of the postwar U.S. science establishment is, resound-
ingly, *to a great extent.* The very first words of *Science: The Endless Frontier,* in the first paragraph of the Summary of the Report,
read as follows:

> Progress in the war against disease depends upon a flow of
> new scientific knowledge. New products, new industries, and
> more jobs require continuous additions to knowledge of the
> laws of nature, and the application of that knowledge to prac-
> tical purposes. Similarly, our defense against aggression de-
> mands new knowledge so that we can develop new and
> improved weapons. This essential, new knowledge can be ob-
> tained only through basic scientific research. [73]

And in a later passage on the importance of basic research,
Bush writes,

> Basic research leads to new knowledge. It provides scientific
> capital. It creates the fund from which the practical applica-
> tions of knowledge must be drawn. New products and new
> processes do not appear full-grown. They are founded on new
> principles and new conceptions, which in turn are painstak-
> ingly developed by research in the purest realms of sci-

ence. . . . *A nation which depends upon others for its new basic scientific knowledge will be slow in its industrial progress and weak in its competitive position in world trade, regardless of its mechanical skill.*[74]

Of course, Vannevar Bush had not seen the economic miracle of Japan and the Pacific rim when he outlined his delicate argument. In it, he forges a firm connection between basic research and such desirable social ends as health, prosperity, and national security, but he also attempts to keep social ends at some distance from the enterprise of basic research. That is, he argues simultaneously that basic research is essential for practical gain and that basic research must be "free," unconstrained by practical demands.

In the following decades the issue arose again and again in many forms. A classic paper by Julius Comroe and Robert Dripps (1976) attempted to connect breakthroughs in the health field with basic biomedical research. The TRACES Report (*Technology in Retrospect and Critical Events in Science*; IIT 1968) did the same for a broader array of technologies. In contrast, their predecessor and progenitor, "Project Hindsight" (1966) had argued that academic research best serves military ends when the research is mission-oriented and targeted by the sponsor.[75] Senator William Proxmire's "Golden Fleece" awards, given in dubious recognition of federally-funded scientific projects that seem inscrutable, and perhaps ridiculous, to the layman, were another element in our national struggle with the proper social and political justification for basic scientific research. Most recently, the growing presence of *engineering* within the National *Science* Foundation, the retitling of *Science Indicators* to *Science and Engineering Indicators*, and the shift at NSF from "peer" review to "merit" review—the latter blending peer evaluations of technical merit with assessments of practical utility—signal a new balance point in the dynamic equilibrium between knowledge and utility. In the summary of NSF's 1986 report on merit review the Committee wrote:

> For an increasing proportion of Federally-sponsored research, however, technical excellence is a necessary but not fully sufficient criterion for research funding. To reach goals such as increasing the practical relevance of research results, or improving the nation's infrastructure for science and engineering, additional criteria are needed. . . . The Committee has adopted the term "merit review" to refer to selection processes which include technical as well as these additional critieria.[76]

Pork-barrelling is far less surprising when considered in this context. Once science has been harnessed to serve practical ends, it is a small step to include political criteria in the selection equation; in effect, political considerations themselves are among the "practical ends" which science may serve, and politics becomes the instrument for choosing among the possible ends which may be served.

Consider as a case in point the twenty-four-year course of research on an implantable artificial heart for humans. The National Heart, Lung, and Blood Institute (NHLBI) spent $240 million on this endeavor until deciding to terminate the program in May 1988. But the decision of Dr. Claude Lenfant, director of NHLBI, did not stick. Senators Orrin Hatch and Edward Kennedy, perhaps in part to preserve contracts to researchers in their states, exerted pressure on the NIH to reinstitute the program. And NIH complied with these powerful senators who sit on the committee that oversees funding for the NIH because, as one NIH official put it, "we felt the Heart Institute better eat a little crow rather than risk the future budgets of all the Institutes."[77]

Or consider the recent experience of the Department of Agriculture (USDA), which had been directed by both House and Senate Appropriations Committees to spend, through its Cooperative State Research Service (CSRS), about $10.75 million on specified research projects in fiscal year 1989.[78] This unprecedented involvement of Congress in the USDA research effort jeopardizes the already threatened competitive grants program, which uses a form of peer review to allocate funds. (The directive was lifted in subsequent legislation but may be reinstated at any time.)

A short-sighted reading of these and similar cases might yield outrage at the intrusion of politics into the inner workings of science. But a more sophisticated view would acknowledge that politics have always been at the heart of allocation decisions in science, and that U.S. science since the second world war has been indebted to the political process.

If federal research funds are expected to yield useful results at the same time that they increase the nation's scientific capacity—to serve economic, political, social, military, and scientific ends simultaneously and efficiently—it is no wonder that the self-regulatory mechanisms of science are overwhelmed, that the peer review process is in disarray, that university presidents are at odds, and that the Congress has entered the fray as peacemaker. As all parties acknowledge, federal research support is inadequate for the array of tasks presented to science. In the words of a *Washington Post* editorial:

The underlying problem is the dual purpose of federal science grants: to get the best possible scientific research for the money (which favors funding projects and buildings with the best facilities and the best talent) and to support and develop the overall research enterprise of the country (which favors funding projects at universities that need economic and technological development). The trouble is that the current competitive review system has given the first goal disproportionate emphasis for many years. . . . To redress the balance, the academic community might . . . take into account other criteria than what the "haves" call pure merit.[79]

In effect, our drive for excellence and desire to reward ability has, in this as in other contexts, run afoul of our commitment to equality and democratic process. AAU President Robert Rosenzweig, replying to the *Post* editorial, makes the case for excellence:

There is a deep and genuine concern among the heads of many of America's leading universities that a very successful system of supporting academic science is being undermined, and that what will replace it will serve the Nation considerably less well.

In a world increasingly dependent on the intellectual achievements that come from university laboratories, it would be unsound policy for the United States to turn away from scientific merit, fairly judged by qualified persons, as the basis for its science policies.[80]

Without relief in the form of a facilities bill (such as H.R. 1905, sponsored by Representative Robert Roe [D, N.J.], which might reduce the pressures on universities to seek direct Congressional allocations), scientists and policymakers will be forced to make a fine distinction between peers and lobbyists, according to *Science* Editor Daniel Koshland:

If a group of chemists decides that there must be more money for instrumentation, if a group of biochemists says that the number of grants must be increased for the National Institutes of Health, if a group of high energy physicists says that we need a new particle accelerator, are they peer reviewers or diligent lobbyists for their own area of science? Are they different from university presidents who are trying to help their institutions, or congressmen watching out for their districts?[81]

This issue highlights the curious triangle formed by the scientific community, universities, and the political institution. The judgment of scientific merit, and the resource allocations that flow from it, can be subordinated, if not subverted, to organizational necessity or political ends. But the victim of such cooptation and control would be the scientific community. For as more institutions pursue pork, the perception grows that academic science is just another interest group. And as science is "leveled" to the plane of other lobbies, the possibility grows that it may be subverted to the purposes of others.

## AUTONOMY, ACCOUNTABILITY, AND THE POLITICS THAT INTERVENE

Lest we forget, a few voices prior to the Reagan Administration chorus protested the involvement of "big" government in science. Economist Milton Friedman, then an advisor to candidate Ronald Reagan, counseled that "the Treasury, the citizenry, and the advancement of science would all be better off without the NSF and other research agencies."[82] Eventually, President Reagan embraced a strategy of weaning science away from federal support. The success of this strategy, of course, is contingent on the private sector's picking up a larger portion of the basic science tab. (Big Science needs big bucks!) This, in turn, depends on incentives like tax credits for such benevolence. Few have been forthcoming. Corporate America kicks in its six percent; doubling that before the end of the George Bush presidency, even in high-tech areas and with a permanent R&D tax credit, seems unlikely.[83]

The Friedman-Reagan thesis is not merely conservative politics. It echoes the argument articulated by sociologist Edward Shils, that since World War II "the Government has ignored the universities' traditional function of searching for truth. It has pushed them into federal programs to train high-level experts, create defense technology and promote national economic growth."[84]

Exacerbating and amplifying the process Shils anticipated are several changes in the organization and operation of research universities. Chief among these are the rise of a cadre of professional managers, increased dependence on federal research support, the growth and institutionalization of research institutes and centers, a quest for profits (in the forms of licensing fees from patents, for example), the regularization of relations with industry, and most fundamentally, changing grounds for legitimizing the university's place in society.[85] These changes have arisen, combined, and reshaped the university with a rapidity that Shils may not have anticipated. (But see Thorstein Veblen, *The Higher Education in America,* and Max Weber, "Science as a Vocation," for evidence that these wise ones might have seen it coming.[86])

Can we separate the lament for science of bygone days from the ideology that underlies it—an ideology predicated on the purity of science residing in an academic house of the holy? Whether or not Friedman, Shils, and others insist on institutional independence for reasons other than the unfettered "search for truth"—for example, perhaps to circumvent affirmative action measures and other policies which apply to those who accept federal research grants—a nagging issue remains. Does the bureaucratization of science—the planning of research—thwart innovation, waste time, divert energy, and generally discourage what it should encourage: the exercise of creativity? Or is it fundamentally irrelevant to the pace and direction of scientists' work?

We do not know. We surmise that if accountability overtakes autonomy, not only will politics intervene in the creative process but it will also divert the apparatus for deciding what is meritorious and what is not. After all, innovativeness, the keystone of merit in science, is bound by paradigm definitions of soluble problems. Peer review becomes a test of permissible innovativeness in puzzle-solving. The "luck of the reviewer draw," for instance, has been shown to be a significant determinant of proposal funding at NSF. This finding attests to the lack of consensus—an elasticity of professional opinion—at the research front of *any* scientific specialty.[87]

Chance and uncertainty go hand in hand. How patient and open-minded are peers in proposing and disposing of "innovative" but inchoate ideas? When they become impatient, the door opens to malpractice. It is thus easy to argue, without cynicism, that almost-wrongs are endemic to the process of knowledge production and the evaluation of research through peer review.

The practice of earmarking has given rise to heated discussion about Public Science. Is it ethically right to support science in this way? Is it efficient, from the standpoint of having good prospects for yielding new knowledge? Is it fair and equitable? Does it level the playing field and enhance institutional competitiveness for peer-reviewed funding? Or does blatantly politicized funding for science taint the entire scientific enterprise?

# 6

# *Augmenting Peer Review:*

## *The Place of Research Evaluation*

Peer review has played an unparalleled role in the evaluation of research performance. Whether the review is binding or advisory, it represents a key input to decision-making by those defined as peers of the scientist undergoing evaluation.

The rationale for peer review, from the perspective of the scientific community, is indisputable: who is better suited, by virtue of training and expert knowledge, to judge the "best" science, either as promised in proposals or as delivered in research reports? In general, the community is bullish about peer review because it delegates a measure of authority to representatives of the community. Professionals agree that like should evaluate like; it takes an elementary particle physicist to evaluate the work of other elementary particle physicists. To scientists, in short, review by peers is an axiom of science.

What we have observed in the previous chapters, however, is that expert evaluation is inevitably plagued by cronyism, elitism, and conflicts induced by self-interested competition. Professionals will be professionals—and then some. Federal policymakers have seized upon this situation, and upon the intellectual development of bibliometrics and science indicators as specialties in their own right, to encourage evaluations of scientists' research perfor-

165

mances by analysts trained in social science, statistics, or other fields outside the scientists' specialties. These analysts are *not* peers of the scientists whose work they evaluate. What they have to offer can be hailed as an antidote to the "reviews" of "good old boys"—an independent baseline of information that participant researchers in an area do not have and may not understand. Regardless, these outside evaluations of scientific research performance have become an input to national decision-making about resource allocations.

We seek here to recount briefly the history of "outside" evaluation of science. First, we outline the contributions of research evaluators, then review the political problems facing them and their clientele as parties potentially at odds with the scientists evaluated. How outsiders' data are weighed against insiders' judgments has become a vital link between peer review and science policy for the 1990s and beyond. This is not merely an empirical issue of quantitative methodology and interpretation applied to science; it is a matter of the politics of knowledge and the divergent epistemologies that guide the ultimate uses of knowledge.

## BIBLIOMETRICS AS RESEARCH EVALUATION: THE PROMISE

The quantitative analysis of science is in its second generation. The first generation, spurred by Eugene Garfield's founding of the *Science Citation Index* and Derek de Solla Price's visionary thought and experimentation, explored the feasibility of understanding science through its literature alone instead of by one's participatory role in its creation.[1] Price boldly named this approach the "science of science" and published demonstrations of its heuristic, if not immediate policy, value.[2]

The second generation, now more than a decade old, sought to develop and exploit publication and citation data as tools for informing decisionmakers, especially in federal agencies and universities.[3] This current generation features all of the trappings of an institutionalized scientific specialty: multi-disciplinary journals and practitioners, a clientele (both consumers and patrons), and numerous claims about the efficacy of "bibliometrics" as a policy tool.[4] The quantitative analysis of science has arguably established its place in the evaluation of research outcomes and as an input to the allocation of resources for research. More fundamentally, bibliometrics and related techniques have inculcated in policymakers the expectation that the growth of scientific knowledge can be measured, interpreted, and managed.

Today there is a second generation of non-economic quantitative measures of scientific "process" and "product"; it evaluates claims of policy relevance and utility against the foreseeable needs of decisionmakers to plan and evaluate R&D performance. The most promising approaches and methods suggest how quantitative data and models could be refined to augment decision-making processes in science. Of course, we do not simply endorse quantitative techniques and advocate future usage; rather, we selectively caution about, criticize, and qualify their usage.

Bibliometrics has a place in science policy deliberations. But numbers possess no inherently magical quality; they are more or less embraced for reasons having to do with social contexts, political purposes, and ideologies—not because they are more "objective."[5] Contrary to the maxim that "the data speak for themselves," the decisionmaker's values endow numbers with meaning, and his or her interpretation becomes a claim about what is known and how that knowledge may be acted upon.

Quantitative data may form the basis for claims. There is surely ample precedent within the history of federal science policy for weighing such claims.[6] But it is the distinctiveness of a quantitative measure, pattern, or trend that makes it appealing or useful. Bibliometrics represents but another systematic means of reducing uncertainty, of providing evidence that complements other data, intuitions, and interpretations. The burden of the bibliometrician, or any quantitative science policy researcher, is to translate the lessons learned through analysis for the government "client." As we shall see, a misfit between the questions asked and decisions to be made, on the one hand, and the data available and analyses undertaken to address them, on the other, can retard the usage of bibliometric indicators and frustrate all concerned. The main challenge for the second generation has been how to evaluate science, and then how to translate evaluations into usable knowledge about research performance and outcomes.

## The First Generation of Bibliometrics (1961–1974)

The pioneers of what today is known as "bibliometrics" groped for ways to understand science independently of the scientists themselves. First-person accounts (found in memoirs and interviews), questionnaires, and historical narratives all require some form of cooperation from or consent of the scientists (or their representatives) involved. This dependence on sentient sources was seen to inhibit what could be learned about science. Thus, the writings of the early 1960s described the need first to reconstruct, then to monitor and predict, the structure and products of science. This had been a gleam in the eyes of Garfield, Derek Price, and others who wished to use formal scientific communication to study "invisible colleges" and to trace patterns of "intellectual influence"—in brief, to hold a mirror up to science, to build a science of science. Unobtrusive study of the scientific literature (that is, study without intruding upon the scientists themselves) would open new vistas, both practical and analytical, once that literature was catalogued, indexed, and made retrievable.

With the creation of the *Science Citation Index* (SCI), the scientific literature became a distinctive data source, a research instrument for the quantitative analysis of science. Early analysts, using data from the SCI, devised the concepts and measurement techniques that today remain the bedrock of bibliometrics.[7] They established that the principal units of analysis would be *publications* (such as papers, articles, journals), *citations* (that is, various counts and treatments of the bibliographic references attached to publications), and their producers (including individual authors, teams of coauthors, or larger aggregations such as projects, programs, centers, laboratories, and institutions). When subjected to the primary methods of analysis—counting, linking, and mapping—these units yield measures of higher-order concepts: coherent social groups, theory groups, networks, clusters, problem domains, specialties, subfields, and fields.

In short, computer-aided imagination led to the increasingly sophisticated manipulation of documents in the growing SCI data base. Journal publications could be counted by author, but also aggregated into schools of thought and whole institutions.[8] Citations could be counted pairwise (i.e., linked via co-citation) to separate the "signal" of core contributors to a research area from the "noise" of occasional (or "transient") authors. The resultant co-citation clusters could be depicted as a "map of science" for a given year showing the strength of links within clusters and the relations, if any, among them.[9]

Hence, by the mid-1970s, bibliometricians were able to represent, structurally and graphically, the domains and levels of research activity in science. Further, these pictures could be compared to other accounts based on biographic, demographic, informal communication, and other informant-centered data, to render an approximation of how research communities—their research foci, intellectual leaders, and specialized journals—change over time. This discernment of patterns afforded a more comprehensive perspective on the growth of knowledge, at least in terms of its outputs, than was ever previously available.[10] Although interpretations of the validity and generalizability of this perspective often differed, and the life of the scientific community responsible for the outputs tended to remain obscure, bibliometric analysis supplied the independent baseline implied in Price's phrase, "the science of science."[11]

## The Second Generation (1975–present)

The transition to the current, second generation of bibliometrics was marked by the appearance of bibliographies, special issues of journals to assess what various editions of the NSF-sponsored series entitled *Science Indicators* had and had not accomplished, and explicit recognition that bibliometrics could be useful to federal policymakers. By the late 1970s, the mood was one of stock-taking, of refining tools and claims through new case studies, and of client-sponsored attempts to apply bibliometric analysis to the policy decisions embedded in R&D budgets and research evaluations.[12] What had been heuristic had become diagnostic and perhaps even prescriptive.

The legacy of the first generation was the promise of its scholarly literature. The second generation would have to deliver on the promise that bibliometric analysis was predictive and reliable for decision-making. That promise—at least in the United States—has yet to be fulfilled. In this section, we discuss why this is so, and highlight growing evidence that the quantitative assessment of science warrants the attention it is now receiving from policymakers, especially in Europe. Finally, we critically review the current approaches, methods, and data that represent the state of the art in the non-economic evaluation of scientific outputs for policy purposes.[13]

## Lessons Learned

One measure of innovation is the audience it finds. In 1975, *Science* announced that "A new way to assess scientific productivity is about to come into its own. Citation analysis, hitherto an arcane tool of historians and sociologists of science, has now been refined to the point where it offers increasingly interesting possibilities to the science administrator."[14] Though the announcement was premature, it was prophetic of the problems that still dog citation analysis today.

"The scientific community," Price predicted, "will at first resist the outside evaluation represented by citation analysis, but will accept the technique when they find it corroborates the judgment of peer review and their own beliefs about who is good and who is bad."[15] Furthermore, "it is likely that all possible applications of the technique will fall within the interest—as narrowly construed—of the scientific community. . . . Some citation analysis studies might point toward painfully radical redistributions of scientific resources."[16]

What is arcane may not be readily adaptable to the needs of a non-technical audience. Their claims notwithstanding, bibliometricians' key concepts—citation rates, doubling times, half-lives, journal influence, impact factors, research fronts—do not provide easy policy handles. As "indicators" they are, by definition, statistical proxies for unmeasured parameters in a complex economic, political, and social system of knowledge production. They were never designed with policy in mind. Thus one challenge lies in juxtaposing interpretations derived from bibliometrics with those based on other, non-quantitative data. This creates the possibility of disagreement over findings: bibliometric data may contradict what the participants in the science under evaluation perceive or have experienced. How is the "outsiders'" interpretation to be weighed against the "insiders'" expertise? This question was raised a decade ago; it remains unresolved.

If bibliometrics represents the opening of the scientific community to such evaluation, then what are the empirical grounds for entertaining outsiders' evaluations? Garfield put the question bluntly in the title of a 1979 paper, asking "Is citation analysis a legitimate evaluation tool?"[17] Unsurprisingly, his answer then was a resounding "Yes." But it smacks as much of self-interest now as would a scientist's gut resistance to outside evaluations on the grounds that the evaluators are neither trained in nor practitioners of X, lack understanding of research in X, and therefore cannot possibly produce valid assessments of X. What, then, is a decisionmaker to do? Ignore such objections? Hardly. Defend the outside evaluations? Why should they? Until very recently, bibliometricians had not offered defensible recommendations and a rationale for their methods. But the accumulated results of bibliometric analysis, coupled with recent changes in bibliometric practice, might incline decisionmakers to intervene on the outsider's behalf (if only to counterbalance the abused power of the anecdote).

First, observed regularities in bibliometric indicators provide empirical support for their potential policy usefulness. Whatever is going on in aggregate publication and referencing practices, it has an appealing empirical lawfulness.[18] But since twenty-five percent of all published scientific papers are never cited and the average annual citation count for cited papers is less than two, the baseline for bibliometric analyses must be sensitive to differences among sciences, and even within them. Global measures must be adjusted for variables such as the size of the literature, its decay and obsolescence (as defined by the decline and eventual absence of citations to seminal papers), and for the degree of coauthorship and self-citation (by individuals and teams). The basis for such adjustments cannot be the literature itself; rather, they must be based on a reading of intellectual histories, or the content analysis of review articles and primary papers. Efforts by bibliometricians in these directions should give heart to the policymakers who support the approach.

Second, the meaning of "citation" has been clarified in terms of type and significance. For example, if one examines the passages in which citations are given, one finds that "perfunctory" references dominate, while "negational" ones are rare.[19] While informative, this attribution of motivation for referencing has been overshadowed by the multitude of measures defined to capture the type of citation: total citations, citations to first-authored papers, citations per year. These arithmetic adjustments have become part of now-familiar calculations of frequency and significance: influence, impact, utility, quality. All are based, however, on the assumption that citations are votes by the entire scientific community, and therefore reflect aggregate peer evaluation.[20] While reasonable and perhaps necessary, these conceptual and methodological developments compromise the "independent baseline" that bibliometrics claims to be, for they reveal the underlying social foundations of referencing behavior. Citation data are subject to the same limitations as any other social indicator: ultimately, the meaning and accuracy of the data reside in the persons who first inscribe them in the archives. Just as the meaning of a community's archives ultimately resides in the quotidian decisions of town clerks, so too are the meanings of citation data ultimately grounded in the referencing decisions of authors and the specialty-specific norms that govern their referencing behavior.

Third, although outsiders can often assimilate enough technical detail to inform their quantitative analyses, some analysts prefer the collaboration of a current or former insider to an exclusively "outsider" interpretation.[21] With either approach, evidence from several case studies suggests that what passes for bibliometric analysis of a discipline or research area is much more. Typically, such studies correlate "cognitive" and "social" structures, asking how the evolution of ideas (intellectual content) can be traced through cultural contexts (institutions, programs) in terms of individual, team, or facility performance.

Notable "insider" examples are the study of referencing patterns in the papers of competing radio astronomy groups in Britain, 1946–66, and a series of citation analyses of post–World War II physics research on weak interactions of elementary particles.[22] The latter show that citation clusters are sensitive to monthly, as well as yearly, changes in intellectual activity such as the episodic interplay between experimentalists and theorists.[23] Congruence with participants' perceptions is the criterion of rigor and accuracy in this approach. The goal is to validate the oral or written record. Departures from this record are seen as flaws or failings of "the statistical reconstruction of events obtained through co-citation analysis."[24]

If the test of a "true" citation-based account is its agreement with participants' views, then the technique is not allowed to generate new information. True, the citation-based method may be quicker or more efficient than consulting informants, but by construction there is no gain in knowledge. It is ironic that citation approaches should be thought to supplant rather than to supplement insiders' accounts.

In the typical social analysis of science, insiders will be consulted as data sources, informants, respondents, or panelists, but very seldom as collaborators. In "outsider" approaches, the issue is whether or not one's statistical time-series of publication and citation levels and linkages will be subjected to the "veto power" of insider accounts. If they are not, then how does one reconcile discrepancies between, say, co-citation clusters indicating the centrality of intramural NIH research, and the claims that "NIH-authored" papers discussing a highly-cited theory are of little intellectual consequence for research in the specialty? Does one discard or downplay the quantitative findings in light of informants' appraisals, or does one duly report the discrepancies and try to explain the sources—be they locational (intramural $v.$ extramural), intellectual (cancer research $v.$ basic virology), or political (research funded under the National Cancer Act of 1971)?[25] If the analyst must live with equivocal data, then the policymaker must learn to accept uncertainty. There may be no "objective" means for reconciling alternative interpretations; reconciliation may be an inherently political matter.[26]

The lessons learned by bibliometricians have established a baseline of analytic units, methods, and interpretations. This baseline presents a range of choices to the audience (or, with the commercialization of research, should we say "market"?) of policy analysts. The promises and doubts associated with these choices become clear once the lessons learned are applied to science policy issues of resource allocation and future research performance. In the sections that follow, we profile a selection of these applications to demonstrate not only their strengths and weaknesses, but also their inheritance from two generations of quantitative tool-making in the social study of science as a system of knowledge production.

## Lessons Applied

The current genre of evaluative bibliometrics qualifies as policy research in accordance with Garfield's second-generation injunction:

> as the scientific enterprise becomes larger and more complex, and its role in society more critical, it becomes more difficult, more expensive, and more necessary to make the evaluations that identify those people and groups who are making the greatest contribution.[27]

So stated, the ingredients of policy analysis seem to consist of retrospective measurement and straightforward extrapolation. But the task is more complicated, for policymakers wish to anticipate the sources of "greatest contributions," to exploit "hot" or "ripe" areas, and to foster (indeed, *accelerate*) scientific research. To do so, policymakers must frame their questions in such a way that answers, if deemed plausible and sound, could be acted upon with confidence.

The analysts discussed below have brought bibliometrics to a state that can nearly bear the weight of policy needs. Their work acknowledges its origins *outside* the scholarly community and educates decisionmakers about the applicability of such methodologies to policy concerns. They have all succeeded to the extent that they "talk the language" of policy and recognize intervention—decisions that affect research communities—as a desirable consequence of their work. They have all been patronized by governments, in the U.S. and elsewhere, to provide empirical inputs to decision-making that can be obtained from no other source. We restrict our focus to three major performers of research evaluation, and their approaches to the question: "How can we characterize the effects of decisions about funding programs as they reverberate into the various levels of the scientific community: up from 'fields' into disciplines and down from 'fields' into research areas or teams?"[28]

## EVALUATIVE BIBLIOMETRICS AND BEYOND

Francis Narin and his company, Computer Horizons, Inc., is the veteran performer in this group, linking the two generations of bibliometricians. Narin's computerized approach is based on the *Science Citation Index* and used in conjunction with other data, such as the National Library of Medicine's Medline and the NIH in-house grant profile system, IMPAC. Although Narin's work tends to focus on macroscopic issues, his methods have grown increasingly sophisticated in their capacity for addressing micro-level questions. There has always been a "brute force"element to Narin's work (for example, his calculations of relative journal influence require massive amounts of data and extended computations), accompanied by an appealing directness and intelligibility. Narin's methodology can provide quantitative answers to the following kinds of questions:[29]

1.  To what extent are articles published in basic journals referenced in clinical and practitioner journals?

2.  Is there a relationship between priority scores on research applications and the number of articles produced and citations received?

3.  Are research grants to medical schools more productive than grants to academic departments?

4.  Are younger researchers more productive than older researchers?

5.  Are grants in support of investigator-initiated proposals (R01 awards, in the NIH terminology) more productive than other support mechanisms?

6.  How often do NIH-supported researchers from one institute cite work supported by other institutes?

From his data base Narin can provide definitive answers to such questions. But what one does with the information is, of course, another matter altogether.

A common criticism of Narin's work is that it is too descriptive (read "superficial") and relies on ad hoc explanation for the observed patterns and trends. In short, it suffers from an outsider's inability to discern fine detail; it is excessively dependent on a literature baseline and unschooled in the sciences it appraises. Narin seems to have realized that he has invested too much in the "numbers," so to speak, and has introduced some innovations into his approach. In a recent project sponsored by the National Cancer Institute, "An Assessment of the Factors Affecting Critical Cancer Research Findings," Narin consciously tries to remedy the problem by working closely from the outset with a panel of cancer researchers. He is tracing key events through participant consensus, the historical record, and various bibliometric indicators. Discrepancies are apparently negotiated as the project unfolds, though the exact negotiation procedure is not specified.[30]

Another departure for Narin stems from his acquisition and computerization of U.S. Patent Office case files that will permit mapping of literature citations in patents at the national, industry, and inventor levels. This spinoff of co-citation methodology should render the stages implicit in the term "R&D" more transparent than ever. An infant literature has crystallized around the notion of "technology indicators" with patents signifying the conversion of knowledge into an innovation with commercial and social value—another tangible return on investment.[31]

**Converging Partial Indicators**

John Irvine and Ben Martin's evaluation programs in "converging partial indicators," conducted at the Science Policy Research Unit of the University of Sussex in Great Britain, has had an unparalleled effect on both the world science policy and "big science" communities. Their evaluations have gained attention (some would say notoriety) for three important reasons:

1.  They claim to assess the basic research performance of large technology-dependent facilities such as the CERN accelerator and the Isaac Newton Telescope.

2.  They make cost-effectiveness the central performance criterion in their input-output schema.

3.  Their "triangulation" methodology is an impressive codification of many separate procedures and measures that have been advocated both by policymakers and by analysts.

Irvine and Martin have been taken quite seriously; they have not only evaluated big science in investment and progress terms, but have tested its power structure with controversial conclusions and recommendations. They have been invited by several Western European governments to apply their methodology to current policy problems and have testified before the U.S. House of Representatives Committee on Science and Technology. They have also been criticized, vilified, and even sued. Their work, now collected in a book and numerous scholarly articles, is a splendid yardstick of how far bibliometrics has come—and how far it has to go—as a tool for science policy.[32]

Our synopsis is based primarily on a review of Irvine and Martin's articles, and four critiques and a reply, which culminated, in 1985, seven years of research and four of publication, mainly in the journals *Social Studies of Science* and *Research Policy*. In one fifty-page exchange, Irvine and Martin separate their purposes from those of their academic critics.

> We have seen our task as one of providing systematic information . . . in a form accessible not just to researchers in the field concerned but also to policymakers, scientists in other fields, politicians and the public, thereby making possible greater transparency in the scientific decision making process.[33]

What also makes their policy-driven studies so appealing to policymakers (and so threatening to scientists) is their acceptance of the current retrenchment mentality as science spending in many nations levels off or becomes concentrated in areas of perceived competitive advantage. Thus the time is right for methodologies that can justify the trimming of "waste" in national R&D.

For Irvine and Martin there is a need "not just for accountability" and the "greater use of output indicators in helping regulate the scientific system," but also for a way to reduce the "increasing strain on the peer-review system."[34] Hence, part of their rationale for developing indicators of past research performance and assessing future prospects is that it provides "a means to keep the peer-review system 'honest' [because] these peers are asked *only* to give advice on the *scientific* performance of *existing* institutions working in the *same* field."[35] Further, Irvine and Martin's structured use of peer-review input differs from "conventional peer-review (involving a small number of referees or 'experts' on a panel)" in that they would draw on "very large numbers of researchers across different countries and based on structured confidential interviews and attitude surveys."[36] In their terms, conventional grants or journal peer review is but a single indicator; when combined with bibliometric data on research performance and other information, peer evaluations become a valuable indicator of likely future performance. If these indicators converge (that is, if they all yield similar results) then we may "regard the results of the evaluation as being relatively reliable."[37]

The crux of Irvine and Martin's method is an institutional focus that only compares "like with like." But this presupposes that the analyst has established that two or more facilities are similar enough to compare; indeed, that the analyst can define operationally what it means to be "similar enough" for the purposes at hand. Merely housing a particular instrument or publishing a particular kind of research (for example, optical astronomy) does not adequately establish that two facilities are alike. We would want to know more about the organization's structure, membership, climate, work style, local environment, and the like. Without such knowledge, facilities are just a black box through which inputs and outputs circulate, and Irvine and Martin's "indicators give a *global measure of the effects of these 'explanatory' factors on scientific output*. To disentangle them, to weigh their importance one against the other, [Irvine and Martin] *need* to refer to peer interviews."[38] Organizational data and qualitative, "subjective" descriptions of the work place and work process fill the gaps between the partial indicators. They would insure that similar facilities are compared and would offer incipient explanations for observed differences in facilities' conversion of resources into outputs. Without such information, we have a report card but no plan of action for improving performance. An historian, commenting on Irvine and Martin's work, said it well: "I wish they had been less ruthless in suppressing their interpretive instincts and more forthcoming in discussing those issues which, after all, give those data meaning."[39]

As proxies, partial indicators must stand for a lot that goes unmeasured (by choice or otherwise). Sometimes the interpretive burden is overwhelming. No matter how systematic, quantitative, and convergent their findings appear, Irvine and Martin's reliance on triangulation is problematic, as they admit:

> The fact that the indicators converge in a given case does not "prove" that the results are 100 percent certain—the indicators may all be 'wrong' together. However, if a facility like the

Lick 3-meter telescope produces a comparatively large publication output at fairly low cost, if those papers are relatively highly cited, . . . and if large numbers of astronomers rate it highly in the course of structured interviews, we would place *more* credibility on the resulting conclusion that this was a successful facility than if the same finding were arrived at by a panel of three or four "experts" without access to the systematic information that we have collected.[40]

Still, what is a policymaker to do when output measures do not converge?[41] There is no straightforward means of resolution except intuition and rhetoric, that is, a judgment based on reason but steeped in values. As one critic observes, "If something has succeeded, with the wisdom of hindsight the risk is thought to have been 'reasonable'; if something has failed, the risk is often considered as having been 'too big.'[42] The maintenance of scientific facilities is a formidable risk. Reducing a budget has tangible repercussions in terms of staff size and knowledge-production capacity. What are the expected payoffs—the key discoveries, the level of productivity, the prestige relative to other facilities, and so forth—and when are they expected?[43] In the case of CERN's particle accelerator, for example, it took fifteen or twenty years for the facility's output to approach that of its U.S. competitors.[44] What would have happened had a decision been forced a decade earlier? How could we ever learn from such mistakes?

Overall, then, what has been Irvine and Martin's contribution to research evaluation? As their critics acknowledge, four benefits accrue from their efforts.[45] Since each of these is both instructive and distinctly problematic, we offer a brief critical commentary on each item.

1. Irvine and Martin have collected, synthesized, and published a colossal amount of original data about the scientific performance of big and expensive scientific institutes. Thus through their efforts we know far more about certain aspects of contemporary "big science" than we would otherwise.

    But we do not know how the Irvine-Martin approach would fare in "smaller science" areas. Is their methodology transportable to different cultural and research contexts, as they claim?[46] Even if "validity" is achieved, that is, even if the indicators of scientific impact do converge, judgments about "applicability" and "quality" do not automatically follow.[47] These are properties of interpretation, shaped by the social and political context, not immutable results of dispassionate analysis. Irvine and Martin tend to confuse the two.

2. They have shown that when peers are assessing their own fields they can be reliable judges of scientific performance.

   Although Irvine and Martin's methodology turns researchers' vested interests into an analytic asset, this method serves only "tactical" purposes, for they focus on peer ratings of facilities in the same science, not knowledge-producing facilities in different sciences. But the strategic choices *between* sciences are the tough ones in a world of limited resources, more so now than when Weinberg first proposed considering both "technical" and "social" criteria of choice in the support of science nearly three decades ago.[48] Like peer review, "converging partial indicators" are useless for strategic choices: each is far better able to compare "like with like" than to choose between dissimilar (and perhaps incomparable) alternatives.[49] Granted, this shortcoming can be accepted as long as it is admitted openly, so that the inherent limitations and avowed purposes of the methodology are clearly understood.

3. Where choices have to be made among several similar research units that are competing for resources, Irvine and Martin provide policymakers with sound information to assist in reaching a rational decision.

   But what is "rational" depends upon whose ox is being gored. While input-output ratios are based on "like-to-like" comparisons, definitions of comparability are bound to vary. To some critics, high-energy physics research in the East and the West are not comparable, regardless of the common journals in which researchers at the respective facilities publish.[50] Nor is a well sited telescope comparable to one operating in a cloudier climate. Some facilities may serve symbolic ends, may be necessary complements to other areas of research excellence, or may represent an emerging or transitional research area or perspective.

   Moreover, critics argue, scientific knowledge is ultimately produced by a community of scientists, not by competing institutionally situated teams. Thus matching and comparing facilities may be an empty exercise: although funds are allocated along organizational lines, policy must be concerned with the health and the output of the entire community. The criticism is a subtle but important one. On the one hand, science policy is charged with sustaining *communities* which collectively—through cooperation and competition—advance knowledge. On the other hand, resources are allocated to specific investigators and teams who congregate at certain sites. It is easy, as Irving and Martin do, to focus on the smaller-scale allocation decisions while losing sight of the knowledge production system. And the implications of their recommendations are clear: reducing or eliminating support for the least cost-effective facilities will have no adverse effect on "progress." Accordingly, diverting scarce resources to more efficient, productive, creative facilities will increase aggregate output.

But this overlooks the organic character of the knowledge-producing system. It views knowledge as a bundled output, not as a cultural activity that intertwines local teams with peers scattered about but achieving solidarity through shared literature, informal communication, and the training of new generations of practitioners. These are not entirely ignored by Irvine and Martin, but they are minimized amidst the short-term measures of things that are taken as forecasting future, longer-term novelty. By restricting their focus to the immediate resource constraints that policymakers face, Irvine and Martin's research addresses the short-term challenge of providing information that is both relevant and usable for decision making.[51] But it leaves many deeper issues untouched.

4. Finally, there have been important "spinoffs" of Irvine and Martin's research. Their book, *Foresight in Science,* is an inspiration in its breadth and in the comparative questions it raises.[52]

Irvine and Martin's research is politically astute; it serves scholarly and policy communities, yet it goes beyond bibliometrics as a necessary and sufficient tool for policy. It explicitly anticipates criticism and sources of error, disarms skeptics, and gets an analytical foot in the right doors—those shielding the offices of policymakers who have come to rely on participant scientists and their own imprecise and self-serving devices for making decisions about whose research prospers and whose does not.[53]

Irvine and Martin's approach cannot tell us how or why research is performed, but it does show us "how much" and "how good" the performances have been, at least in the near term. Though it may have been oversold and is subject to the qualifications we have noted, it is credible analysis that has taken bibliometrics and its associated social methods to a new plane, and more importantly, marketed it to a powerful audience.

What is more apparent than ever, however, is Irvine and Martin's lack of reflection on how their work is ultimately used by decisionmakers. Technical virtuosity is not enough; greater ethical sensitivity to misuses of their data and interpretations might by now have altered their approach or promoted them to remind us all that as researchers we have only limited control over the applications of our analyses. By doing more of the same, by uncritically applying a methodology without regard for its consequences, Irvine and Martin have sidestepped a crucial ethical issue. For every government they have served, some would claim, a research community has been disserved. As evaluators they need to look back over their work and ask how it has shaped *their* future plans and reshaped the circumstances of those they have studied. Their silence on these matters creates a gap that the second generation of bibliometricians must fill.[54]

## Qualitative Scientometrics

Qualitative (or "cognitive") scientometrics is noteworthy for two reasons: (1) the research team responsible for the methodology is French-based but international with collaborative ties to Dutch and British analysts (Michel Callon, Jean-Pierre Courtial, William Turner, John Law, and Arie Rip, among others), while (2) its intellectual roots are an amalgam of the co-citation algorithm and a professed concern for theory-based interpretation.[55]

One focus of co-word analysis has been the disciplinary base of biotechnology, particularly the relative contributions of "in-house" French laboratories both within the country and in the international arena. The co-word approach is motivated by the need for strategic policy decisions that face the ultimate difficulty of "translation" into action. As Callon et al. put it:

Our study of French efforts to program research shows
clearly how policy objectives are progressively redefined
through the complex negotiation process that political scientists and sociologists have started to analyze. . . . Perhaps to
a greater extent than in other sectors of the economy, the dynamics of scientific and technological change depends upon
the decisions taken by a multitude of actors, rather than
upon those taken by a small and visible elite.[56]

Using the data files of a department in the French Research
Ministry, these researchers seek to assist the department "to monitor academic and industrial research and use the results as input
into the existing peer review system for awarding grants."[57] Their
tool is applied both to the scientific and the patent literature to
address questions such as: What subjects are appropriate for international cooperation? How do publications of the French Research Institute compare with articles published elsewhere?

Maps of research activity are constructed by treating the
number of co-occurrences of keywords as a measure of the proxim-
ity of two keywords, then generating a map that "best" (according
to mathematical criteria) reflects the relative proximities of the
entire set of keywords. For clarity, a frequency threshold of linkages among keywords is established, so keywords that are not
strongly connected with others are excluded from the maps. (The
level of detail in a map may be adjusted by changing this threshold.) Thus, a map of co-word linkages represents a topological map
of a city: The analyst's challenge is then to explain the overall pattern and the specific intersections of main thoroughfares. By increasing the breadth of source documents and the time frame,
maps may be altered to show regions of keywords and patterns of
stability and change. Maps can be restricted to various levels of
aggregation and types of performer (for example, universities may
be compared to government laboratories).[58]

The advantages of the co-word technique originate with the
titling practices of authors. Their words "signal" what is important
in the research (unlike bibliographic citations, which reflect consumer interest, not author intention). As an instrument to measure developments in spheres of scientific discourse, the technique
rests on map interpretations. Rip and Courtial, for example, invoke the "center-periphery" model as a way of explaining core concepts and contributors. But they admit that "there seems to be no
systematic way of going about the interpretation of the maps . . .
[and] interpretation remains intuitive."[59]

Co-word analysts have recognized from the outset the "actor-analyst dilemma" and in their most recent work they have moved inside research organizations to enlist actors in resolving the analyst's dilemma. Thus Callon and his colleagues use the co-word technique to identify the "problem areas which mobilize the resources of their departments" and to specify areas "of common interest to laboratories working in different departments."[60] This is quintessentially client-centered analysis. It throws the light of local context on the shadowed production of research. By getting inside the black box, co-word analysis clarifies "practical day-to-day problems such as how to organize discussions . . . which mix together indiscriminately social, political, economic and cognitive considerations."[61]

Co-word analysts underscore the translation and application problem at the micro-level that is virtually ignored in Irvine and Martin's input-output schema. The very premise that like-to-like can be compared is rendered dubious: no two facilities *are* culturally alike. Perhaps this contentiousness is fortunate because, taken together, converging partial indicators and co-word analysis render complementary pictures of local knowledge production. Yet they, like the more purely bibliometric approach used by Narin, aspire to placing research evaluation into an international context. Each approach illuminates a dimension of research performance; thus each invites other inputs into the decision-making process. And each has taken a somewhat different path to applying—both retrospectively and prospectively—the lessons learned from bibliometric analysis. Finally, we can say that the choices of methodology and modes of interpretation have expanded along with efforts in this genre.[62]

## CHALLENGES AND NEW DIRECTIONS

Research evaluation is on the world science policy agenda because quantitative analyses of science can inform the resource allocation decisions faced by policymakers. But what must happen to usher in the next generation of evaluative bibliometrics and indicators of scientific progress? Which are the most constructive ideas that warrant additional investment, both intellectual and fiscal, to maximize their usage as a policy resource?

Since science and technology are intimately linked to the economic, social, and political life of a nation, science and technology indicators can take on a variety of contextual meanings. Research—pure, applied, and developmental—is embedded within complex cultural arrangements. What we blithely call a hierarchy of units of analysis or stages of development is in fact part of a techo-scientific system.[63] Little of this systemic character is captured by current approaches. As analysts have discovered, the chief product of science, "knowledge," is rather intangible, ephemeral, and hard to measure. Similarly, constructs such as "impact" and "utilization" (and their relatives) are not universals but instead are limited in time and space to a particular society, industry, sector, type of organization, historical configuration, and economic circumstance, for example. Studies of science and technology may have too eagerly shed such interpretive contexts in the course of becoming a "science of science" that may serve policy interests. We need to restore those contexts, and to do so requires demolishing barriers between "basic" and "policy relevant" studies of science and technology. The distinction is artificial and anachronistic: no sound study of science or technology can ignore policy, and useful policy analysis must be grounded in our knowledge of the social organization of science and technology.

This means, for example, that we can no longer talk loosely about a "science and technology system," but must instead specify exactly what sort of system it is, how it is structured, and how it functions. In doing so, we should consider the full range of resources upon which the system depends, including knowledge, political power, legitimacy, money, and the like. Characteristics of the social organization of science and the careers of scientists must be integrated with bibliometric indicators. It simply will not do to have bibliometric studies performed without regard for the basic demographic, social, and political properties of fields of science.

Another new challenge for policy-relevant studies of science and technology arose at a May 1983 workshop on "Federal Funding and Knowledge Growth," sponsored by the National Science Foundation. The central issue for the workshop was, "How do the amount, timing, and form of resources the federal government provides affect the intellectual development of specific scientific fields?"[64] Thus the workshop showcased the critical problems confronted by the program officer with limited resources to expend. As Susan Cozzens put the issue:

Between the confidence that the investment in science as a whole is a wise one and the uncertainty about the payoffs of specific efforts lies a range of intermediate issues which arise again and again in the process of making budgets for science here in Washington. These questions all assume that funding somehow affects knowledge growth, and ask how. They are thus concerned, not with *a* relationship but with the *multitude* of *relationships* which the funding system has with science.[65]

Not only is science more complicated than our simple models, but policy is more complicated, too, and their interface is not simple and linear but complex and interactive. While easy to assert, these principles are hard to incorporate into the basic input-output framework that underlies much science policy research.[66] One commentator at the NSF workshop, Program Officer Carlos Kruytbosch, seized the opportunity to direct analysts' attention to three classes of "policy relevant variables": science push, application pull, and broker roles.[67] These same categories can be profitably used to frame the challenges and indicate the new directions that we see in the future of policy-relevant science studies.

### Science Push—Application Pull

"Science push" refers to the driving force of changes in knowledge and techniques that provide opportunities—perhaps even *create* opportunities—for their application. In the case of science studies, science push derives from the "ripeness" of concepts, theories, data, and techniques available for use by policymakers.[68] Much of this chapter testifies to the near-ripeness of quantitative analysis for research evaluation. Yet there is work to be done before the research tools are ready for the policy applications. In the words of Derek Price, though the tools are at hand, the "next step must involve some integration of the various types of indicators into a comprehensive system ... [for this is] the prime desideratum of interpretation."[69] For Price, the science push demands more than the "production of well-mannered indicators," but also requires "integrating measures of money, people and output into a single system that, so to speak, criticizes and explains itself in the process of integration."[70]

Of course, this conceptual and empirical science push awaits the application pull. What are, to use Kruytbosch's phrase, the "articulated societal needs"? Do they merely correspond to missions such as health and national defense or are they more elusive? As science and technology studies evolves as a discipline, science policymakers will have to learn to ask more sophisticated questions. Cozzens suggests as much:

> It is intuitively obvious that the same resources will not bring the same benefits, either for science or society, if they are spent in different areas. Where will the benefits be greatest? On the one hand, reliable answers to a question such as this cannot be produced through research, since the problem itself is a political one of weighing the many different desirable outcomes of research (for example, stimulating technological innovation, producing scientific advance, and improving quality of life). On the other hand, it might be possible to specify social or intellectual conditions under which equal investments might produce unequal intellectual returns for the fields in question.[71]

While policymakers must not ask unanswerable questions of research (and must accept inherently political questions as such), they might find that sharper conceptualizations and analyses open new avenues for policy formulation. As Price warned, bibliometrics cannot supply the context for interpretation and action. But policymakers must do so; their deliberations would benefit from the analysts' empirical models and underlying theory. The science push of bibliometrics, for all its cumulative vigor, so far amounts to little more than a nudge.

Converting nudges into pushes demands not just keen marketing, but connecting with "pulls" that have policy value. Several commentators have recognized this and asked "Science for what?" Manfred Kochen puts the push-pull relationship this way: "The art of constructing science indicators, and the science of S&T and S&T planning shape each other as both become more sophisticated, and thus could even affect the growth of science itself."[72] The receptivity of national governments to the bibliometric approaches reviewed above is undeniable. Even if the conclusions and recommendations are ignored, they have expanded the scope of decision-making by illuminating hitherto unknown quantitative properties, and thereby creating policy options.

As an information scientist, Kochen is acutely sensitive to the translation of analysts' findings into policymakers' judgments and ultimate actions. He distinguishes types of research, types of performer, and types of utilization. And he does so in terms of "models of science planning":

For each model of science planning, at least two criteria of significance can be used in judging the adequacy of various measures of output. . . . The first criterion is the extent to which the output measure helps to assess the achievement of the major purpose of S&T assumed by the model. The second criterion is the extent to which the output measure helps to assess errors of omission and commission.[73]

Models—whether implicit or explicit, the analysts's or the decisionmaker's—contain the extrinsic values attached to elements of the knowledge production system. For our purpose, it is the match between criteria and "sample methods of measuring output," and not the embracing of one or another model, that matters. This evaluation is practical because it moves us beyond the tactical choices that quantitative analysis so readily informs to the more policy-urgent issue of strategic choices. Kochen's prescription is tripartite: examine the existing time-series that measures scientific output, search for causal relations, then apply a system or model for planning and policy-making.[74]

Short-circuiting the process by eliminating the search for causal relations (and proceeding directly from output measures to policy actions) can be very dangerous. Consider Price's observation that

it could happen [on the basis of empirical evidence] that we decide that we wish to underplay Chemistry and to a lesser extent Physics because we have less use than most nations from the side benefits of engaging in the international pursuit of knowledge.[75]

Certainly not an unlikely policy decision, particularly if one substitutes "sociology" and "psychology" for chemistry and physics. But as Cozzens advises,

Coherent areas of scientific inquiry cross-cut the basic units of the funding system . . . [so] any change in the size or funding mode of one program is likely to interact with the activities of others in its influence on "the field." It also poses a challenge to the researcher, who must be able to think back and forth between the viewpoint of the planner who deals in programs and the scientists who "make knowledge grow."[76]

In any case, the development of models to help policymakers think about such matters can occur if policymakers "attach strings" to the research evaluation projects they fund, adding on an element of basic research as overhead on the applied work. Simultaneously, researchers must be reminded that interpretive frameworks tied to systemic goals, purposes, or criteria ("articulated societal needs"), in addition to quantitative indictors, will command the attention of policymakers.[77]

## Broker Roles

Negotiating the pushes and pulls of research evaluation is the responsibility of those who are accountable, in Kruytbosch's schema of policy relevant variables, for project selection, design, and budgeting. There is a division of labor between "the way societal needs become articulated, and the way the representatives of the scientific community become involved with helping to articulate those needs with a view to generating future resources.[78]

Peer review has been the traditional mechanism of brokerage; it advises decisionmakers about who is deserving, who is not, and to what degree. Though generally desirable from the perspective of the peer community (acting as representatives of an autonomous profession), this mechanism entails deference to specialized, expert knowledge; therefore it is anti-democratic and often plagued, as we and others have discussed, by cronyism, elitism, and conflicts of interest.[79]

Bibliometrics constitutes a supplement, some might say s counterweight or antidote, to the way S&T policymakers reach or justify resource allocation decisions. As Harvey Brooks observes:

> The expertise required to identify and formulate sociotechnical goals, and to relate research objectives to social objectives, is different from the expertise required to assess the opportunities and prospects for advances in a scientific discipline or a technological development.[80]

There is room for the exercise of both kinds of expertise in science policy; competitors and claims abound. Outside research analysts without credentials in the science they are evaluating have a role to play in assessing "opportunities and prospects for advances." Of course, they have less legitimacy than policymakers and elected officials "to identify and formulate sociotechnical goals." The question is how the policymaker circumscribes the analyst's role and whether outsiders' data (and models for interpreting them) are introduced, along with other inputs (especially the insiders' own), into the decision-making process.

Evidence (which may be quantitative, historical, simulational, anecdotal) is inextricably tied to its source, and is amplified or discounted accordingly. Bibliometricians come bearing evidence that may be counterintuitive, couched in a foreign analytical language, and lacking the source credibility that participants in the community under evaluation, by definition, possess. So what is a policy broker to do?

For one thing, the brokers must translate the arcane into the intelligible. More importantly, brokers must promote face-to-face exchanges between insiders and outsiders to extricate *themselves* from the "analyst-actor" dilemma. Defending various points of view in public forums becomes an essentially educational function. It builds trust and makes accountability more palatable to all concerned. But it especially conveys to evaluators that their role is valuable.

Quantitative analysis of science outputs is a new instrumentality; it will therefore require a new style of science policy brokerage, one that supports the production of independent assessments as a legitimate research activity, and secures its place as a unique and competent cog in the decision-making apparatus. Quantitative analysis of science, with all the qualifications attendant to any policy tool, has earned that place.

## CONCLUSIONS

Can we measure research performance? Yes, but the measurements cannot forecast strategic plans and tactical choices for investments in science. Can such measurements improve science policy? Yes, but only if they can overcome the resilient ideology of peer review and can be shaped into a form useful to policymakers. Quantitative indicators, like other data produced or adapted for policy usage, do not speak for themselves. Indeed, they can be easily coopted. It is the policymaker who will impose extrinsic values on analyses to anchor or undermine conventional wisdom.

In this chapter, we have traced two generations of bibliometric analysis to distill for the policy consumer and actor the lessons learned in, and applied to, research evaluation. The evolution of these instrumentalities has pushed and pulled outside evaluators into the dialogue over past performance and future priorities. This dialogue has given both the resource brokers and the participant researchers good reason to heed those lessons and incorporate them into their planning and practice, respectively. But there is also good reason for them to expand the dialogue by exerting conceptual and empirical influence on the ways research evaluators execute, report, and interpret their work.[81]

Finally, we have suggested that the assessment of knowledge production and progress in science can be turned on its head. Policymakers can expect a greater return on their investment in bibliometrics if they can formulate the right questions and position themselves to utilize the evidence they receive to answer the following questions: Are we getting our money's worth from R&D? How does knowledge grow? Can we anticipate the locus (if not the form and timing) of innovations in research? No longer need they rely on peer review alone. The evolution of quantitative measures of research performance and outcomes has already made them, as well as others with a stake in the science policy system, more responsive to their respective clients. Even if outside evaluation of science has not come of age, it has experienced an important rite of passage: it is not an impetuous and "promising" upstart activity but an innovative contribution of savvy and increasingly sophisticated policy researchers.

# Peer Review

## and

# Unauthorized Science Policy

One of the reasons biomedical research has progressed so well in this country is that we have an efficient and effective system based upon peer review.

David Baltimore (1989)

The controversy is no longer whether there will be public participation and control of science, but over who will take part in the establishment of controls, how such controls will be organized, and how far they will influence detailed decisions concerning the nature and procedures of research.

Maurice Goldsmith (1986)

## IMPEDIMENTS AND NAGGING ISSUES

David Baltimore's remark reflects the thinking of many scientists, even scientists who are quite critical of peer review: at bottom, they are reluctant to change the peer review system. When changes are proposed, three sorts of responses tend to dominate the discussion:

191

1. Denial: Peer review is not a problem, the system works reasonably well in its current configuration, and to say otherwise is to make "much ado about nothing." Those who complain are simply incapable of competing successfully; their complaints are motivated by the unpleasant taste of sour grapes. There is nothing to worry about and nothing to fix.

2. Privilege: Science deals with a "higher" rationality that is inaccessible to the lay population. Only scientists have access to this privileged information, others cannot possibly understand scientific matters, and so only scientists can govern science. Peer review is much ado about something, but scientists have it under control.

3. Elitism: We scientists may not play by the rules but we know where the best scientists are trained, where they work, what they study, and where they publish. There is no need to study peer review because it is irrelevant to the important decisions that are made, correctly, despite "peer" input. Study the work and careers of the scientific elite, if you must, and forget the problems that bedevil the rank and file. Better yet, do not study any of this, as it is an unrespectable form of navel-gazing.

With such entrenched commitment to peer review, it is no wonder that efforts to study and amend it are foiled at every turn. No matter what is proposed, some "vital" interest of some stakeholder is threatened. Recall from chapters 3 and 4 how difficult it was to obtain the sample of scientists for the survey of NCI applicants and how reluctant editors and program managers were to allow access to their files. And, because of such difficulties, many studies of peer review must be undertaken by insiders, such as Stephen Lock or Rita Simon and Clark McPhail, who are in a position to "entrust" themselves with sensitive data about their own editorial behavior.

Recent evidence suggests that the rank-and-file scientist may be growing impatient with peer review. In a 1988 survey of members of Sigma Xi, The Scientific Research Society (with a 40 percent response rate, rather lower than the NSF survey reported in chapter 3), peer review "came in for a startling indictment."[1] Only 8 percent agreed that "peer review works well as it is." But the vast majority thought that "Congress is too political to set a proper agenda for research" and a majority (58 percent) agreed that "scientists should try to develop a ranking of fields and programs to present to Congress." These findings imply that scientists "would rather submit to the prejudices of their fellow scientists than the political fashions of the country at large." Survey director Jack Sommer concluded:

> Scientists are indeed saying they know better. They want to be funded and don't want to be held accountable. They have Ph.D.s in their pockets and hands in the public till. . . . Scientists have a responsibility to help the public understand why their research is worthwhile. . . . The canons of science are to ask questions; the canons of politics are to seek answers.[2]

Thus the pressing problem for the future is to reconcile scientific and political imperatives, and peer review is at that interface.

Scientists' attitudes and experiences aside, there are other inherent difficulties with peer review. Chief among these is the changing definition of a "peer." Social criteria have now joined technical specialization in determining who will be asked to review a manuscript or proposal. In a 1980 review of the Cole et al. Phase I study of peer review at NSF, one of us wrote:

> Gender and current geographical location are dominant factors in the selection of panel members. The implication is that panel members who are female or, say, reside in the southern U.S., conceptualize the world in a particular way, and thereby endow the panel or mail reviews with a balanced perspective otherwise missing.[3]

Nothing has changed in this regard, only intensified. Add these proxy social (status) characteristics to the epistemological variations that distinguish disciplinary or technical "peers" and an altogether new dimension emerges, that of "cognitive style."[4]

Even if we restrict our focus to social characteristics and treat cognitive styles as a random element in the review process, we find the notion of "peer" a misnomer. According to Lyle Groeneveld and his colleagues, grants peer reviewers are older, more accomplished, and more likely to work at prestigious institutions than are the rank and file of a field.[5] These reviewers are certainly not every scientist's *peers,* just as the members of a jury are exceedingly unlikely to be the defendant's "peers," except in the very loosest sense in which we are all one another's peers. In both cases the idea of peer decision making is a rhetorical device that lends legitimacy to the proceeding.

While reviewers may, on average, be more accomplished than those whose work they review, they are sometimes less accomplished:

> For the most advanced scientists only a few or no peers exist. In their research new areas are explored, often with special techniques and approaches. There is thus a high probability that one or several aspects of a proposal will not be appreciated by the judging "quasi-peers."[6]

For the "best" scientists *peer* review is unlikely.

Scientists are at the mercy of peer review systems that may offer neither "peers" nor "review." Instead, applicants must compete with others' intellectual capital, positional advantage, and political clout. Luck of the reviewer draw or mere chance may matter nearly as much as measurable features of the manuscript or proposal. Under current conditions of high competition for research funds and space in first-rate journals, such nonmeritocratic criteria make a decisive difference at the margin. Transcendently brilliant science will generally be funded or published and arrant nonsense usually will be turned away, but between those extremes chance and its less respectable relatives will play important roles in allocation decisions. Under these circumstances, the strategy of pouring more and more proposals into the review hopper (and shipping more and smaller manuscripts to journals) may be the most sensible way to increase one's probability of success.[7] But, as we have argued, this strategy also strains the review system, burdening its managers with more reviews and increasing the workloads of their trusted reviewers. Such pressures, in turn, encourage application of bureaucratic criteria of success, reduce reviewers' tolerance for new ideas, erode the quality of their reviews, and increase the opportunities for conflicts of interest to arise. After all, the standards of judgment most easily replicated and defended may not be the most effective. Objectivity and fairness in selection procedures do not guarantee creativity in the work selected.

Looking at the process from another perspective, how does the proposal writer respond to rejection? Does he or she write riskier, bolder, more imaginative proposals that challenge the reader or "safer" proposals that cleave as closely as possible to the best available model of a winner? Risk aversiveness may be built into the U.S. research funding system, with scientists unwilling or unable (due to their conditions of employment) to take risks while agencies and their reviewers are unable to evaluate risky ideas.[8] Ironically, as scientists become ever less able to undertake innovative but risky research, policymakers increasingly call for scientific excellence. Current peer review practices may be at odds with our society's need for high-quality science. Can federal agencies, for example, devise an allocative mechanism able to meet these needs? Can they balance the inconsistent desiderata of peer review that were presented in chapter 2? Who should participate in these important decisions about the structure and operation of peer review? In the next section we consider some proposals for reform, then present our own modest proposals for improvement.

## REFORMING PEER REVIEW: SLOUCHING TOWARD ICONOCLASM

Whatever their criticisms of peer review, scientists and their employers and research sponsors find a comforting predictability in current review practices. This predictability has bred inertia and resistance to change. While many proposals to change peer review have been offered—and some will be offered here—the major stakeholders in the current system for awarding research support and selecting manuscripts for publication are unreceptive to change. Often whatever urge they feel for improvement is overwhelmed by their fear of the unknown. But in other instances this resistance may reflect well-considered pessimism about a proposed change. Let us consider critically some proposals for changing the peer review system.

Milton Friedman and Edward Shils, expressing a longing for times past that only a romantic or a reactionary could embrace, have called for a return to the days when universities were not dependent on federal largesse. But today major research universities are mainlining federal research support; abrupt termination of their supply of this peculiar opiate could be fatal. In the past three decades, university research and development expenditures have increased fivefold, while the federal share of these expenditures has fluctuated within the narrow range of 60 to 70 percent. Whatever growth there has been in private and state support for universities, it remained a constant share of university research budgets. Dependence on federal support is even greater at the top:

somewhat more than a third of the top research universities receive more than 70 percent of their research support from federal sources.[9] Indirect costs, chiefly for administrative and maintenance expenses necessary for research, have risen from 16 percent of the national academic research and development budget in 1966 to about 28 percent in 1986.[10]

Numbers aside, universities have undergone substantial structural change to accommodate the growth of their research component, adding vice-presidents (or vice-chancellors) for research and government relations, enlarging offices of sponsored research, creating research institutes and centers, devising faculty incentive schemes to encourage research activity, and constructing new forms of academic employment that are almost wholly dependent upon external funding for support.[11] Through such changes universities have transformed themselves to suit their resource environment. The withdrawal of federal research support would deeply scar many universities and might cause others to collapse. U.S. science policy cannot abjure the dependency it has unwittingly created.

Similarly, Deborah Shapley and Rustum Roy's call for a "reconfiguration" of the U.S. university science system is equally improbable.[12] They propose that only the top institutions should devote their energies to performing "world-class basic science at the frontier."[13] Other universities should concentrate on varieties of applied work, with perhaps a soupçon of basic research as "overhead" (or seasoning?) on the meat and potatoes of applications.

This proposal assumes that someone, somewhere, knows indisputably where excellence can be found and that others will concur with their evaluations and not contest the allocations that follow. But there is currently no indisputable measure of scientific excellence. Worse, as one moves from the esoteric research front of science studies and the evaluation of scientific research into the muddle of application, the quality of the research erodes with alarming rapidity. For example, a straightforward effort to evaluate an innovative research program of the National Heart, Lung, and Blood Institute crumbled in the hands of a contract research company, so the program has gone unevaluated. And a congressional committee (that shall remain nameless), interested in developing a national perspective on the geographic dispersion and intensity of research activity, scraped together an appallingly amateurish "study" that could serve no discernible policy purpose. Indeed, the "science indicators" used in that study would have been faulted by professionals in the field fifteen years ago.

Such folly is part of a larger tragedy. In recent years the federal government has sharply weakened the nation's ability to do sound science policy research—and many other forms of social assessment and research—by decimating in-house research staffs, reducing support for external research efforts, and withdrawing support for national data bases. Ironically, while the field of science studies—including degree programs, basic research, and policy-relevant work—seems healthy today, the U.S. is hardly disposed to use those resources as the basis for science policy decisions. Other nations, including Britain, France, and the Netherlands, may be more successful in nurturing and benefiting from science studies.

There are other flaws in Shapley and Roy's proposal. They treat universities as the unit about which decisions would be made, implicitly assuming that universities are homogeneous—that at the best schools a fine physics or chemistry program, for example, would be accompanied by strong engineering and economics. While there is a tendency for good-quality departments to cluster together on campuses, the relationship is neither perfect nor immutable. Strong and weak departments may be mixed on any given campus, and the relative status of departments may change over time. But it would not do merely to shift the unit of evaluation from the university to the department. Departments are interactive, interdependent, changing social organizations. Much of the excitement in science today is taking place at the interstices of academic departments and traditional disciplines, in research institutes, centers, interdisciplinary programs, and emerging departments and fields. A top-flight physics department may benefit from the research activities of lesser-rated chemistry, geology, astronomy, archaelogy, biology, mathematics, and computer science departments, and it may perish in isolation from these cognate fields. A policy of supporting and developing "steeples of excellence" to the exclusion of other parts of the university may erode the foundations upon which new steeples are built.

*Scientists,* not *universities,* are the key actors in the science system. The rhetoric of their presidents and development offices notwithstanding, it is scientists, not their universities, who research, discover, educate, innovate, and disseminate. Scientists also move from school to school during their careers. Restricting the research activities of "lesser" institutions would limit the research opportunities of their faculty, at least some of whom make significant contributions to science. While there may be some merit to providing block grants to the best universities, such a policy also has serious pitfalls.

A third option is to replace peer review with a lottery system that would award funds at random. Every scientist would be given a "ticket," and a few winning tickets would be drawn and awarded support. Cynics might argue that the current grants peer review system already operates much like a lottery, at least for some scientists, and the preceding chapters have provided partial support for this view.

Yet most scientists would be uncomfortable with a lottery system. It would be difficult to define the population of researchers eligible to participate, so the boundary between scientists and non-scientists, between science and non-science, so carefully constructed and defended in the past three centuries, might again become indistinct. Worse, the merit of ideas in a proposal or the quality of a scientist's work would be flushed from the system, removing the last vestiges (or, cynics might say, pretenses) of meritocratic decision making. This would intensify the anomic conditions already present in contemporary science. And the "quality assurance" function of peer review would also be abandoned, perhaps replaced by the simple warning, "caveat lector." Each reader of a scientific report or user of a scientific result would be individually responsible for ascertaining its validity. Finally, societal notions of fairness would be offended, for the achievement ideology of the U.S. does not readily accept luck as a cause of success. Instead, talent, hard work, persistence, and dedication are believed to be the keys to success. It would be politically unacceptable and cruel to devise a funding system that worked otherwise. Thus, for reasons that range from threats to the professional identity of scientists through the practical benefits of (admittedly modest levels of) quality assurance to consideration for the norms of science and society, it would be unwise to replace the peer review system with a lottery.

For many of the same reasons it would not work to replace peer review mechanisms with a sort of proportional allocation system, based on population or level of economic activity. While this was a live issue in the early years of the National Science Foundation, and has recurred periodically in congressional and agency policy discussions, it would probably seem punitive and disruptive to impose such criteria of equity on the highly concentrated research system of today. In effect, it would raze the steeples of excellence that have been so carefully constructed on campuses across the nation.

An imaginative alternative to the NSF merit review system was proposed in March 1989 by physicist Richard Muller, of the

University of California at Berkeley, in testimony before the House Science, Space, and Technology Committee. Muller suggested that funds be allocated according to a scientist's reputation, and that reputations be evaluated using a networking or "snowball" approach. In his words,

> Ask all the U.S. scientists for their list of the best working scientists. Then ask the members of that list for *their* lists of the best. Repeat once again. Then, take the 1000 top scientists from the final list and give each $1 million a year to spend on any kind of research he or she desires.[14]

Before evaluating Muller's "modest proposal," consider his rationale for offering it:

> Money spent in this fashion would be far more productive in producing innovation than by doling it out for proposals that achieved the consensus of their "peers." . . . The problem . . . is that NSF is set up to support only ongoing, mainstream research projects and can't identify, much less support, forefront research.[15]

Under Muller's plan, half the annual NSF budget would still be reserved for peer-reviewed awards. The other half, in effect, would be committed to innovative research (or to whatever the "best" wanted to do). While his motives are laudable, Muller's proposal does not solve many of the most trenchant problems that plague the federal research system: How is the "best working scientist" defined? Each judge may have an idiosyncratic perspective grounded in iconoclastic criteria. What if there is not much agreement among judges after three iterations? And why stop after three iterations? What about the relative sizes and levels of visibility of disciplines? Would not larger and more visible disciplines and specialties, overrepresented among the population of scientists and unduly prominent in the minds of scientists, be disproportionately successful? And once successful, how would they be displaced by newer fields? What about logrolling and other forms of collusion among nominators? What guarantees do we have of accountability to sponsors and society for funds received? And what of the social characteristics of the final, fortunate thousand—particularly their sex, race, ethnicity, age, institutional affiliation, geographic distribution, and other such characteristics that NSF considers, implicitly or explicitly, in award decisions?

Should these now become irrelevant decision criteria? It would be most surprising if the reputational approach gave a fair shake to scientists who happen to be young, female, minority, or employees of less prestigious institutions. That is, the approach probably suffers from the same biases that plague the current system: it would surely spend the money in our science budgets but with little assurance about the quality of the work supported.

There are deeper flaws as well. Muller presupposes that under such terms scientists would innovate, that they have an innate drive to innovate that is limited only by social bonds of accountability but would be liberated by autonomy. Yet there is little evidence that this is so, and some evidence that a balance of freedom and accountability is more conducive to innovation.[16] Further, depending upon what sorts of research output are required to sustain a scientist's reputation (and, thus, his or her funding), Muller's proposal may generate volumes of humdrum publications that keep a prolific scientist in the top thousand. Ultimately, some form of traditional peer review must intervene to decide which manuscripts are published in which journals, thereby displacing the decision from grants peer review to journal peer review.

Social and historical studies of science show that discovery and innovation are context-bound, that they are at least as much *declared* by an appreciative community of scientists as they are unearthed or invented, in isolation, by brilliant scientists.[17] By further concentrating support for science and removing incentives for scientists to weave their research into the work of others, Muller's proposal creates the conditions under which "discoveries" may go unnoticed and unexploited—that is, undiscovered. Finally, how does a scientist recover from a dud, from a project that yielded little and thus diminished his or her reputation? In Muller's system the traditional peer review competition would be fiercer than today's, because half the money has been allocated according to reputation. A scientist who falls from the aristocracy of the fortunate thousand back into the scrambling masses should not expect gentle treatment by those "peers." Hence, under this plan top scientists will have an incentive to be conservative, just as they do today.

Despite these important shortcomings, the virtues of Muller's approach should be recognized. Foremost among them are administrative efficiency and promise of enhanced freedom. Everyone favors increased efficiency, particularly in these days of tight science budgets, but that is only one value among many competing values. Innovativeness is also a rallying cry today, and Muller's observation that NSF is unable to support "forefront" research may be a signal that federal agencies can no longer take the lead in supporting innovative science but must instead be content with supporting follow-ons, mops-ups, and maintenance activities. In the end, there may be no system for picking "winners," and a policy of "laissez-rechercher" may be as good as any other.

Taking such limitations to heart, the federal government might reverse the trend of past decades by substantially reducing its direct support for research—including projects, programs, and centers—and instead devoting funds to infrastructure, equipment, and the training of predoctoral, postdoctoral, and mid-career scientists. This would insure a certain base level of national preparedness for science without compelling the federal government to place bets about social and economic needs. Instead, let foundations, industries, state governments, and other interests (that putatively have a sharp eye for innovation) provide direct support for projects.

Alternatively, federal agencies may try to encourage innovative research by taking risks themselves. An example of this strategy is the recent decision by NSF allowing each program to set aside up to 5 percent of its budget for one-time grants of no more than $50,000 to be awarded, without external review, in support of risky, innovative proposals.[18]

Industry and private foundations find and fund many visionaries in the laboratory today and may well have done so yesterday, too.[19] The Howard Hughes Medical Institute (HHMI), located in the shadow of NIH, has become a shadow organization as well, quietly selecting and bankrolling the best biomedical scientists. But HHMI is also reputedly ruthless is cutting off those who are seen as not making sufficiently rapid progress in their research programs. Perhaps the decision rules of HHMI selection committees should be shared and compared with those of their neighbors on the Bethesda campus.

But HHMI is not alone in its impatience with sluggish research progress. According to the physics grapevine, shortly before Paul Chu made his startling discovery of "warm superconductivity," his NSF grant was in jeopardy of not being renewed. Thus, there appears to be a statute of limitations on the "promise" of basic research: if promise does not yield product within some unspoken interval, the implicit contract is terminated and the investigator's funds are reduced. Chu came perilously close to exceeding

NSF's patience; NSF came equally close to forfeiting its claim as a patron of innovative, leading-edge, basic research—jeopardizing its reputation as a patron for "pure science."

To summarize, we believe that the academic research enterprise should not be dismantled in an effort to re-enter a golden age of innocence, where science was not so competitive, resources not so scarce, and choices not so difficult. The current perils are reciprocal: not only is it difficult for potential patrons to identify and funnel support to the "truly excellent" institutions, but it is also impossible to evaluate research performers readily and accurately. If one could, with certainty, recognize excellent science, trace its sources, and provide exactly the right mixture of resources necessary to sustain it, then peer review would function flawlessly and allocation decisions would be utterly simple. Funding mechanisms should not be replaced by a lottery that awards support at random or by a proportional allocation system that insures economic, political, or demographic equity. A reputational system that supports scientists nominated by their colleagues is also deeply flawed. Acknowledging all that, can we hope to reform our mechanisms for allocating resources for science? Is it possible to improve traditional peer review with new mechanisms?

Thus far, this chapter has discussed impediments to study and reform of the peer review system and has criticized reforms suggested by others. The tone has been critical, perhaps strident. But the time has come when argumentation must yield to other creative impulses: we must now deliver on *our* promise to propose improvements in the peer review system.

We have no simple answers. Indeed, we think it important to forswear effortless but ill-informed solutions to such complex problems. But we do wish to propose some modest steps toward improving peer review systems and to suggest a process of thinking about allocative decisions that might eventually lead to substantially better decision-making.

This is a most revealing activity for, in Harold Orlans's words,

> The most childishly simple way to determine if an investigation is partisan is to see if it offers any recommendations. . . .
> Recommendations put the matter baldly. They avow support of particular interests or of the general interest which everyone espouses and cannot agree upon.[20]

To the extent that our partisanship has remained concealed, despite our best efforts to the contrary, the veil will now be lifted boldly. Our recommendations are in three parts: first, three specific procedural changes for current peer review practices; next, two ideas for redirecting the "professional education" of scientists and the professional conduct of program managers; finally, a call for fashioning a new analytic role and stance toward policy for science and society.

## Modest Improvements at the Margin

We recommend three changes in peer review procedures that, while admittedly neither radical nor original, would nonetheless change practices for the better.

1. Principal investigators and authors should be allowed to write a rejoinder to their reviews *before* the award or publication decision. In practice, many resubmitted proposals and revised manuscripts embody or are accompanied by such a rejoinder. Often a program manager or journal editor will subtly solicit such responses, after the initial decision, by asking the proposer to outline plans for responding to the reviews or inviting the author to enter into negotiations about the revisions that will transform a manuscript into a publication.

   Unfortunately, according to current practice, these rejoinders are prepared after a formal declination or rejection has been issued. The process could be streamlined by making such rejoinders the rule rather than the exception. Instead of resubmitting full-blown proposals (in twelve to twenty copies, complete with a half-dozen signatures) to be reviewed (by roughly five reviewers plus a panel or by a Study Section plus a National Advisory Council) these bodies could instead consider a five- to ten-page rejoinder and reply, or might even delegate this duty to the program manager. This happens today in some programs at NSF, when a prospective principal investigator is asked to respond to some questions or comments from the panel. Then, upon receipt of satisfactory responses, the program manager recommends that an award be made. In our experience, the request for such responses signals that an award is very likely. According to our suggested procedure, unfortunately, that inference would be unwarranted: some proposals would be declined, even after a reply. The paperwork savings of manuscripts would be less dramatic but equally liberating. Simply reducing the transaction costs for obtaining a grant or publishing a paper will be a modest but noticeable (and welcome) improvement.

But we seek more than a reduction in paperwork from this suggestion. We hope peer review can become a dialogue, a collective decision with somewhat less of the adversarial tone it now has. Reviewers are sometimes mistaken in their understandings or judgments; the procedure we propose will allow such mistakes to be undone more gracefully than the current appeals system permits. Authors and proposal writers also err at times; a more extensive exchange may make such flaws easier to identify, understand, accept, and repair.

2. Reviewers and referees should sign their reviews and should be openly associated with the work they approve or disapprove. This would hold reviewers publicly accountable for their decisions and would take a step toward acknowledging the value of reviewers' work. No longer would it be convenient for a reviewer to trash another's work. Nor would it be advisable to endorse unexamined work.

   Yes, we understand that removing the shield of anonymity may reduce reviewers' candor and put them at risk of reprisals. But the current practice is semi-open, with authors and proposers free to speculate about their critics' identities and, inappropriately, to reply in kind. To the extent that some of these reprisals are certain to be in error, our proposal will eliminate such mistakes. Better still, by making open review the usual practice, all would live in glass houses, not just those with tell-tale points of view, writing styles, or typefaces. Most importantly, the communal character of science would be openly recognized and reinforced, the tide of covert careerism would be stemmed (or brought into the open), and the opportunities for communication among scientists would be improved.

   At bottom this suggestion is motivated by two questions: Is it appropriate to allow comments in a review that one would not write directly to the author? and How many essential, accurate, critical comments about a manuscript or proposal *cannot* be expressed in language that could be directly communicated to the author? Criticisms that must be anonymous probably should not be written, and it would be a very rare criticism that could not be phrased in civil language.

3. Reviewing is an important professional activity that demands time, care, and intelligence, and therefore deserves to be openly rewarded. Yet today it is often bootlegged, squeezed into the small spaces of a crowded schedule. Under such circumstances we would be surprised to find thorough, careful, balanced reviews undertaken in good time and with good will. Worse, the most substantial "rewards" for reviewing are those universally regarded as unethical or degenerate: theft or plagiarism of ideas, inside information that provides an advantage over colleagues, and a chance to forestall competitors or settle old scores. Such undesirable rewards must be driven out by the desirable ones of professional recognition and perhaps pay. Recognition could be awarded through the open review process suggested above; pay is harder to come by. Nonetheless, it is fatuous to complain about the costly errors of peer review and to argue for the economic, social, and military necessity of science while insisting upon simple, guaranteed, and cost-free solutions.

## Changing Roles and Rules

In addition to these changes in peer review procedures, we also recommend changes in graduate education and in the evaluation of scientific work. Scientists must reconsider the values and principles of conduct that are being taught to the next generation of scientists. If long bibliographies and entrepreneurial zeal are rewarded with power and prestige, while thoroughness and deliberation go unrewarded, it is unlikely that any tinkering with peer review procedures will effect the necessary changes. As long as specialization, deference to gatekeepers, and solidarity with allies in research are favored over comprehensive understanding, skepticism, and independent thinking, then conformity to the petty rules of the game will overwhelm research. If stonewalling to protect professional prerogative prevails where openness and public scrutiny are needed, then others may step into the breach, as demonstrated by the assortment of congressional hearings on research fraud and conflict of interest.

Sadly, there is much evidence—offered in the preceding chapters and elsewhere—that the scientific career is fundamentally changing in ways that threaten the research enterprise, and that the new rules of conduct are being well learned by graduate students and postdoctoral fellows. Sensitivity to the problems of professional socialization has led to at least one major study, conducted by Judith Swazey, Karen Seashore Louis, and Rosemary Chalk (with support from NSF) to identify the most significant ethical issues facing young scientists and to survey the reference points and resources available to resolve them. More such studies are needed, and they must be accompanied by efforts to change the contingencies of the scientific career and revise programs of graduate education.

We also recommend that the connection between science evaluation and peer review be improved. To do this the insular secrecy of peer review must be broached: peer review should be supplemented with bibliometric information, allowing our understanding of science "outputs" to inform the functioning of peer review. The science studies community should be invited to enter and examine the peer review system.

Since evaluation is an accountability tool, a research tool, and a way of measuring how close one has come to program objectives, it is fair to wonder why measures of research output, using bibliometric or other evaluation techniques, are not used to supplement the traditional peer review of proposals. The latter assesses intentions and promises, while the former weighs outcomes and products, so that they would seem to complement one another. While it would not be easy to combine these data, the potential benefits are substantial. Yet program managers seldom make the effort.

Beyond the program managers, there is also work for the agencies and the bibliometrics community. Agencies must foster a climate of open evaluation of the efficacy and performance of peer review, encouraging an ongoing dialogue between outside researchers or evaluators and inside administrators. Both parties must share data and interpretations, and they must question one another's assumptions and assertions.

The science studies community must become more client-oriented, moderating its preoccupation with an arcane research agenda and scholarly publication so as to entertain the needs of the decisionmakers. By doing so the researcher stands to gain a fuller understanding of the political, organizational, and interpersonal forces that shape the daily world of science through access to previously concealed events and decisions. For their part, science policymakers and administrators would gain an independent perspective on the inner workings of science, an organized sounding board for new practices, and a growing reservoir of knowledge and information about contemporary science to assist in the development of new funding strategies.

## Toward a Process of Reform

It is very unlikely that a brief book, based upon the sketchy available evidence, idiosyncratically chosen and arranged, could propose a definitive and successful revision of peer review procedures and, more generally, improve the mechanisms through which resources for science are allocated. Indeed, we have freely castigated others for doing so. But we wish our modest suggestions for improvement to be accompanied by processes that could yield more fundamental, thoroughgoing change. We will suggest such processes in the closing sections of this book.

## META-ANALYSIS, THE SCIENCE CRITIC, AND SCIENCE POLICY

The policy researcher wields imperfect tools in an uncertain world. Yet policy research is expected to explain how past actions produced present conditions and to predict how various policy proposals will yield alternative futures. Not only must the policy researcher consider unpredictable physical phenomena, but he or she must also reckon with the intersecting social worlds of scientists and engineers, politicians and their assorted (and interested) constituencies, and the varieties of publics and interests that populate modern societies.[21] Unfortunately but understandably, policy research tends to focus on the physical phenomena while ignoring or grossly simplifying the social world. The result is a researcherless, context-free, aseptic analysis where "the social" is presumed unrelated either to the research and development processes or to their projected consequences. In this world, policy research comes "vacuum packed," insulated from the confounding nuisances and nuances of "social factors."

In this book we have advanced an alternative approach to policy research that critically examines scientists' behavior, especially their values, customs, procedures, and standards of evidence. Some might consider this a call to reflexivity, urging scientists, policy analysts, and others to call into question their values and presuppositions about what science should be and how science should be done. But we want more than reflexive scientists. We are also calling for "meta-philosophical" analysis, a systematic inquiry into the world view underlying current philosophies of science.[22]

As a prefix, "meta-" denotes that a layer of analysis and criticism has been added to an existing intellectual discipline. In this context, the purpose of a meta-analysis of science is to uncover the hidden assumptions that convenient labels conveniently obscure, and thus to make explicit the values, ethical principles, and mechanisms through which experts negotiate and defend their world views.

Philosopher Marx Wartofsky has christened the philosophy, history, and sociology of science "metasciences" because their subject matter has to do with other sciences. To Wartofsky, metasciences are, by definition, "applied" sciences that produce "applied" knowledge:

> What the metasciences can do . . . is to provide a critical understanding of the relations between the state and science, between social class and science, between ideology and scientific rationality. Insofar as such a study remains . . . a descriptive account of such relations, it is useful for a critical study; but only as a groundwork.[23]

The metasciences can play a distinctive role in science policy, improving its methods, assessing its consequences, and redirecting its focus. By scrutinizing scientific rationality and applying this knowledge to social ends, the reflexive social analyst—the metascientist—becomes a part of the policy-making process. As science and technology become increasingly important elements of society, such organized, systematic, and reflexive analysis and criticism become indispensable.

For Maurice Goldsmith the metascientist would be a "science critic . . . a public policy generalist alerting us to the growing pains of future worlds through the day-to-day discoveries of the present."[24] The critic's missions are "to see the whole picture," anticipate the future, discern recurring issues, and "uphold the integrity of science." To flesh out the science critic's role we will present an extended account of one recent issue that would merit the attention of a science critic and provide a sampling of the issues a critic might raise.

## The Science Critic in Action

Metascientists and science critics should have sprung into action when, at a University of Utah press conference in the spring of 1989, researchers announced that their tabletop experiment demonstrated nuclear fusion at room temperature, a discovery promising widespread commercial prospects as a new energy source. Scientific excitement aside, it is somewhat surprising that scientists would choose to announce a major new discovery through the media rather than through publication in a peer-reviewed journal. In effect, the researchers were establishing priority for their discovery and commanding the attention of scientists, policymakers, and business interests worldwide without benefit of the criticism and validation of the peer review process.

Biomedicine has the "Ingelfinger rule" to discourage such announcements: researchers who announce their discoveries through the media forfeit their claim to space in the *New England Journal of Medicine,* one of the most prestigious biomedical research journals. Apparently, chemistry and physics lack such a prohibition. But shortly after the press conference a manuscript submitted to *Nature* by the researchers, B. Stanley Pons and Martin Fleischmann, was returned to them for extensive revision. They refused to make the changes and withdrew the manuscript, claiming to be too busy to undertake revisions while caught up in the swirl of activities that followed their announcement. (At one point they declined an invitation to address the American Physical Society admittedly, an unreceptive, perhaps even hostile audience— during its annual meeting in Baltimore because they had a prior engagement to talk with the House Science, Space, and Technology Committee. In the course of those talks, the president of the University of Utah requested $25 million for a center to study cold fusion.) It is ironic that while newspaper stories contained requests by scientists for more information about the Utah researchers' experiments, some also featured a photograph of Fleischmann explaining the apparatus to a member of Congress. What is going on here, the science critic must ask? (Indeed, some *were* asked, for attribution, by both the popular and the science presses.) Have the traditional norms of science given way to new, entrepreneurial rules of conduct? Has a new system of scientific communication replaced the peer-reviewed journal?

Perhaps so. But perhaps the change lies not exclusively within the rules of professional conduct that scientists profess and sometimes practice but in their working environments and the structure of rewards. Why did the researchers announce their discovery when and how they did (which putatively violated an agreement they had made with Steven E. Jones, a physicist at nearby Brigham Young University, who had been studying a similar phenomenon and whose results were published in *Nature* in early 1989)? According to James J. Brophy, vice-president for research at the University of Utah, Pons and Fleischmann

> really wanted another 18 months. They really were not comfortable with announcing something they didn't completely understand.[25]

Understandably so. But they nonetheless made the announcement at the urging of University of Utah officials, who were concerned about the consequences that would result "if the story got out in such a way that it would preclude any kind of commercialization."[26] Another said,

> Had we waited on the assumption that we could keep it secret and somebody else then published the information before us, we could have lost incredibly significant patent rights.[27]

For "significant" read "lucrative." Now that the university has applied for several patents and feels somewhat secure about its financial stake in the new technology, we might expect communication to be more open. Once the cash is not a problem, perhaps science can take place. Not so, according to this article. Researchers at the Los Alamos National Laboratory in New Mexico, who were hoping to examine the Utah researchers' apparatus so they could work together to devise a more definitive experiment, had had difficulty in gaining access to the laboratory. Why the delay? Lawyers at the University of Utah were postponing the joint work until they could sort out who would own the rights to any inventions that might result from the collaboration.[28]

The science critic would note that, whatever the norms of science might dictate, direct intervention by employing institutions may have an overriding influence on the conduct of scientists. In many respects scientists are ceasing to be independent professionals and increasingly resemble engineers, not in the problems they address or the methods they employ (although resemblances in those areas are growing), but in their extensive obligations to employers. Unlike the "free" professions of law and medicine with their ethic of individual responsibility, engineers and scientists have become increasingly beholden to the organized interests that fund, equip, and employ them. The cold fusion case also warns us not to confuse situationally-determined changes in scientists' behavior with more fundamental changes in the scientific culture. Enduring situational pressures may lead to cultural change, but transient conditions may produce only a transient accommodation. The analyst's problem is to tell the difference.

Cold fusion is the best current example of the heat generated by the "fusion" of scientific and commercial interests in the laboratory. A science critic might ask of such arrangements to "transfer technology" from the university to industry the same question others are asking of the cold fusion experiments: Could it be that the amount of energy necessary to bring about the reaction is too great in proportion to its yield? That is, have the circumstances and principles governing science been so transformed in the quest for rapid commercial application that the ability to do science has been jeopardized?

The cold fusion case holds even more work for the science critic. After a Georgia Tech team recanted its replication of the Utah experiment due to an error in interpreting the data, the Atlanta *Journal and Constitution* ran as front-page headlines "Premature 'Discovery' May Hurt Georgia Tech" and "Georgia Tech Learns Risks of Going Public Too Soon." Good, dramatic press but dubious analysis? In the words of Melvin Kranzberg, an historian of technology at Georgia Tech who was quoted in one story, "The world is changing. Peer review, which has worked very well, is obviously not quick enough. People are going to get ahead of you if you wait to announce." Has Georgia Tech lost credibility through premature disclosure or is Kranzberg correct in asserting that the rules have changed?

Science critics must sort out these and related issues: Do early announcements of new discoveries diminish scientists' credibility or are they an essential new device for establishing priority claims? How does the prospect of commercial development influence the disclosure of scientific results? Does public cynicism grow with each new correction and retraction, or does it appear that error—as in "trial and error"—is a part of normal scientific practice that is becoming better understood and accepted by the public?

In *Megatrends*, John Naisbitt had warned that the "information float"—the amount of time it takes for information to be communicated—was collapsing, so that decisions must be made more speedily.[29] Shapley and Roy wondered if this means that science and innovation must now be more tightly coupled, that "discoveries" must become "inventions" more speedily.[30] Citation and patent indicators confirm this, suggesting that "discovery" and "application" are becoming more tightly coupled. The science critic might ask if the collapse of the information float could impair science, strangling the "discovery machine" in a tangled web of intersecting interests.

Media attention adds fuel to the race for priority, but the history of science teaches us that priority disputes have been fought for centuries.[31] A central issue in the cold fusion dispute is the familiar tension between priority and thoroughness in science. Thus the science critic asks, how are the new circumstances of scientific work shaping scientists' resolution of this longstanding tension?

Does the cold fusion case teach us that peer review is antiquated, sluggish, losing its moral force? Probably not. Are scientists eager to bypass the blessings of their peers for the accolades of the media? Not usually. But when science is gripped by a new lead, such as cold fusion or warm superconductivity, the rules may be temporarily suspended or superseded. Scientists sense the headlines, excitement, institutional visibility, career capital, and cold cash that major discoveries can yield. Perhaps more significantly, scientists' bosses—the department chairs, deans, and provosts—and those new arrivals in the academic menagerie—the vice-presidents for research or government relations, patent lawyers, and "technology transfer" experts—sense the rewards at stake and insist that the game be played according to the rules of the business world.

Hundreds of scientists in the U.S. alone tried to confirm or refute the Utah findings. Chemists and physicists, who seldom speak to one another or read the same journals, jointly focused on a phenomenon that fell between the cracks. This interdisciplinarity, coupled with the intensity of the competition, the magnification of media scrutiny, and the magnitude of the rewards at stake, combine to open the laboratory doors and allow the public—and the science critic—to look inside. Pious calls for the rigor that only peer review can provide are still heard, but so too are the frolicking, winking, and groaning of competition.[32]

### Policy Research and the Public Interest

The "knowledge utilization" literature recognizes the need for the science critic a) to bridge the diverse cultures that intersect in the realm of science policy, and b) to translate policy *research* into policy *analysis* and implementation. Many of those who currently attempt to span these boundaries are seen as well-intentioned captives of their training and habits, further constrained by the powerful institutions they serve. They interact as much out of professional necessity as out of conviction. They listen, but often hear only what they wish; they talk, but often shape their words to the interests of their audiences. As one veteran policy analyst observes, "both research and policy rest largely on preconceptions and faiths that are beyond the purview of either."[33]

Closer to meta-analysis than this brittle characterization of cynical or impotent resignation is the call for a "sociology of knowledge application"[34] that

> would investigate the conditions under which knowledge is produced, diffused, and applied. [There is a] need for understanding the multiple frames of reference with which people perceive knowledge and the discrepancies between the frames of reference of knowledge producers and knowledge users.[35]

Consigning this function to a single discipline—sociology—is inadequate because the issues that arise at the juncture of science and policy entail questions of history, economics, politics, values, ethics, and morally defensible normative decisions about preferred futures. Moreover, the focus must extend beyond the production and exchange of "disciplinary" knowledge to include questions about the application of knowledge, its beneficiaries, and the characteristics of parties included in and excluded from the negotiation of future directions for science. An intellectual convergence or coalition such as that represented by the metasciences is needed, with its focus on the mutual accommodation of science, technology, and society.[36]

The "larger problem," according to Orlans,

> is that the policy research community has no common understanding of its public responsibilities, that there are no agreed codes or conventions by which to distinguish research conducted and administered in the public interest from that entirely legitimate and indispensable research which serves special interests. . . . Such conventions would not be easy to define or administer; if it proves impossible to define them, then we must confess that "policy research in the public interest" has no operational meaning.[37]

This "confession" makes two main assertions: first, that policy research is done without reference to "the pubic interest;" second, that the public interest is exceedingly difficult to discern. As Prewitt suggests, "Instead of asking what the public knows or should know about science, we might ask what the scientists know or should know about the public."[38] This observance gives new meaning to the notion of "science literacy." It is the science critic's job to develop shared understandings of the public interest, to distinguish between public and partisan research, and to educate scientists about the public as well as teach the public about scientists.

The science critic, as a peer among unequals, can make a unique contribution to public deliberations about science. But the critic's work must be relatively free of institutional entanglements, lest he or she become another entrenched interest with some special disciplinary or organizational issue to advance. To be effective, critics must be geographically dispersed—not simply more Washington insiders jostling with lobbyists for position on the Hill. And the critics must have resources—resources that have become increasingly scarce during the past decade for reasons that have less to do with budgetary strictures and far more to do with a failure of our nation's will to engage in thorough, critical self-examination.

## SCIENCE POLICY AND THE FLYWHEEL OF PEER REVIEW

The study of peer review is the study of science policy and the environment in which research funding decisions are made. Today's catchwords are "competitiveness" and "priority-setting." They are shorthand expressions for subtler, deeper issues in a complicated, pluralistic debate that is itself embedded in an ongoing tug-of-war between the executive and legislative branches of the federal government. To say that the executive proposes and the legislative disposes only hints at the process that produces policy, which is largely budget-driven.

Science has never been an effective political force. If anything, it has had some moral authority, derived chiefly from its willingness to remain above the political fray. Since the early years of the Reagan presidency this perception has changed, and, in the eyes of both branches of government, science has taken on the character of an interest group like any other. The frenzy over earmarking has surely reinforced this perception. Weakened both politically and morally, science must nonetheless stand up to a daunting agenda of issues in the coming years.

Some of these are questions of tradeoffs, such as striking a balance between civilian and military research, big science and little science, centers (or other forms of collective research activity) and individual investigators, commercial or targeted research versus "pure," curiosity-driven research. Such tradeoffs are commonplace in the policy discourse about how to fund, organize, manage, and optimize U.S. investments in scientific research. All retain a link to peer review. As the federal budget deficit intrudes ever more rudely into decisions of resource allocation, not only between science and other national needs but within science itself, scrutiny of that link intensifies. One of the least tractable issues has to do with establishing funding priorities across areas of science. For example, how can we choose among the human genome project, a space station, and the superconducting supercollider? Having chosen, how can we establish a reasonable timetable and pattern of investment? How can we sustain such projects once they've begun?

Peer review is better suited to setting priorities *within* a research community—comparing "like with like"—and has not been systematically applied to the problem of allocating resources *across* communities. Scientists have been reluctant to engage in such work. In part their reluctance might derive from mutual respect for one another's expertise. Part of their reluctance may stem from unwillingness to open the Pandora's box of "lay" decisions about scientific matters, for fear that if chemists help set priorities for physics this year, soon sociologists and perhaps even classicists will be consulted in the future. Such self-interested considerations aside, scientists may also recognize the intrinsic difficulties of setting such priorities on *scientific* (as opposed to economic, political, practical, or moral) grounds. Scientists know that basic research is unpredictable—the war on cancer provided a lesson about this, and AIDS research is adding a contemporary chapter to the text—so they may be wary of promising specific results from a process that demands redundancy, latitude, and slack resources. In effect, the priority-setting issue revisits Alvin Weinberg's discussion of "technical" versus "social" criteria in choosing among scientific projects and Harvey Brooks's distinction between "truth" and "utility."[39] Peer review can assist with decisions based on technical criteria or standards of truth, but is not up to the task of choosing on the basis of social criteria or utility. Those criteria belong to other realms.

Peer review *is* the flywheel of science, if for no other reason than that it symbolizes the professional autonomy *and* the accountability of science to the society that sustains it. Peer review communicates and enforces the terms of a social contract. It is also a foil for the apparatus and process that dominates science policy: science advice. The flywheel function of peer review slows the more partisan workings of presidential science advice. The science advisor, to exert any influence, must be a political insider. Peer review, to retain credibility as a decision tool, must function as a "technical insider," reflecting the best judgment of those researchers competent to judge promise.

In the political realm, there is a range of actors—Congress, the courts, the president's science advisor, lobbyists, businesses, and other interests—pulling and tugging on science policy. At its best, peer review should be a flywheel that moderates such forces, dampening their impact on science. But should peer review instead be harnessed to the task of priority setting, its ability to moderate other forces will be at an end, for it will have openly crossed the boundary that separates the technical realm from the political. In fact, peer review may well serve to amplify partisan influences on science, adding "scientific" justifications to the political, economic, and social rationales offered by others.

## Inventing Tools for Perception and Foresight

Enter the new science advisor to the President, physicist Allan Bromley. Science advisors, too, are prisoners of the bureaucracy. We wonder: Can new vision be wrought from such an appointment? How well can he negotiate the policy apparatus and competing interests *within* the science community? Will he discover "new ways of analyzing complex information" and satisfy the urgent "need for S&T (science and technology) coordination at the top of the executive branch?" Can he stave off what one university president has decried as the American public's "alarming level of mistrust about our [the scientific enterprise's] motives?"[40]

A vacuum may have been filled at the Office of Science and Technology Policy with Bromley's appointment, but it remains to be seen, in one science writer's words, "whether the tools for perception and foresight can be invented."[41] The 1980s have been a time of surging recognition that science and technology underlie national, regional, and local economic development, development that requires cross-sectoral cost-sharing and collaboration, and that will inherit, and therefore must invest in, the quality of the future U.S. work force.[42] All the while, malaise gripped science policy and nobody was home at the White House.

After the 1988 election, out of desperation and anticipation, inventions such as the new Carnegie Commission on Science, Technology, and Government became another point of light among the constellation of constituencies vying to offer science advice to the science advisor, Congress, and virtually anyone else with significant resources and a willingness to listen. A more "holistic" approach to science policy and improved foresight are welcome prescriptions. But can they change the process and its decisions by expanding or refining the quality of information upon which decisions are based? What of the knowledge base, the theories, models, and other interpretive frameworks that give shape and sense to information? Who will create such knowledge? Who will use it?

These are timeless questions. They reflect the context in which peer review is carried out and how decisions based on it are used to defend, redirect, accelerate, and curtail the science that is funded (and, ultimately, disseminated through journals and reports). For example, NSF's success is supporting science, we have observed,

> has attracted so many participants that it has lost efficiency, then clarity, and perhaps, according to some, its mission. Peer review . . . is burdened with too much responsibility and too few resources to satisfy the formidable demands of our research work force. This system is being overwhelmed by its participants.[43]

Paradoxically, if the flywheel of peer review is to be a steadying device, it must also be disturbing, if not disruptive, of conventional thought and unimaginative action. Peer review is an old dog; U.S. science needs some new tricks.

# Appendix: Survey of NCI Applicants

## The Sample

The sample was stratified according to the disposition of the applicant's proposals in fiscal year 1980, which was determined by standard NIH review procedures (as described in chapter 2). For grant proposals subjected to this review process, three outcomes are possible: approved and funded, approved but not funded, and disapproved and declined funding. The "approved" and "disapproved" categories are self-explanatory. The "approved but not funded" category came into existence as constraints on the NIH budget grew, causing some projects that were judged to deserve support on their merits to remain unsupported because their priority scores were below the threshold for support (or "payline" in NIH jargon). The printouts from NIH listed 7609 investigators in all three categories.

Limited resources did not allow us to sample from each category, so the extremes of the distribution were sampled: individuals whose proposals were approved and funded and those whose proposals were disapproved (and therefore not eligible for funding). The third category of approved but not funded proposals, which included 4009 (52.7%) of the applicants, was not sampled. Because scientists often submit more than one proposal to NIH during a given year, some of those in our sample experienced more than one of the possible outcomes. Of the 719 investigators to whom the survey was sent, more than a quarter submitted two or more proposals during the year. Of these, the proposals of 43% were uniformly approved and funded, those of 31% were uniformly disapproved, while 26% (53 investigators or 7.3% of the total) saw their proposals meet both fates, funded *and* disapproved for funding during fiscal year 1980. In our analysis we examine how such experiences shape scientists' attitudes toward the NIH funding system.

## Response rate

Overall, 336 (47%) of the scientists surveyed returned usable questionnaires. This is a good response rate, as only a single mailing (with no follow-up reminders) had been sent in order to preserve respondents' anonymity. The response rate did vary by sampling stratum, with higher rates among the more successful applicants. Of those who were uniformly successful, 52% (205 people) completed and returned the survey. Those who experienced mixed success had a response rate of 47% (25 responses); uniformly unsuccessful investigators had a response rate of 39% (106 responses). These differences in response rate, while modest, are noteworthy because the cover letter stated that, "If we do not receive your completed questionnaire, we will assume that your satisfaction with the present peer review system precluded it." That provocative statement was expected to elicit responses from dissatisfied scientists, perhaps at some risk of under-representing those who were satisfied.

These response rates may be better understood within the context of similar studies conducted by others. A recent NSF survey of prospective principal investigators had a 67% response rate, with completed questionnaires returned by 88% of the funded applicants, but only by 52% of those not funded.[1] Similarly, in an interview study performed under contract to the NIH, 85% of those whose applications were approved but *not* funded agreed to participate in the study, whereas 68% of those whose applications were disapproved chose to participate.[2] It is not surprising that studies under the official sponsorship of a funding agency elicit higher response rates than do studies conducted by academic social scientists: such surveys have an aura of authority and offer respondents an opportunity to "speak" directly to policymakers.

More puzzling is the universal tendency for less successful scientists not to respond. One would expect them to have much to say, perhaps in an effort to alter the system, send a message, or offer a quasi-public explanation for their failure. Instead, successful scientists—those most likely to be supportive to the status quo—are also most likely to respond. For this reason, when reading averages and aggregated percentages (such as, "X% of all respondents were enthusiastic about Y") one should bear in mind that such figures combine the responses of two quite different subpopulations which are generally not equally represented in the sample.[3]

# Notes

## CHAPTER 1

1. Marcel C. La Follette, "Journal Peer Review and Public Policy," *Science, Technology, and Human Values* 10 (Winter 1985): 3–5.

2. Kenneth Prewitt, "The Public and Science Policy," *Science, Technology, and Human Values* 7 (Spring 1982): 5–14.

3. La Follette, op. cit., p. 4.

4. Two reports issued by the Twentieth Century Fund highlight these disputes and how they compromise the autonomy of science: Task Force on Communication of Scientific Risk, *Science in the Streets*, background paper by Dorothy Nelkin (New York: Priority Press, 1984); Task Force on the Commercialization of Scientific Research, *The Science Business*, background paper by Nicholas Wade (New York: Priority, 1984).

5. James C. Petersen, ed., *Citizen Participation in Science Policy* (Amherst: University of Massachusetts Press, 1984).

6. Daryl E. Chubin, "Values, Controversy, and the Sociology of Science," *Bulletin of Science, Technology, and Society* 1 (1981): 427–37; Daryl E. Chubin and Sal Restivo, "The 'Mooting' of Science Studies: Research Programs and Science Policy," in Karen D. Knorr-Cetina and Michael J. Mulkay, eds., *Science Observed* (London and Beverly Hills: Sage, 1983), pp. 54–83.

7. Daryl E. Chubin and Ellen W. Chu, eds., *Science Off the Pedestal: Social Perspectives on Science and Technology* (Belmont, CA: Wadsworth, 1989); Bruno Latour, *Science in Action* (Cambridge, MA: Harvard University Press, 1987).

8. Harriet Zuckerman and Robert K. Merton, "Institutionalized Patterns of Evaluation in Science," in Robert K. Merton, *The Sociology of Science* (Chicago: University of Chicago Press, 1973) pp. 460–96; D. A. Kronick, "Authorship and Authority in the Scientific Publications of the Seventeenth Century," *Library Quarterly* 48 (1978): 255–75.

9. On points (1) and (2) see General Accounting Office, *Better Accountability Procedures Needed in NSF and NIH Research Grant Systems,* Report to the Congress (Washington, D.C., 1981); and Howard J. Sanders, "Peer Review: How Well is it Working?" *Chemical & Engineering News,* March 15, 1982, pp. 32–43. On the more general point (3) of public understanding of science as public policy, see Dorothy Nelkin, "Science and Technology Policy and the Democratic Process," in *The Five-Year Outlook: Problems, Opportunities, and Constraints in Science and Technology,* vol. 2 (Washington, D.C.: National Science Foundation, 1980), pp. 483–92.

10. National Science Foundation Advisory Committee on Merit Review, *Final Report* (1986), p. 2.

11. Vannevar Bush, *Science: The Endless Frontier* (U.S. Office of Scientific Research and Development, July 1945, rpt. NSF, 1960), p. 12.

12. Ibid., p. 19.

13. American Association for the Advancement of Science, "Board Statement on Politics and Science," *Science* 224 (January 6, 1984): 27.

14. Henry B. Gonzalez, "Scientists and Congress," *Science* 224 (April 13, 1984): 127–29.

15. Orrin Hatch, "Amendment of Title IV of the Federal Food, Drug, and Cosmetic Act," U.S. Congress, Senate, *Congressional Record,* 98th Cong., 1st sess., October 6, 1983, p. S13789.

16. Michael J. Mahoney, "Psychology of the Scientist: An Evaluative Review," *Social Studies of Science* 9 (1979): 349–75; Ian I. Mitroff and Daryl E. Chubin, "Peer Review at NSF: A Dialectical Policy Analysis," *Social Studies of Science* 9 (1979): 199–232.

17. Gerald Holton and Robert S. Morison, eds., *Limits of Scientific Inquiry,* (Cambridge: American Academy of Arts and Sciences, 1978) pp. 171–90.

18. Deborah Shapley and Rustum Roy, *Lost at the Frontier* (Philadelphia: ISI Press, 1985).

19. Ibid., pp. 102–3.

20. Ibid., pp. 99, 54, 103–4.

21. D. H. Osmond, "Malice's Wonderland: Research Funding and Peer Review," *Journal of Neurobiology* 14 (1983): 95–112.

22. For example, see Grace M. Carter, *What We Know and Do Not Know about the Peer Review System,* Rand Corporation report N-1878-RC/NIH, June 1982; Stephen Cole, Leonard Rubin, and Jonathan R. Cole,

*Peer Review in the National Science Foundation: Phase I of a Study,* (Washington, D.C.: National Academy of Sciences, 1978).

23. Arie Rip, "Peer Review Is Alive and Well in the United States," *Science, Technology, and Human Values* 10 (3) (Summer 1985): 82–86.

24. Rustum Roy, "Peer Review of Proposals—Rationale, Practice, and Performance," *Bulletin of Science, Technology, and Society* 2 (1982): 402–22.

25. National Commission on Research, *Reviewing Processes: Assessing the Quality of Research Proposals,* (Washington, D.C.: 1980).

26. Erich Bloch, "Science Policy and Tight Budgets," *Science* 227 (March 1, 1985): 991; Barbara J. Culliton, "NIH Proposes Extending Life of Grants," *Science* 226 (December 21, 1984): 1400–1402.

27. Donald Kennedy, "Government Policies and the Cost of Doing Research," *Science* 227 (February 1, 1985): 480–84; Daryl E. Chubin, "Research Malpractice," *Bioscience* 35 (February 1985): 80–89; John Maddox, "Privacy and the Peer-Review System," *Nature* 312 (December 6, 1984): 497; "Secrecy in University-Based Research: Who Controls? Who Tells?" *Science, Technology, and Human Values* 10 (special issue, Spring 1985): 3–114.

28. Rustum Roy, "An Alternative Funding Mechanism," *Science* 211 (March 21, 1981): 1377.

29. Richard C. Atkinson and William A. Blanpied, "Peer Review and the Public Interest," *Issues in Science and Technology* 2 (Summer 1985): 101–14.

30. Ibid, p. 110.

31. U.S. Congress, House, Committee on Science and Technology, Task Force on Science Policy, *An Agenda for a Study of Government Science Policy,* 98th Cong., 2d sess., December 1984 (Washington, D.C.: USGPO, 1985); Barbara J. Culliton, "Fine-Tuning Peer Review," *Science* 226 (December 21, 1984): 1401.

## CHAPTER 2

1. *Grants Peer Review: Report to the Director, NIH Phase I,* NIH Grants Peer Review Study Team, (Washington, D.C.: December, 1976), pp. 3, 4.

2. Ibid., p. 4, emphases added.

3. Rustum Roy, "Alternatives to Review by Peers: A Contribution to the Theory of Scientific Choice," *Minerva* 22 (3, 4) (Autumn-Winter 1984): 316–28.

4. NSF Advisory Committee on Merit Review, *Final Report* (Washington, D.C.: NSF, 1986), p. 2.

5. Eugene Garfield, "Refereeing and Peer Review," part 4, *Current Contents,* February 2, 1987, p. 8.

6. Harriet Zuckerman and Robert K. Merton, "Institutionalized Patterns of Evaluation in Science," in Robert K. Merton, *The Sociology of Science* (Chicago: University of Chicago Press, 1973 [1971]), p. 463.

7. U.S. General Accounting Office, *University Funding: Information on the Role of Peer Review at NIH and NSF* (Washington, D.C.: USGAO, March 1987), p. 5.

8. Rustum Roy, "Funding science: The *real* defects of peer review and an alternative to it," *Science, Technology, and Human Values* 10 (3) (Summer 1985): 74.

9. Ibid.

10. J. Merton England, *A Patron for Pure Science: The National Science Foundation's Formative Years, 1945–57.* (Washington, D.C.: National Science Foundation, 1982), p. 165.

11. Ruth L. Kirschstein, testimony before the Task Force on Science Policy of the Committee on Science and Technology, U.S. House of Representatives, 99th Cong., 2d sess., no. 134, April 8–10, 1986, p. 64.

12. Ibid., p. 71.

13. Ibid., p. 65.

14. Grace Carter, citing a 1980 GAO report in *What We Know and Do Not Know about the NIH Peer Review System* (Santa Monica, Calif.: RAND, June 1982), p. 4.

15. Kirschstein, op. cit., p. 88.

16. Carter, op. cit., p. 4.

17. Carlos E. Kruytbosch, "The Role and Effectiveness of Peer Review," Ciba Foundation Symposium No. 142, "The Evaluation of Scientific Research," London, June 5–8, 1988; NSF Advisory Committee on Merit Review, op. cit., p. 21 and passim; Roy, "Funding Science."

18. NSF Advisory Committee on Merit Review, p. 21.

19. Ibid.

20. Ibid.

21. Kruytbosch, op. cit.; U.S. General Accounting Office, op. cit.

22. Mary Clutter, testimony before the Task Force on Science Policy (see note 11), p. 137.

23. U.S. General Accounting Office, op. cit., p. 11.

24. NIH, *Peer Review Trends 1975–1985* (Bethesda, Md.: Statistics and Analysis Branch, Division of Research Grants, NIH), p. 13.

25. U.S. General Accounting Office, op. cit., p. 9, citing Mary Clutter's testimony.

26. NIH, *Peer Review Trends,* p. 8.

27. NSF, *Proposal Review at NSF* (Washington, D.C.: NSF Report 88-4, 1988), Appendix D. It is surprisingly difficult to calculate success rates, as proposals are often carried over from year to year, and the same proposal may appear more than once in a year.

28. Data provided by Thomas Quarles, NSF.

29. James W. Symington and Thomas R. Kramer, "Does Peer Review Work?" *American Scientist* 65 (January-February 1977): 18.

30. Ibid., p. 19.

31. Ibid., pp. 18–19.

32. Stephen Cole, Leonard Rubin, and Jonathan R. Cole. *Peer Review in the NSF: Phase I of a Study* (Washington, D.C.: National Academy of Science, 1978) pp. 12–13.

33. House Task Force on Science Policy, April 8–10, 1986, op cit., p. 83 (Fuqua).

34. Ibid., p. 86 (Brown).

35. Ibid., p. 88 (Packard).

36. David Baltimore, "Limiting Science: A Biologist's Perspective," *Daedalus,* Summer 1988 [Spring 1978], p. 334.

37. Ibid., pp. 339–40.

38. Rosalyn S. Yalow, "Is Subterfuge Consistent with Good Science?" *Bulletin of Science, Technology, and Society* 2 (1982): 401.

39. Richard A. Muller, "Innovation and Science Funding," *Science* 209 (22 August 1980): 881.

40. Ibid., p. 883.

41. C. P. Rhoads, quoted in John C. Burnham, John E. Sauer, and Ronald D. Gibbs, "Peer-Reviewed Grants in U.S. Trade Association Research," *Science, Technology, and Human Values* 12 (2) (Spring 1987): 48.

42. Ronald E. Paque, "Overhaul Peer Review," letter to *The Scientist,* 5 October 1987, p. 10.

43. Roy, "Alternatives to Review by Peers," p. 316.

44. Ibid., 317.

45. Roy, "Funding Science," p. 74.

46. Ibid., p. 73.

47. Roy, "Alternatives to Review by Peers," p. 317.

48. Ibid, p. 317 (emphases added).

49. Ibid, p. 318.

50. Deborah Shapley and Rustum Roy, *Lost at the Frontier* (Philadelphia: ISI Press, 1985), p. 18.

51. See, for example, Julius H. Comroe, Jr., and Robert D. Dripps, "Scientific Basis for the Support of Biomedical Science," *Science* 192 (9 April 1976): 105–11; C. W. Sherwin and R. S. Isenson, *First Interim Report on Project Hindsight* (Washington, D.C.: Office of Director of Defense Research and Engineering, 30 June 1966, revised 13 October 1966); Illinois Institute of Technology, *Technology in Retrospect and Critical Events in Science* (Washington, D.C.: National Science Foundation, 1968).

52. Shapley and Roy, op. cit., p. 11.

53. Ibid., p. 13 (emphases added).

54. Ibid., p. 12.

55. Ibid., p. 13.

56. Roy, "Alternatives to Review by Peers," p. 317.

57. Ibid., p. 318.

58. Robert K. Merton, "The Matthew Effect in Science," in Robert K. Merton, *The Sociology of Science,* pp. 439–59; Paul D. Allison and John A. Stewart, "Productivity Differences among Scientists: The Evidence for Accumulative Advantage," *American Sociological Review* 39 (1974): 596–606.

59. Shapley and Roy, op cit., p. 9.

60. For a partial attempt, see Office of Technology Assessment, *Research Funding as an Investment: Can We Measure the Returns?,* (Washington, D.C.: U.S. Congress, April 1986).

61. See Comroe and Dripps, Sherwin and Isenson, and Illinois Institute of Technology, op. cit.

62. One such report is entitled "An Analysis of Research Publications Supported by NIH 1970–1976: NIH and NIAMDD," available through the Office of Program Planning and Evaluation, NIH, Bethesda, Md. Separate reports have been prepared for each institute, and each report has a distinctively colored cover, hence "rainbow reports."

63. A. Carl Leopold, "The Peer-Review System: Pique and Critique," *The Scientist,* July 11, 1988, pp. 11–12; D. H. Osmond, "Malice's Wonderland: Research Funding and Peer Review," *Journal of Neurobiology* 14 (2) (1983): 95–112.

64. Stephen Cole, Jonathan R. Cole, and Gary A. Simon, "Chance and Consensus in Peer Review," *Science* 214 (20 November 1981): 881–86.

65. U.S. General Accounting Office, op. cit., pp. 35–36.

66. Stevan Harnad, "Rational Disagreement in Peer Review," *Science, Technology, and Human Values* 10 (3) (Summer 1985): 59.

## CHAPTER 3

1. See, for example, *Washington Research Project v. Department of Health, Education, and Welfare,* cited in NIH Peer Review Study, 1976, vol. 2, p. F-5-1, which allowed access to the funded proposals but denied access to site visit reports and Summary "pink" Sheets.

2. NIH Grants Peer Review Study Team, *Grants Peer Review: Report to the Director, NIH Phase I* (Washington, D.C.: December, 1976); Lee Sigelman and Frank P. Scioli, Jr., "Retreading Familiar Terrain—Bias, Peer Review, and the NSF Political Science Program," *PS* Winter 1987, pp. 62–69; David Klahr, "Insiders, Outsiders, and Efficiency in a National Science Foundation Panel," *American Psychologist* 40 (2) (February 1985): 148–54; Stephen Cole, Leonard Rubin, and Jonathan R. Cole, *Peer Review in the National Science Foundation: Phase I of a Study* (Washington, D.C.: National Academy of Sciences, 1978); Jonathan R. Cole and Stephen Cole, *Peer Review in the National Science Foundation: Phase II of a Study,* (Washington, D.C.: National Academy of Sciences, 1981); NSF, *Proposal Review at NSF: Perceptions of Principal Investigators* (Washington, D.C.: NSF Report 88-4, 1988). A summary of the main findings in this last report is available as Jim McCullough, "First Comprehensive Survey of NSF Applicants Focuses on their Concerns about Proposal Review," *Science, Technology, and Human Values,* 14 (1) (Winter 1989): 78–88.

3. Rustum Roy, "Funding Science: The *Real* Defects of Peer Review and an Alternative to It," *Science, Technology, and Human Values* 10 (3) (Summer 1985): 74.

4. Cole, Rubin, and Cole, op. cit., pp. 17–19.

5. Cole and Cole, op. cit., pp. 6–11.

6. Examples of archival studies are Klahr, op. cit., and Sigelman and Scioli, op. cit. Grace Carter combines archival data with interview material and citation analyses in "Peer review, Citations, and Biomedical Research Policy: NIH Grants to Medical School Faculty," Rand Report R-1583-HEW, December 1974, and in "The Consequences of Unfunded NIH Applications for the Investigator and his Research," Rand Report R-2229-NIH, October 1978. NSF, op. cit., is a good example of the survey approach.

7. Alan L. Porter and Frederick A. Rossini, "Peer Review of Interdisciplinary Research Proposals," *Science, Technology, and Human Values* 10 (3) (Summer 1985): 33–38.

8. Edward J. Hackett, "Funding and Academic Research in the Life Sciences: Results of an Exploratory Study," *Science and Technology Studies* 5 (3/4) (1987): 134–47.

9. Gilbert W. Gillespie, Jr., Daryl E. Chubin, and George M. Kurzon, "Experience with NIH Peer Review: Researchers' Cynicism and Desire for Change," *Science, Technology, and Human Values* 10 (3) (Summer 1985): 44–53.

10. This and all quotations in this section not otherwise attributed are taken from the "Brief of the Appelles" submitted to the First Circuit Court of Appeals (No. 80-1695) and heard on February 12, 1981.

11. There was a third affidavit submitted in support of the government by a high-ranking official of the Association of American Medical Colleges. The plaintiff's case was supported by a single affidavit from Professor Rustum Roy, a materials scientist at Pennsylvania State University.

12. This is an error: heart disease is the leading cause of death in the U.S.; cancer is second.

13. Perhaps this statement was inspired by an address to the Endocrine Society by Nobel laureate Rosalyn S. Yalow (which the plaintiff attached to his brief). In this address, Yalow commented:

> If you will forgive a mixed metaphor, the peer review system as currently constituted should not be more a sacred cow than is the gas-guzzling monster we thought necessary to our transportation. We always hope for and expect a revolution in science; to make that feasible it may be necessary first to revolutionize our mechanisms for funding science.

14. Reported in L. J. Carter, "A New and Searching Look at NSF," *Science* 204 (8 June 1979): 1064; Thomas M. Vogt, "Szent-Gyorgi's Research," *Science* 203 (30 March 1979): 1293; Daniel S. Greenberg, "A Conversation with Vincent T. DeVita, Jr., M.D.," *The New England Journal of Medicine* 303 (23 October 1980): 1014.

15. Chubin has had first-hand experience with such issues: see Jonathan R. Cole and Stephen Cole, "A Comment on an Ethical Issue," and Daryl E. Chubin, "Reply to the Coles," *Contemporary Sociology* 9 (September 1980): 603–5.

16. Dorothy Nelkin, "Changing Images of Science: New Pressures on Old Stereotypes," *Newsletter 14, Program on Public Conceptions of Science* (Cambridge: Harvard University, 1975), pp. 21–31.

17. While the study of interests is central to the "strong programme in the sociology of knowledge," there are at least some skeptics about. For example, see Steve Woolgar, "Interests and Explanation in the Social Study of Science," *Social Studies of Science* 11 (1981), pp. 365–94.

18. See Gillespie et al., op. cit., for details.

19. Karl Mannheim, *Ideology and Utopia* (New York: Harcourt-Brace, 1936), p. 265.

20. McCullough, op. cit., p. 78.

21. On the NIH experience see James B. Wyngaarden, "The National Institutes of Health in its Centennial Year," *Science* 237 (21 August 1987): 871; for NSF, see NSF, op. cit., Appendix D.

22. Wyngaarden, op. cit., p. 870.

23. NIH, *Grants Peer Review,* p. 140.

24. NSF, op. cit., Appendix G, Questions 37A and 37B.

25. Ibid., p. 13.

26. Carter, "Consequences of Unfunded NIH Applications," p. 9.

27. Hackett, op. cit.

28. NSF, op. cit., p. 14.

29. Ibid., p. 15.

30. Hackett, op. cit., pp. 140–41.

31. NSF, op. cit., p. 16.

32. Hackett, op. cit., pp. 144–46.

33. Wyngaarden, op. cit., 869.

34. Hackett, op. cit., 140–41.

35. Porter and Rossini, op. cit.; NSF Advisory Committee on Peer Review, *Final Report;* NSF, *Proposal Review at NSF.*

## CHAPTER 4

1. For example, see Michael Gordon, *Running A Referee System* (Leicester, England: Primary Communications Research Center and A. B. Printers Ltd., 1983); Marcel C. La Follette, "Beyond Plagiarism: Ethical Misconduct in Scientific and Technical Publishing," *Book Research Quarterly* 4 (1989): 65–73; and idem, "Journal Peer Review and Public Policy," *Science, Technology, and Human Values,* 10 (Winter 1988): 3–5; Stephen Lock, *A Difficult Balance: Editorial Peer Review in Medicine* (London: The Nuffield Provincial Hospitals Trust, 1985).

2. For the classic work on the reward system of science, see Robert K. Merton, *The Sociology of Science* (Chicago: University of Chicago Press, 1973), and Warren O. Hagstrom, "Competition in Science," *American Sociological Review* 39 (1) (1974): 1–18. Empirical studies working in this vein include Jonathan R. Cole and Stephen Cole, *Social Stratification in Science* (Chicago: University of Chicago Press, 1973), and Jerry Gaston, *The Reward System in British and American Science* (New York: Wiley, 1978). Empirical work that raises questions about this framework and its universalistic presuppositions has been done by J. Scott Long, Robert McGinnis, and Paul D. Allison. A good point of entry is Paul D. Allison and J. Scott Long, "Interuniversity Mobility of Academic Scientists," *American Sociological Review* 52 (October 1987): 643–52. The fundamental work on the exponential growth of science is Derek J. Price, *Science Since Babylon,* enlarged edition (New Haven: Yale University Press, 1975).

3. David L. Hull, *Science as a Process: An Evolutionary Account of the Social and Conceptual Development of Science* (Chicago: University of Chicago Press, 1988).

4. This account is based on Harriet Zuckerman and Robert K. Merton, "Patterns of Evaluation in Science: Institutionalisation, Structure, and Functions of the Referee System," in Merton, op. cit., pp. 460–496, especially 462–70.

5. Henry Oldenburg, *Correspondence* 4: 223–4, quoted in Merton, op. cit., p. 468. Thomas Sprat is believed to have added authentication to reviewers' tasks. Similarly, "the members of the French Academy took authentication as one of their chief functions. Authors submitted their work,

and members of the academy actually repeated the relevant observations and experiments." (Hull, op. cit., pp. 323–4).

6. Merton, op. cit., p. 468.

7. Merton, op. cit., p. 469.

8. They have recently returned to the scene of the crime, so to speak, in analyzing misconduct in research. See Harriet Zuckerman, "The Sociology of Science," in N. Smelser, ed., *Handbook of Sociology,* (Newbury Park, Calif.: Sage, 1988), pp. 520–26.

9. Greg Myers, "Texts as Knowledge Claims: The Social Construction of Two Biology Articles," *Social Studies of Science* 15 (4) (November 1985): 593–630. See also our discussion of the "Baltimore case" in chapter 5.

10. Myers, op. cit., p. 609.

11. Merton, op. cit., pp. 491ff.; John C. Bailar III and Kay Patterson, "Journal Peer Review: The Need for a Research Agenda," *New England Journal of Medicine* 312 (10) (March 7, 1985): 654–57.

12. Lowell L. Hargens, "Patterns of Evaluation of Manuscripts Submitted to Three Scientific Journals," paper presented at the joint meetings of EASST and 4S, Amsterdam, November 1988.

13. Myers, op. cit. No better is this dramatized than by the recent agony over publication of a controversial article on AIDS. See Anthony Liversidge, "PNAS Publication of AIDS Article Spurs Debate over Peer Review," *The Scientist* 3 (3 April 1989): 1, 4–5, 19, and Igor V. Darvid et al., "PNAS Reviewing Procedures," *Science* 243 (17 March 1989): 1419.

14. The classic work is S. C. Gilfillan, *The Sociology of Invention* (Cambridge: MIT Press, 1970 [1935]), recently updated by Richard S. Campbell and A. L. Nieves, *Technology Indicators Based on Patent Data: The Case of Catalytic Converters* (Richland, Wash.: Battelle Pacific Northwest Laboratories, 1979).

15. Merton, op. cit., pp. 491ff.; Bailar and Patterson, op. cit., p. 654.

16. Merton, loc. cit.; Sheila Jasanoff, "Peer Review in the Regulatory Process," *Science, Technology, and Human Values* 10 (3) (1985): 20–32.

17. Leah Lievrouw, "Four Programs of Research in Scientific Communication," *Knowledge in Society* 1 (2) (1988): 6–22.

18. On the function of dogma in the reception and evaluation of research (foreshadowing the better-known, paradigm-driven discussion of *The Structure of Scientific Revolutions*) see Thomas S. Kuhn, "The Essential Tension: Tradition and Innovation in Scientific Research," in his col-

lection *The Essential Tension: Selected Studies in Scientific Tradition and Change* (Chicago: University of Chicago Press, 1977), pp. 225–39.

19. This rhetoric of progress permeates researchers' oral reports as well. See Daryl E. Chubin, "Scientific Progress: An Interim Report," *Bio-Science* 36 (April 1986): 234–35.

20. An excellent empirical review and critique appears in Michael J. Mahoney, "Psychology of scientists: An evaluative review," *Social Studies of Science* 9 (1979): 349–75. An extensive psychological treatment is available in Mahoney's edited volume, *Scientist as Subject* (Cambridge: Ballinger, 1976).

21. Some of these general principles were first presented in Daryl E. Chubin, "Open Science and Closed Science: Tradeoffs in a Democracy," *Science, Technology, and Human Values* 10 (2) (Spring 1985): 73–81.

22. Merton, op. cit., p. 482.

23. S. J. Ceci and D. Peters, "How Blind is Blind Review?" *American Psychologist* 39 (1984): 1491–94.

24. Hull, op. cit., p. 123; Nicholas C. Mullins, *Theory and Theory Groups in Contemporary American Sociology* (New York: Harper and Row, 1973), pp. 18, 19, 32.

25. Mullins's notion of "trusted assessorship" is apt here, as it encompasses both authors who seek presubmission commentary and editors in need of candid evaluation.

26. Merton, op. cit.

27. Hull, op. cit., pp. 168ff. The most infamous contemporary case of rolling (that is, endless) review is that accorded Stewart and Feder's analysis of errors in publications coauthored by John Darsee. See Daryl E. Chubin, "Allocating Credit and Blame in Science," *Science, Technology, and Human Values* 13 (1,2) (1988): 53–63.

28. Bailar and Patterson, loc. cit.

29. "Panel Urges Researcher be Censured over Ethics," *New York Times,* December 20, 1988; for a fuller account of the research effort, see "Researcher is Criticized for Test of Journal Bias," *New York Times,* September 27, 1988. Epstein's experience had been shared by others; see Michael J. Mahoney, "Scientific Publication and Knowledge Politics," *Journal of Social Behavior and Personality* 2 (2; Part 1) (1987): 168–9 for a brief account of his experiences and those of Peters and Ceci.

30. In 1988 the Council of Biology Editors designed and distributed for comment a series of scenarios, soliciting ingenious suggestions for re-

solving the editorial quandaries in the most ethically sound ways. They will publish a collection of scenarios and commentaries in 1990.

31. For example, see Duncan Lindsey, *The Scientific Publication System in Social Science* (San Francisco: Jossey-Bass, 1978); Janet Chase, "Normative Criteria for Scientific Publication," *American Sociologist* 5 (1970): 262–65; Domenic V. Cicchetti, Harold O. Conn, Leonard Eron, and Sandra Scarr, "The Reliability of Journal Peer Review in Behavioral and Biomedical Science" (New Haven, Conn.: Yale University, mimeo, n.d.); Lock, op. cit.

32. Domenic V. Cicchetti, "We have Met the Enemy and He is Us," *The Behavioral and Brain Sciences* 5 (1982): 205.

33. See Duncan Lindsey, "Assessing Precision in the Manuscript Review Process: A Little Better than a Dice Roll," *Scientometrics* 14 (1,2) (1988): 75–82, and Cicchetti et al., op, cit., Lowell Hargens and Jerald Herting, "Neglected Considerations in the Analysis of Agreement among Journal Referees," (mimeo, August 1989) point out the importance of using *composite* reliability to evaluate peer review.

34. We are indebted to Lowell Hargens for providing a draft of the Hargens and Herting manuscript from which these figures were taken. That manuscript, in turn, improves upon and corrects the work of Lindsey, op cit., p. 77; Arthur L. Stinchcombe and R. Ofohc, "On Journal Editing as a Probabilistic Process," *American Sociologist* 4 (1969): 116.

35. Thomas Stossel, "Reviewer Status and Review Quality," *New England Journal of Medicine* 312 (10) (7 March 1985): 658–59.

36. Gordon, op. cit.; but see Zuckerman and Merton, op. cit., pp. 489–91 for a contrasting finding.

37. Cicchetti, op. cit.

38. Janice B. Lodahl and Gerald A. Gordon, "The Structure of Scientific Fields and the Functioning of University Graduate Departments," *American Sociological Review* 37 (1972): 57–72.

39. Lowell Hargens, "Scholarly Consensus and Journal Rejection Rates," *American Sociological Review* 53 (1988): 139–51.

40. Stephen Cole, Gary Simon, and Jonathan R. Cole, "Do Journal Rejection Rates Index Consensus?" *American Sociological Review* 53 (1988): 152–56; Stephen Cole, "The Hierarchy of the Sciences?" *American Journal of Sociology* 89 (1983): 111–39.

41. Cognitive style is a component of each explanation. This intrapersonal trait influences authors, reviewers, and editors to act in a certain way. Unfortunately, cognitive style and its effects are seldom studied, so we have little idea of the distribution of such attributes and their cor-

relations with other behaviors. A thorough discussion of cognitive style in science is available in Ian I. Mitroff, *The Subjective Side of Science: A Philosophical Enquiry into the Psychology of the Apollo Moon Scientists* (New York: Elsevier, 1974).

42. Michael Mahoney, "Publication Prejudices: An Experimental Study of Confirmatory Bias in the Peer Review System," *Cognitive Therapy and Research* 1 (2) (1977): 161–75.

43. Ibid, p. 164.

44. Ibid, p. 173.

45. Lowell Hargens made this point in a personal communication. We are grateful that he urged us to reexamine technical aspects of Mahoney's study.

46. Hull, op. cit., p. 335; see also pp. 172–73 for a similar instance in which referees encouraged publication so they could "execute" the author, "blast him out of the water."

47. Bailar and Patterson, op. cit.

48. See Douglas P. Peters and Stephen J. Ceci, "Peer-Review Practices of Psychological Journals: The Fate of Published Articles, Submitted Again," *The Behavioral and Brain Sciences* 5 (1982): 187–255, for these results and an extended presentation of peer commentary on the research, its findings, and the general issues it addresses.

49. Ibid, p. 190.

50. Ibid, pp. 192–93. Note that this conclusion is quite controversial and that even Peters and Ceci offer extended qualifications. The interested reader should examine the peer commentary appended to the Peters and Ceci article for an airing of these issues.

51. Von Bakanic, Clark McPhail, and Rita J. Simon, "The Manuscript Review and Decision-making Process," *American Sociological Review* 52 (1987): 631–42.

52. Ibid, table 1, p. 636.

53. Our argument must be tempered somewhat in light of the low reliability of referees' evaluations. In a multiple regression framework, low reliability means that the "signal" of the average rating is surrounded by the substantial "noise" of random (and, perhaps, nonrandom) error. This will reduce the validity and reliability of average rating as a measure of the "true" quality of a manuscript and will attentuate the correlation between average rating and final disposition. Briefly stated, it is possible that editors' apparently particularistic judgments are necessary remedies for reviewers' misjudgments. Perhaps so. But there is no evi-

dence that editors' judgments are any more reliable or valid than referees' judgments. And Bakanic et al. offer neither the measurement error argument nor the superior judgment argument in support of their conclusions.

54. Ibid, p. 637.

55. Ibid, p. 640.

56. Lock, op. cit., p. 30.

57. Hull, op. cit., p. 168–9.

58. Maurice Crosland, "Assessment by Peers in Nineteenth Century France: The Manuscript Reports on Candidates for Election to the Academie des Sciences," *Minerva* 24 (Winter 1986): 413–32.

59. Ina Spiegel-Rosing, *"Science Studies*: Bibliometric and Content Analysis," *Social Studies of Science* 7 (February 1977): 97–113. This article profiles all full-length articles published in the first four volumes of *Science Studies* (n = 66) or, as the author puts it, "one aspect of its collective self-presentation: this is what the authors want and claim to be relevant for; what the Editors of *Science Studies* get; and what they and their referees approve of" (p. 110). Our analysis complements this work, representing the other side of the refereeing coin.

60. Methodological deficiencies were offered as grounds for rejecting the "recycled" manuscripts submitted to psychology journals in the Ceci and Peters experiment.

61. Bailar and Patterson, op. cit., make a similar call for research.

62. G. Nigel Gilbert, "Refereeing as Persuasion," *Social Studies of Science* 7 (1977): 113–22; Michael J. Mulkay, "Methodology in the Sociology of Science," *Social Science Information* 13 (1974): 107–19.

63. Zuckerman and Merton, op. cit.

64. Thomas Stossel, "Beyond Rejection: A User's View of Peer Review," paper presented at the Conference on Ethics and Policy in Scientific Publication, sponsored by the Council of Biology Editors, Inc., held at the National Academy of Sciences, Washington, D.C., October 18, 1988.

65. Mary Glenn Wiley, Kathleen S. Crittenden, and Laura D. Birg, "Why a Rejection? Causal Attribution of a Career Achievement Event," *Social Psychology Quarterly* 42 (1979): 214–22.

66. Charles McCutcheon, "An Evolved Conspiracy," *New Scientist*, April 29, 1976, p. 225.

67. For a spectacular example of vicious language, see Hull, op. cit., p. 325; see also Lock, op. cit., p. 55.

68. Stevan Harnad, "Creative Disagreement," *The Sciences,* September 1979, p. 18.

69. Nicholas Wade, "Medical Journal Draws Lancet on Rival," *Science* 211 (February 6, 1981): 561.

70. James E. Lloyd, "Male Photuris Fireflies Mimic Sexual Signals of their Females' Prey," *Science* 210 (November 7, 1980): 669–71.

71. Hull, op. cit., pp. 181–82.

72. Leroy P. Zorn, Jr., and Albert D. Carson, "Effect of Mating on Response of Female Photuris Firefly," *Animal Behavior* 26 (1978): 843–47.

73. James E. Lloyd, "Selling Scholarship down the River: The Pernicious Aspects of Peer Review," *The Chronicle of Higher Education* 30 (June 26, 1985): 64.

74. Daryl E. Chubin, "Research Malpractice," *Bioscience* 35 (February 1985): 80–89; Daniel Herxheimer, "Make Scientific Journals More Responsive—and Responsible," *The Scientist* (20 March 1989): 9–11; Murray Saffran, "On Multiple Authorship: Describe the Contribution," *The Scientist* 3 (20 March 1989): 9.

75. Daryl E. Chubin and Sheila Jasanoff, "Peer Review and Public Policy," *Science, Technology, and Human Values* 10 (3) (1985): 3–5.

76. This elite has become increasingly reflective about peer review in recent years. The latest evidence is a 1989 conference, sponsored by the American Medical Association, which brought together a variety of interested parties to consider the journal peer review system. See Marjorie Sun, "Peer Review Comes Under Peer Review," *Science* 244 (26 May 1989): 910–12; Tabitha Powledge, "Now It's the Journals' Turn on the Firing Line," *AAAS Observer* (Supplement to *Science* 7 July 1989 No. 6): 1.

77. Daryl E. Chubin, "Scientific Progress," op. cit.

## CHAPTER 5

1. Patricia K. Woolf, "Deception in Scientific Research," *Jurimetrics: Journal of Law, Science, and Technology* 29 (Fall 1988): 67–95; Daryl E. Chubin, "Research Malpractice," *BioScience* 35 (February 1985): 80–89; Chubin, "Misconduct in Research: An Issue of Science Policy and Practice," *Minerva* 23 (Summer 1985): 175–202.

2. Barbara J. Culliton, "Random Audit of Papers Proposed," *Science* 242 (4 November 1988): 657–58; Adil E. Shamoo, "We Need Data Audit," *AAAS Observer* no. 2 (4 November 1989): 4.

3. Division of Policy Research and Analysis, National Science Foundation, *Distribution of U.S. Academic Research Activity: An Economic View,* Working Draft (Washington, D.C.: NSF, September 1988).

4. Arnold Relman, "Lessons from the Darsee Affair," *New England Journal of Medicine* 308 (23) (9 June 1983): 1415–17.

5. J. R. Ravetz, *Scientific Knowledge and Its Social Problems* (Oxford: Oxford University Press, 1971).

6. Michael Polanyi, *The Tacit Dimension* (Garden City, N.Y.: Doubleday-Anchor, 1966).

7. Daryl E. Chubin and T. Connolly, "Research Trails and Science Policies: Local and Extra-Local Negotiation of Scientific Work," in N. Elias et al., eds., *Scientific Establishments and Hierarchies,* Sociology of the Sciences Yearbook, vol. 6, (Dordrecht: D. Reidel, 1982), pp. 293–311.

8. Daryl E. Chubin, "Scientific Malpractice and the Contemporary Politics of Knowledge," forthcoming in S. E. Cozzens and T. F. Gieryn, eds., *Theories of Science in Society* (Bloomington, Ind.: Indiana University Press, 1990).

9. Sal Restivo, "Modern Science as a Social Problem," *Social Problems* 35 (3) (June 1988): 206–25.

10. The norms of science were originally formulated by Robert K. Merton in "Science and the Social Order" (1938) and "The Normative Structure of Science" (1942), which are most accessible in Merton, *The Sociology of Science* (Chicago: University of Chicago Press, 1973), pp. 254–78. Ian I. Mitroff, in "Norms and Counternorms in a Select Group of the Apollo Moon Scientists: A Case Study of the Ambivalence of Scientists," *American Sociological Review* 39 (1974): 579–95, proposes that these norms are in tension with a set of counternorms, and invokes the notion of sociological ambivalence to explain how scientists experience and resolve the conflict.

11. Michael J. Mulkay, "Norms and Ideology in Science," *Social Science Information* 15 (1976): 637–56; Daryl E. Chubin, "Research Missions and the Public: Overselling and Buying the U.S. War on Cancer," in J. C. Petersen, ed., *Citizen Participation in Science Policy,* (Amherst: University of Massachusetts Press, 1984), pp. 101–29; Chubin and Alan L. Porter, *Measuring Scientific Output: A Collective Biography Approach,* final report to the National Science Foundation, Grant No. PRA84–13060, 1986.

12. Chubin, "Scientific Malpractice."

13. Charles Babbage, *Reflections on the Decline of Science in England and on Some of Its Causes,* (London: B. Fellowes and J. Booth, 1830).

14. See Woolf, op. cit., for a summary of cases.

15. William Broad and Nicholas Wade, *Betrayers of the Truth,* (New York: Simon and Schuster, 1982); Daryl E. Chubin, "They Blinded us with 'Science'?" *Science, Technology, and Human Values* 8 (1983): 23–29; Dorothy Nelkin, *Science as Intellectual Property,* (New York: MacMillan, 1984).

16. R. A. Knox, "Study Says Schools Lack Means to Deal with Research Fraud," *Boston Globe,* 21 June 1985.

17. Judith P. Swazey and S. R. Scher, eds., *Whistleblowing in Biomedical Research* (Washington, D.C.: USGPO, 1982).

18. P. J. Greene et al., "Policies for Responding to Allegations of Fraud in Research," *Minerva* 23 (Summer 1985): 203–15.

19. National Institutes of Health, "Policies and Procedures for Dealing with Possible Misconduct in Science," *NIH Guide for Grants and Contracts* 15 (11) (18 July 1986); Institute of Medicine, *The Responsible Conduct of Research in the Health Sciences,* (Washington, D.C.: National Academy Press, 1989); Responsibilities of Awardee and Applicant Institutions for Dealing with and Reporting Possible Misconduct in Science," *NIH Guide* 18 (1 September 1989): 1–18.

20. Daryl E. Chubin, "Misconduct in Research: A Congressional Perspective," presented at the conference on Trust, Misconduct, and the Integrity of Biomedical Research, College of Physicians and Surgeons of Columbia University, October 1988.

21. *New York Times,* "Scientists Who Hog Data," 28 July 1985, p. 22; S. E. Fienberg et al., *Sharing Research Data,* (Washington, D.C.: National Academy Press, 1988).

22. Broad and Wade, op. cit., pp. 171–80.

23. Kim McDonald, " 'Ethical Offenses' by Scholars Said to Harm Science and its Journals," *The Chronicle of Higher Education* 30 (5 June 1985): 7, 9.

24. Relman, op. cit.

25. Barbara J. Culliton, "Baltimore Cleared of All Fraud Charges," *Science* 243 (10 February 1989): 727–28.

26. David Baltimore, letter, 17 May 1988. The publications are "Baltimore's Travels," *Issues in Science and Technology* (Summer 1989), 48–54 and "Self-Regulation of Science," *Technology Review* (August/September 1989), 20.

27. Margot O'Toole, "Scientists Must be Able to Disclose Colleagues' Mistakes without Risking their Own Jobs or Financial Support," *The*

*Chronicle of Higher Education,* 25 January 1989, p. A44. For more detail see Philip Weiss, "Conduct Unbecoming," *The New York Times Sunday Magazine,* October 29, 1989: 40.

28. Baltimore, op. cit., p. 3.

29. Ibid., pp. 4–5.

30. Ibid., p. 5.

31. O'Toole, op. cit.

32. Baltimore, op. cit., p. 7.

33. Ibid., p. 6.

34. Ibid., p. 7.

35. Ibid., pp. 7–8.

36. Ibid., p. 7.

37. Ibid., p. 8.

38. Ibid.

39. O'Toole, op. cit.

40. David L. Wheeler, "Nobelist Found Guilty of Errors in Paper, but Innocent of Fraud," *The Chronicle of Higher Education,* 8 February 1989, pp. A1, A9.

41. Culliton, "Baltimore Cleared."

42. Wheeler, op. cit.

43. Culliton, "Baltimore Cleared"; Wheeler, op. cit.

44. Baltimore, quoted in Culliton, "Baltimore Cleared," p. 727.

45. O'Toole, quoted ibid.

46. Ibid.

47. Wheeler, op. cit., p. A9.

48. O'Toole, op. cit.

49. Ibid.

50. Sheila Slaughter, "Academic Freedom and the State: Reflections on the Use of Knowledge," *Journal of Higher Education* 59 (3) (1988): 241–62; Edward J. Hackett, "Science as a Vocation in the 1990s," *Journal of Higher Education,* forthcoming (1990).

51. Baltimore, op. cit., p. 9.

52. Max Weber, "Science as a Vocation," in Hans Gerth and C. Wright Mills, eds., *From Max Weber: Essays in Sociology,* (New York, Oxford University Press, 1946 [1918]), pp. 29–58.

53. See David E. Drew, *Strengthening Academic Science* (New York: Praeger, 1985), pp. 22–43 for a summary.

54. This position was attributed to Senator Kilgore. See Drew, op. cit., p. 23.

55. Quoted in Drew, op. cit., p. 23.

56. Drew, op. cit., pp. 23–24.

57. Ibid., p. 25 (emphasis added).

58. Pp. 14–15 of the report, quoted in Drew, op. cit., pp. 25–26.

59. P. 28 of the report, quoted in Drew, op. cit., p. 26.

60. See Drew, op. cit., for a summary and evaluation of these programs.

61. Colleen Cordes, "Colleges Received about $289 Million in Earmarked Funds," *The Chronicle of Higher Education,* 1 February 1989, pp. A1, A20–21; Cordes, "Congressional Practice of Earmarking Research Grants Does Not Broaden Allocation of Funds, Study Says," *The Chronicle of Higher Education,* 1 March 1989, pp. A17–A18.

62. Kin Ha, David Lipin, and Bruce Cain, "Pork-Barrelling of Science Funds," mimeo, 1989; Cordes, op. cit., both works cited.

63. Quoted in Cordes, "Colleges Received . . . ," p. A20.

64. Ibid.

65. Constance Holden, "Lobbying Urged for Facilities Funds," *Science* 229 (9 August 1985): 540.

66. "Direct University Facility Funding by Congress," *The Blue Sheet,* 3 July 1985, p. 5.

67. Eamon Kelly, president of Tulane University, quoted in Cordes, "Congressional Practice," p. A18.

68. Colin Norman, "AAU Renounces Pork," *Science* 236 (22 May 1987): 909.

69. *Washington Post,* "Merit and Money," 1 June 1987, p. A11.

70. Colin Norman, "When Did We Agree that Peers Would Cut the Melon?" *Science* 233 (11 July 1986): 146.

71. Colin Norman, "House Endorses Pork Barrel Funding," *Science* 236 (8 August 1986): 617.

72. Lois Ember, "Research Porkbarrel: Senator Assails Lobbying Practices," *Chemical & Engineering News* (7 August 1989): 4.

73. Vannevar Bush, *Science: The Endless Frontier* (Washington, D.C.: National Science Foundation, 1960 [1945]), p. 5.

74. Ibid., p. 19 (emphasis original).

75. Julius H. Comroe, Jr., and Robert D. Dripps, "Scientific Basis for the Support of Biomedical Science," *Science 192* (9 April 1976): 105–11; C. W. Sherwin and R. S. Isenson, *First Interim Report on Project Hindsight* (Washington, D.C.: Office of Director of Defense Research and Engineering, 30 June 1966, revised 13 October 1966); Illinois Institute of Technology, *Technology in Retrospect and Critical Events in Science* (Washington, D.C.: National Science Foundation, 1968).

76. NSF Advisory Group on Merit Review, *Final Report* (Washington, D.C.: NSF, 1986).

77. *New York Times*, "The Dracula of Medical Technology," and "(Senators) Doctors Kennedy and Hatch," 15 July 1988.

78. Mark Crawford, "USDA Grants Program Threatened," *Science* 241 (1 July 1988): 21.

79. *Washington Post*, op. cit.

80. Robert Rosenzweig, "Which Policy for High-Quality Science?" *Washington Post*, June 8, 1987, p. A12.

81. Daniel E. Koshland, "Addons and Catchons," *Science* 229 (2 August 1985): 5.

82. Nicholas Wade, "Why Government Should Not Fund Science," *Science* 210 (3 October 1980): 33. *Free to Choose*, the book and the television series, presents the Friedman world view.

83. This is elaborated in Wil Lepkowski and Daryl E. Chubin, "U.S. Science Policy in the Reagan Era: Some Critical Thoughts," American Association for the Advancement of Science, Los Angeles, May 1985. Also see Wil Lepkowski, "Tax Policy Effect on High Tech Assessed," *Chemical and Engineering News* 63 (12 August 1985): 26.

84. *Time*, "A Jeremiad from Academe," 30 April 1979, p. 52.

85. Examples of work in this vein include Slaughter, op. cit., Hackett, op. cit., Stuart W. Leslie, "Playing the Education Game to Win: The Military and Interdisciplinary Research at Stanford," *Historical Studies in the Physical Sciences* 18 (1) (1987): 56–88.

86. Weber, op. cit.; Thorstein Veblen, *The Higher Learning in America: A Memorandum on the Conduct of Universities by Business Men* (New York: Viking, 1918).

87. These matters are discussed in chapters 2 and 3. See also Allan H. Clark, "Luck, Merit and Peer Review," *Science* 215 (1 January 1982): 11; C. H. E. Weatherbee, "Peer Review and Chance," *Clinical Chemistry News* 8 (January 1982): 4.

## CHAPTER 6

1. For a first-person retrospective, see E. Garfield, *Essays of an Information Scientist,* vol. 1, 1962–73, and vol. 2, 1974–76 (Philadelphia: ISI Press, 1977). For examples, see E. Garfield, I. Sher, and R. Torpie, *The Use of Citation Data in Writing the History of Science* (Philadelphia: Institute for Scientific Information, 1964); D. de Solla Price, "Networks of Scientific Papers," *Science* 149 (30 July 1965): 510–515; and de Solla Price, "Is Technology Historically Independent of Science? A Study in Statistical Historiography," *Technology and Culture* 6 (Fall 1965): 553–68.

2. The benchmark is D. de S. Price, *Little Science, Big Science* (New York: Columbia University Press, 1963).

3. For reviews, see Y. Elkana et al., eds., *Toward A Metric of Science: The Advent of Science Indicators* (New York: Wiley-Interscience, 1978); F. Narin, "Objectivity Versus Relevance in Studies of Scientific Advance," *Scientometrics* 1 (September 1978): 35–41. The use of projected citation data in a controversial promotion and tenure case is described in N. L. Geller, J. S. De Cani, and R. E. Davies, "Lifetime-Citation Rates to Compare Scientists' Work," *Social Science Research* 7 (1978): 345–65.

4. Co-founded in 1978 by Garfield and Price, *Scientometrics* became the flagship journal of bibliometrics. Its contributors seem to come primarily from information science, psychology, and sociology. Other spurs to the institutionalization and visibility of bibliometrics have been the National Science Board's biennial *Science Indicators* series (begun in 1972 and renamed *Science and Engineering Indicators* in 1987) and the ongoing work of the Institute for Scientific Information (especially Henry Small) and Francis Narin's Computer Horizons, Inc. (discussed below). For historical perspectives on the development of this specialty, see D. E. Chubin, "Beyond Invisible Colleges: Inspirations and Aspirations of Post-1972 Social Studies of Science," *Scientometrics* 6 (1985): 221–54; Chubin and S.

Restivo, "The 'Mooting' of Science Studies: Strong Programs and Science Policy," in K. D. Knorr-Cetina and M. Mulkay, eds., *Science Observed* (London and Beverly Hills: Sage, 1983), pp. 58–83. Also see the special issue of *Scientometrics* 6 (1985) dedicated to the memory of Derek Price.

5. Various policy literatures—distinguished as evaluation research, educational research, knowledge utilization, R&D management, etc.—make this point. For discussions of how context, content, and actors interact—more or less successfully—in the policy process, consult D. Krathwohl, *Social and Behavioral Science Research: A New Framework for Conceptualizing, Implementing, and Evaluating Research Studies* (San Francisco: Jossey Bass, 1985); C. E. Lindblom and D. K. Cohen, *Usable Knowledge: Social Science and Social Problem Solving* (New Haven: Yale University Press, 1979); L. Lynn, ed., *Knowledge and Policy: The Uncertain Connection* (Washington, D.C.: National Academy of Sciences, 1978); A. Majchrzak, *Methods for Policy Research* (Beverly Hills: Sage, 1984); M. Rein, *Social Science and Public Policy* (New York: Penguin, 1976).

6. Project Hindsight, the TRACES study, the aforementioned *Science Indicators* series, and related efforts supported by the U.S. National Science Foundation, as well as by the National Institutes of Health and the Department of Defense can be cited. See F. Narin, *Evaluative Bibliometrics: The Use of Citation Analysis in the Evaluation of Scientific Activity* (Cherry Hill, N.J.: Computer Horizons, Inc., 1976).

7. These are touted, debated, and assailed in D. E. Chubin, "The Conceptualization of Scientific Specialties," *The Sociological Quarterly* 17 (Autumn 1976): 448–76; Chubin, "Constructing and Reconstructing Scientific Reality: A Meta-Analysis," *International Society for the Sociology of Knowledge Newsletter* 7 (May 1981): 22–28; S. E. Cozzens, "Taking the Measure of Science: A Review of Citation Theories," *ISSK Newsletter* 7 (May 1981): 16–21; D. Edge, "Quantitative Measures of Communication in Science: A Critical Review," *History of Science* 17 (1979): 102–134; and in various chapters of Elkana et al., op. cit.

8. The seminal work here is D. Crane, *Invisible Colleges: Diffusion of Knowledge in Scientific Communities* (Chicago: University of Chicago Press, 1972); B. C. Griffith and N. C. Mullins, "Coherent Social Groups in Scientific Change," *Science* 177 (15 September 1972): 959–64; N. C. Mullins, "The Development of a Scientific Specialty: The Phage Group and the Origins of Molecular Biology," *Minerva* 10 (1972): 52–82; Mullins, *Theories and Theory Groups in Contemporary American Sociology* (New York: Harper and Row, 1973); and the Garfield/ISI "Corporate Index" that lists publications by institution of author.

9. The methodological groundwork for co-citation analysis is presented in B. C. Griffith et al., "The Structure of Scientific Literatures II: Toward a Macro- and Micro-Structure for Science," *Science Studies* 4

(1974): 339–65; H. G. Small, "Co-citation in the Scientific Literature: A New Measure of the Relationship between Two Documents," *Journal of the American Society for Information Science* 24 (1973): 265–69; Small, "Multiple Citation Patterns in Scientific Literature: The Circle and Hill Models," *Information Storage and Retrieval* 10 (1974): 393–402; Small and B. C. Griffith, "The Structure of Scientific Literatures I: Identifying and Graphing Specialties," *Science Studies* 4 (1974): 17–40.

10. Noteworthy illustrations are discussed in Chubin, "The Conceptualization of Scientific Specialties," and G. N. Gilbert, "Measuring the Growth of Science: A Review of Indicators of Scientific Growth," *Scientometrics* 1 (1978): 9–34.

11. For example, in 1969, Price's "Measuring the Size of Science," *Proceedings of the Israeli Academy of Sciences and Humanities* 4: 98–111, tied national publication activity to percent of GNP allotted to R&D. By 1975, Narin and Carpenter ("National Publication and Citation Comparisons," *JASIS* 26: 80–93) were computing shares, on a nation-by-nation basis, of the world literature, and characterizing interrelations among journals (F. Narin, M. Carpenter, and N. C. Berlt, "Interrelationship of Scientific Journals," *JASIS* 23 [1972]: 323–31), as well as the content of the literature in broad fields (Narin, Carpenter, G. Pinski, and H. H. Gee, "Structure of the Biomedical Literature," *JASIS* 27 (1976): 25–45. These analyses employed algorithms for tallying, weighing, and linking keywords in article titles to citations aggregated to journals and authors' nation of affiliation at the time of publication. Some would call this methodology "crude", while others would herald its "sophistication" for discerning patterns in an otherwise massive and perplexing literature. The latter is precisely the mentality guiding the *Science Indicators* volumes and foreshadowed in two other pioneering papers of the first generation: E. Garfield, "Citation Indexing for Studying Science," *Nature* 227 (1970): 659–71; D. de S. Price, "Citation Measures of Hard Science, Soft Science, Technology and Non-Science," in C. Nelson and D. Pollock, eds., *Communication among Scientists and Engineers* (Lexington, Mass.: D.C. Heath, 1970), pp. 3–22. As we learn more about the role of interests in shaping science, the term "science of science" seems less complimentary.

12. An important forum was the Institute for Scientific Information Conference on the Use of Citation Data in the Study of Science, Elkridge, Md. April 1975. Representative publications include M. J. Ivory et al., *Citation Analysis: An Annotated Bibliography* (Philadelphia: Institute for Scientific Information, 1976); H. Zuckerman and R. B. Miller, eds., "Science Indicators: Implications for Research and Policy (Special Issue)," *Scientometrics* 2 (1980): 327–448; and E. Garfield, M. V. Malin, and H. Small, "Citation Data as Science Indicators," in Y. Elkana et al., eds., op. cit., pp. 179–207.

13. A one-person campaign to measure the economic returns on investment is being waged by E. Mansfield; for example, see Edwin Mans-

field, Anthony Romeo, Mark Schwartz, David Teece, Samuel Wagner, Peter Brach, *Technology Transfer, Productivity, and Economic Policy* (New York: Norton, 1982). See also Harvey Averch, *A Strategic Analysis of Science and Technology Policy* (Baltimore, Md.: Johns Hopkins Press, 1985), and U.S. Congress, Office of Technology Assessment, *Research as an Investment: Can We Measure the Returns?* (Washington, D.C.: U.S. Government Printing Office, 1986).

14. N. Wade, "Citation Analysis: A New Tool for Science Administrators," *Science* 188 (2 May 1975): 429.

15. Ibid., p. 430.

16. Ibid., p. 431.

17. E. Garfield, "Is Citation Analysis a Legitimate Evaluation Tool?" *Scientometrics* 1 (1979): 359–75.

18. Ibid., p. 360.

19. D. E. Chubin and S. Moitra, "Content Analysis of References: Adjunct or Alternative to Citation Counting?" *Social Studies of Science* 5 (1975): 423–41; M. J. Moravcsik and P. Murugesan, "Some Results on the Function and Quality of Citations," *Social Studies of Science* 5 (1975): 86–92; H. G. Small, "Citation Documents as Concept Symbols," *Social Studies of Science* 8 (1978): 427–40; H. Small and E. Greenlee, "Citation Context Analysis of a Co-Citation Cluster: Recombinant DNA," *Scientometrics* 2 (1980): 277–301.

20. Multiple operationalizations of citation are rationalized and discussed in Cozzens, op. cit., Garfield, op. cit., and Narin, *Evaluative Bibliometrics*. Their application to the evaluation of individual scientists (in this case, physicists), and a proposed recommendation as to the distribution of research funds based on the twenty-percent minority that is both highly published and highly cited, is found in a controversial paper—overwhelmingly repudiated by physicists in "letters to the editor" (e.g., *Science* 183 [1974])—by J. R. Cole and S. Cole, "The Ortega Hypothesis," *Science* 178 (1972): 368–75. For a fuller treatment of citations, see Cole and Cole, *Social Stratification in Science* (Chicago: University of Chicago Press, 1973).

21. Some *insist* on this insider collaboration—needlessly, we think. See, for example, David Edge's explanation of his collaboration with Michael Mulkay on their history of radio astronomy as presented in "Quantitative Measures of Communication," *History of Science* 17 (1979): 102–34.

22. D. O. Edge and M. J. Mulkay, *Astronomy Transformed: The Emergence of Radio Astronomy in Britain* (New York: Wiley, 1976).

23. D. Sullivan, D. H. White, and E. J. Barboni, "The State of a Science: Indicators in the Specialty of Weak Interactions," *Social Studies of Science* 7 (1977): 167–200; Sullivan, White, and Barboni, "Co-Citation

Analyses of Science: An Evaluation," *Social Studies of Science* 7 (1977): 223–40; D. Sullivan et al., "Understanding Rapid Theoretical Change in Particle Physics: A Month-by-Month Co-Citation Analysis," *Scientometrics* 2 (1980): 309–19.

24. H. G. Small, "A Co-Citation Model of a Scientific Specialty: A Longitudinal Study of Collagen Research," *Social Studies of Science* 7 (1977): 139–66.

25. This quandary appears in D. E. Chubin and K. E. Studer, "Knowledge and Structures of Scientific Growth: Measurement of a Cancer Problem Domain," *Scientometrics* 1 (1979): 171–93; and Chubin and Studer, *The Cancer Mission: Social Contexts of Biomedical Research* (Beverly Hills: Sage, 1980). For a contrasting approach to the same research specialty (reverse transcriptase)—starting with co-citation clusters and blockmodeling or partitioning members to reveal social structure—see N. C. Mullins et al., "The Group Structure of Co-Citation Clusters: A Comparative Study," *American Sociological Review* 42 (1977): 552–62.

26. Outsider analysts with a policy orientation typically compare their "independent" findings against a panel of insiders' expert judgments. This recourse to authority is politically savvy, and for example, has become standard in Narin's methodology (discussed below). For an early effort, see G. M. Carter, *Peer Review, Citations, and Biomedical Research Policy: NIH Grants to Medical School Faculty*, Rand Report R-1583-HEW (Santa Monica: Rand Corporation, 1974). Recent discussion can be found in A. F. J. van Raan, ed., *Handbook of the Quantitative Study of Science and Technology* (Amsterdam: Elsevier, 1988).

27. Garfield, "Is Citation Analysis . . . ," p. 373.

28. S. E. Cozzens, Editor's Introduction, in "Funding and Knowledge Growth," Theme Section, *Social Studies of Science* 16 (1986).

29. "Evaluation Proposals, Phases I and II," NIMH Memoranda, 1983 and 1985.

30. The objective of this project is to estimate knowledge returns from the U.S. war on cancer. What has been the extent and character of NCI funding in the cancer literature: are highly-cited papers and authors supported by NCI grants and contracts? More on this genre of study is presented below. See also F. Narin and R. T. Shapiro, "The Extramural Role of the NIH as a Research Support Agency," *Federation Proceedings* 36 (October 1977): 2470–75.

31. See M. P. Carpenter, F. Narin, and P. Woolf, "Citation Rates to Technologically Important Patents," *World Patent Information* 3 (1981): 161–63, and various case study reports on patent activity emanating from Battelle's Pacific Northwest Laboratories, for example, R. S. Campbell

and L. O. Levine, *Technology Indicators Based on Citation Data: Three Case Studies*, Phase II Report Prepared for the National Science Foundation, Grant PRA 78-20321 and Contract 2311102578, May 1984.

32. J. Irvine and B. R. Martin, *Foresight in Science: Picking the Winners* (London: Frances Pinter, 1984). See especially B. R. Martin and J. Irvine, "Assessing Basic Research: Some Partial Indicators of Scientific Progress in Radio Astronomy," *Research Policy* 12 (1983): 61–90.

33. The quotation is from B. R. Martin and J. Irvine, "Evaluating the Evaluators: A Reply to Our Critics," *Social Studies of Science* 15 (1985): 561. The critics to whom Irvine and Martin reply are J. Krige and D. Pestre, "A Critique of Irvine and Martin's Methodology for Evaluating Big Science," *Social Studies of Science* 15 (1985): 525–29; H. F. Moed and A. F. J. van Raan, "Critical Remarks on Irvine and Martin's Methodology for Evaluating Scientific Performance," *Social Studies of Science* 15 (1985): 548–54; and H. M. Collins, "The Possibilities of Science Policy," *Social Studies of Science* 15 (1985): 554–58.

34. Krige and Pestre, op. cit., p. 526.

35. Ibid., p. 533.

36. Irvine and Martin, "Evaluating the Evaluators," p. 566.

37. Krige and Pestre, op. cit., p. 527.

38. Ibid., p. 530 (emphases original).

39. J. W. Servos, "Trends of Chemistry [Review of Thackray et al.'s *Chemistry in America, 1876–1976: Historical Indicators*]," *Science* 230 (November 1985): 800.

40. Irving and Martin, "Evaluating the Evaluators," p. 568.

41. Collins, op. cit., p. 558.

42. Krige and Pestre, op. cit., p. 531.

43. Ibid., p. 530.

44. Ibid., p. 529.

45. Ibid., p. 537.

46. Irvine and Martin, "Evaluating the Evaluators," p. 563.

47. Moed and van Raan, op. cit., pp. 541–42.

48. A. Weinberg, "Criteria of Scientific Choice," *Minerva* 1 (1962): 159–71. Also see H. Brooks, "The Problem of Research Priorities," *Daedalus* 107 (Spring 1978): 171–90.

49. Krige and Pestre, op. cit., p. 533.

50. Moed and van Raan, op. cit., p. 541.

51. Irvine and Martin, op. cit., p. 573.

52. Such as the classification of types of R&D and the longer-term "noncognitive" aims of science policy.

53. For an unacknowledged forerunner of Irvine and Martin's approach, coming out of a different intellectual tradition and context (management science at the National Cancer Institute) but with a similar orientation, see L. M. Carrese and C. G. Baker, "The Convergence Technique: A Method for the Planning and Programming of Research Efforts," *Management Science* 13 (1967): 420–38. Compare Krige and Pestre, op. cit., p. 536; and Moed and van Raan, op. cit., p. 547.

54. Despite its cross-cultural reflections, Martin and Irvine's latest book, *Research Foresight:* Priority-Setting in Science (London: Frances Pinter, 1989), also seems not to have closed this gap.

55. See Michel Callon, John Law, and Arie Rip, eds., *Mapping the Dynamics of Science and Technology* (London: MacMillan, 1986) for an overview of this work.

56. M. Callon et al., "The Translation Model and Its Exploration through Co-Word Analysis: Using Graphs for Negotiating Research Policies," mimeo: Centre de Sociologie, Ecole des Mines de Paris, and Centre National de la Recherche Scientifique, CDST, Paris, (mimeo, 1985) p. 1.

57. Ibid., p. 5.

58. Arie Rip and Jean-Pierre Courtial, "Co-Word Maps of Biotechnology: An Example of Cognitive Scientometrics," *Scientometrics* 6 (1984): 385.

59. Ibid., pp. 394–95.

60. See the program statement in M. Callon et al., "From Translations to Problematic Networks: An Introduction to Co-Word Analysis," *Social Science Information* 22 (1983): 191–235; Callon, et al., "The Translation Model," p. 2.

61. Ibid., pp. 8–9.

62. This point is stressed in D. E. Chubin, "Evaluating Research Programs: Design Decisions and their Consequences—A 'Science Studies' Approach," Final Report to the Research Planning and Evaluation Branch, National Institute of Mental Health, July 1985.

63. Derek J. Price, "The Science/Technology Relationship, the Craft of Experimental Science, and Policy for the Improvement of High Technology Innovation," *Research Policy* 13 (1984): 3–20.

64. S. E. Cozzens, "Introductory Remarks, Background Materials, and Executive Summaries," Workshop on Federal Funding and Knowledge Growth in Subfields and Specialties of Science, Division of Policy Research and Analysis, National Science Foundation, May 1983.

65. Ibid., p. 2.

66. Efforts to grapple with the policy framework are reflected in European conferences, such as that resulting in the Ciba Foundation, *The Evaluation of Scientific Research* 1989, in volumes such as *Science and Technology Policy Outlook 1988* (Organization for Economic Co-operation and Development, 1988), and the current surge of interest in priority-setting for science in the U.S. (On this see the National Academy of Sciences report, *Federal Science and Technology Budget Priorities: New Perspectives and Procedures* [Washington, D.C.: National Academy Press, 1988].)

67. Carlos Kruytbosch, "Comments," *Social Studies of Science* 16 (1) (1986): 142–44.

68. This is also the spirit of the "finalization" thesis, the policy direction of theoretically mature science, championed in the 1970s by West German sociologists of science. See, for example, G. Boehme, W. van den Daele, and W. Krohn, "Finalization of Science," *Social Science Information* 15 (1976): 306–30; and W. van den Daele and P. Weingart, "Resistance and Receptivity of Science to External Direction: The Emergence of New Disciplines under the Impact of Science Policy," in G. Lemaine et al., eds., *Perspectives on the Emergence of Scientific Disciplines* (The Hague: Mouton, 1976), pp. 247–275.

69. D. de S. Price, "Towards a Comprehensive System of Science Indicators," presented to the conference on "Evaluation in Science and Technology—Theory and Practice," Dubrovnik, Yugoslavia, July 1980, and "Quality Indicators Seminar," mimeo, M.I.T., October 1980, p. 1. For some this has been seen as undue optimism, if not hubris: see B. Mazlish, "The Quality of 'the Quality of Science': An Evaluation," in "On Developing Indicators of Quality of Science," op. cit., pp. 42–52.

70. Price, "Quality Indicators Seminar," p. 5.

71. Cozzens, "Introductory Remarks," p. 3.

72. M. Kochen, "Models of Scientific Output," in Elkana et al., op. cit., p. 98.

73. Ibid., pp. 116–17.

74. Ibid., p. 131.

75. D. de S. Price, "Science Indicators of Quality and Quantity for Fine Tuning of United States Investment in Research in Major Fields of

Science and Technology," paper prepared at the request of Commission on Human Resources, National Research Council, April 1980, mimeo, p. 13.

76. Cozzens, "Introductory Remarks," p. 8.

77. One commentator at the NSF workshop, NSF Program Officer Roger Noll, urged policy researchers to take Delbruck's advice: "to err on the side of too much theory and not enough empirical work [because] . . . we lack a really first-class theory about how fields of research develop and atrophy." See Noll, "Comments," *Social Studies of Science* 16 (1) (1986): 135–42.

78. Kruytbosch, op. cit.

79. In addition to earlier chapters that reviewed theoretical and empirical investigations, see the special issue, "Peer Review and Public Policy," *Science, Technology, and Human Values* 10 (Summer 1985): 3–86.

80. Brooks, op. cit., p. 22.

81. For an example, see D. E. Chubin, "Analyzing Basic Research for the U.S. Congress" in *Managing Science in a "Steady State",* 1990, proceedings of a NATO Advanced Study Institute (October 1989).

## CHAPTER 7

1. All quotations from the Sigma Xi survey are drawn from William Hively, "Survey Probes Tensions between Science and Democracy," *American Scientist* 77 (January-February 1989): 24–26.

2. Quoted in Hively, op. cit., p. 26.

3. Daryl E. Chubin, "Competence is Not Enough," *Contemporary Sociology* 5 (March 1980): 204–7.

4. Ian I. Mitroff and Daryl E. Chubin, "Peer Review at NSF: A Dialectical Policy Analysis," *Social Studies of Science* 9 (May 1979): 199–232; also see John H. Noble, "Peer Review: Quality Control of Applied Social Research," *Science 185* (13 September 1974): 916–21; Gabriel Bar-Haim, "Problem Solvers and Problem Identifiers—The Making of Research Styles," *International Journal of Science Education* 10 (1988): 135–150.

5. Lyle Groeneveld, Norman Koller, and Nicholas C. Mullins, "The Advisers of the United States National Science Foundation," *Social Studies of Science* 5 (1975): 343–54.

6. Walter E. Stumph, " 'Peer' review," *Science* 207 (22 February 1980): 822–23.

7. Stephen Cole, Leonard Rubin, and Jonathan R. Cole, *Peer Review in the NSF: Phase I of a Study* (Washington, D.C.: National Academy of Sciences, 1978).

8. Edward J. Hackett, "Funding and Academic Research in the Life Sciences: An Exploratory Study," *Science and Technology Studies* 5 (1987): 34–47.

9. Division of Policy Research and Analysis, National Science Foundation, "Distribution of U.S. Academic Research Activity" (Washington, D.C.: National Science Foundation, September 1988), p. 8.

10. Ibid., p. 4.

11. Hackett, op. cit.; see also Hackett, "Science as a Vocation in the 1990s," *Journal of Higher Education* forthcoming (1990).

12. Deborah Shapley and Rustum Roy, *Lost at the Frontier: U.S. Science and Technology Policy Adrift* (Philadelphia: ISI Press, 1985), p. 152.

13. Ibid.

14. Gregory Byrne, "A Modest Proposal," *Science* 244 (21 April 1989): 290.

15. Ibid.

16. Among the studies that examine the connection between autonomy and scientific work are Donald C. Pelz and Frank M. Andrews, *Scientists in Organizations: Productive Climates for Research and Development* (New York: Wiley, 1966); Gerald A. Gordon and Susan Marquis, "Freedom, Visibility of Consequences, and Scientific Innovation," *American Journal of Sociology* 72 (1966): 195–202; John R. Sutton, "Organizational Autonomy and Professional Norms in Science: A Case Study of the Lawrence Livermore Laboratory," *Social Studies of Science* 14 (1984): 197–224.

17. The classic statement on multiples is Robert K. Merton, "Singletons and Multiples in Science," in Robert K. Merton, *The Sociology of Science* (Chicago: University of Chicago Press, [1961] 1973), pp. 343–70. See also his "Priorities in Scientific Discovery" (1957), in the same volume, pp. 286–324. The theme is carried in two otherwise quite dissimilar works: Augustine Brannigan, *The Social Basis of Scientific Discoveries* (Cambridge, England: Cambridge University Press, 1981), and Dean Keith Simonton, *Scientific Genius: A Psychology of Science* (Cambridge, England: Cambridge University Press, 1988).

18. Eliot Marshall, "A Fast Track for High-risk Science," *Science* 244 (19 May 1989): 764.

19. Several studies of foundation patronage for science have been published recently. This literature may be entered through the following works: Pnina Abir-Am, "The Assessment of Interdisciplinary Research in the 1930s: The Rockefeller Foundation and Physico-Chemical Morphology," *Minerva* 27 (1988): 35–58; Stephen P. Turner, "The Survey in Nineteenth-Century American Geology: The Evolution of a Form of Patronage," *Minerva* 25 (1987): 282–348; Steven C. Wheatley, *The Politics of Philanthropy: Abraham Flexner and Medical Education* (Madison, Wisc.: University of Wisconsin Press, 1989); and Gerald Jonas, *The Circuit Riders: Rockefeller Money and the Rise of Modern Science* (New York: Norton, 1989).

20. Harold Orlans, "Neutrality and Advocacy in Policy Research," *Policy Sciences* 6 (1975): 107–19.

21. Interactive problem solving is discussed in Charles E. Lindblom and David K. Cohen, *Usable Knowledge: Social Science and Social Problem Solving* (New Haven: Yale University Press, 1979).

22. Clifford A. Hooker, "Philosophy and Meta-Philosophy of Science: Empiricism, Popperianism and Realism" *Synthese* 32 (1975): 177–231.

23. Marx Wartofsky, "The Critique of Impure Reason II: Sin, Science, and Society," *Science, Technology, and Human Values* 5 (1980): 5–23.

24. Maurice Goldsmith, *The Science Critic* (London and New York: Routledge & Kegan Paul, 1986), p. 10.

25. Gilbert Fuchsberg, "Prospect of Commercial Gain from Unconfirmed Discovery Prompted Utah U. Officials to Skirt Usual Scientific Protocol," *The Chronicle of Higher Education,* May 17, 1989, p. A5.

26. Ibid., p. A8.

27. Ibid.

28. Ibid.

29. John Naisbitt, *Megatrends: Ten New Directions Transforming Our Lives* (New York: Warner Books, 1982).

30. Shapley and Roy, op. cit., p. 140.

31. Merton, op. cit.

32. Social scientists' ardor for exploring the interactions sparked by cold fusion is typified by a Cornell University archive consisting of the downloaded messages from various electronic bulletin boards. A project to analyze the messages is now underway. See Bruce V. Lewenstein, "Cold Fusion and Science Communication?" *Beckman Center News* 7 (Spring 1990): 6–8.

33. Quoted in Carol H. Weiss and Michael J. Bucuvalas, *Social Science Research and Decision-Making* (New York: Columbia University Press, 1980).

34. Burkart Holzner and John H. Marx, *Knowledge Application: The Knowledge System in Society* (Boston: Allyn and Bacon, 1979). The book signals a break from the longstanding tradition of indifference by sociologists of knowledge to policy questions. This new-found sensitivity also appears in Michael Mulkay, *Science and the Sociology of Knowledge* (London: Allen and Unwin, 1979).

35. Weiss and Bucuvalas, op. cit.

36. Stephen Toulmin, "From Form to Function: Philosophy and History of Science in the 1950s and Now," *Daedalus* 106 (1977): 143–62. To quote Toulmin:

> For a time, the different academic professions march forward separately but in parallel, each in its own special way; then, for a time, they join hands and work together on the general problems arising in the areas where their techniques overlap.

37. Orlans, op. cit.

38. Kenneth Prewitt, "The Public and Science Policy," *Science, Technology, and Human Values* 7 (1982): 5–14.

39. Alvin M. Weinberg, "Criteria for Scientific Choice," *Minerva* 1 (1963): 159–171; Harvey Brooks, "The Problem of Research Priorities," *Daedalus* 107 (1978): 171–190.

40. Stanford's Donald Kennedy, quoted in Wil Lepkowski, "The Reshaping of White House Science Advice," *Chemical & Engineering News,* April 3, 1989, pp. 7–8.

41. Ibid.

42. Colleen Cordes, "More Partnerships to Boost Technology Sought for Academe," *The Chronicle of Higher Education,* April 9, 1989, pp. A21–23.

43. Daryl E. Chubin and Edward J. Hackett, "Commentary: On the Virtues of Self-Study," *Science, Technology, and Human Values* 14 (1989): 96–99.

## APPENDIX

1. National Science Foundation, *Proposal Review at NSF: Perceptions of Principal Investigators* (Washington, D.C.: NSF Report 88-4, 1988), p. 3.

2. Grace Carter, "The Consequences of Unfunded NIH Applications for the Investigator and his Research," Rand Report R-2229-NIH, October 1978, p. 9.

3. The NSF 1988 study used a weighting procedure to make the sample proportions of funded and unfunded scientists equal those of the population.

# Glossary

| | |
|---|---|
| **AAU** | Association of American Universities |
| **ACS** | American Chemical Society |
| **FOIA** | Freedom of Information Act |
| **GNP** | gross national product |
| **HHMI** | Howard Hughes Medical Institute |
| **IRG** | Initial Review Group |
| **NCI** | National Cancer Institute |
| **NIAID** | National Institute of Allergy and Infectious Diseases |
| **NHLBI** | National Heart, Lung, and Blood Institute |
| **NIH** | National Institutes of Health |
| **NSF** | National Science Foundation |
| **PI** | principal investigator |
| **R&D** | research and development |
| **RO1** | category of NIH grants (individual investigator-initiated) |
| **S&T** | science and technology |
| **SCI** | Science Citation Index |
| **USDA** | U.S. Department of Agriculture |

# Index

academic institutions
  dependence of, on federal funding, 195–97
  lobbying by, for federal funding, 154–58
Académie des Sciences, France, 107
accountability in scientific research, 129, 131
  politics, scientific autonomy, and, 162–63
accountability of peer review, 44–45, 91
Advisory Committee on Merit Review, National Science Foundation, 19
Agriculture, U.S. Department of, 160
Albanese, C., 138
Alvarez, Luis, 13
American Physical Society, 209
anomie, conditions of, in scientific world, 77
applied research, R. Roy on, 38–43
applied results of scientific research
  funding and, 158–62
  science push and, 185–88
Association of American Universities (AAU), 156–57
Atkinson, Richard, 14
Atlanta *Journal and Constitution*, 211
autonomy, scientific, 151, 153
  accountability of science, politics, and, 162–63

Backus, Charles E., 155
Bakanic, Von, 104, 105, 106
Baltimore, David, 30, 32, 33, 191
  role of, in *Cell* misconduct affair, 138–53
Baltimore scientific misconduct affair, 138–53
  Congressional hearings on, 146–49
  dispute becomes a public affair, 141–46
  due process issues in, 147–48
  NIH investigation of, and results, 148–53
  original charges against *Cell* article, 138–41
  public oversight issues in, 151–52
  scientific self-correction issues in, 142–43, 145, 150–51
Barber, Benjamin, 148
Barrett, Michael F., Jr., 147
basic research, R. Roy on, 38–43
*Behavioral and Brain Sciences, The*, open peer commentary in, 94–95
Berliner, Robert M., 54–55
bibliometrics, 88, 106, 166–74
  broker role of, 188
  converging partial indicators in, 175–81
  first generation of, 167–69
  lessons applied from, 173–74
  lessons learned from, 169–73
  F. Narin's work linking generations of, 174–75

257